LIGHTNING
STRIKES TWICE
THE STORY OF THE
ENGLISH ELECTRIC LIGHTNING

LIGHTNING STRIKES TWICE

THE STORY OF THE ENGLISH ELECTRIC LIGHTNING

MARTIN W. BOWMAN

AMBERLEY

First published 2009

Amberley Publishing
Cirencester Road, Chalford,
Stroud, Gloucestershire, GL6 8PE

www.amberley-books.com

British Library Cataloguing in Publication Data.
A catalogue record for this book is available from the British Library.

ISBN 978 1 84868 493 5

Printed in Great Britain

Contents

Introduction

It is difficult for younger readers reared on the Jaguar and Tornado to believe that the Lightning was born of an idea in 1946 and that it progressed as a result of 1950s/60s airframe, engine and weapons technology – all of it British – into the thoroughbred that it is. If, during school holidays, in the far-off, halcyon days of the '60s, you stood, like me, at the end of the brick road by the yellow crash gate to witness the last all-British fighter take off with full re-heat, then you too would recall these times with affection. Let us not forget that the Cold War years were dangerous years, too. No one, though, can ever take away the vivid memories and the cacophony of sound generated by the twin Avon engines, which reverberated around an airfield at take-off time like a violent storm. Visions such as this, albeit in words and pictures, are featured together with pictorial images and vivid recollections of the pilots and their ground crews, in what I hope you will agree is a refreshingly different approach. The Lightning may be gone, but it certainly is not forgotten. There never has been, and never will be, another aircraft like it.

Acknowledgements

J. Adams; Captain A.M. Aldridge; Brian Allchin; John Arnold; Diana Barnato Walker MBE; Rex Barrett; Group Captain Antony I. Barwood OBE; Richard C. Basey; Chris Bassham; Mike Baxter; Captain Martin Bee; Squadron Leader Dick Bell; Anthony 'Bugs' Bendell; John Bexfield; Ray Biddle MBE; AVM George P. Black; Steve Bowes; Alan A. Brain; Roly Bray; Wing Commander John Bryant; John Brindle; Colin W. Brock; Ray Brooks; Flight Lieutenant Peter Brown; Trevor Brucklesby; Squadron Leader E.H. Bulpett; Wing Commander Ken Burford; RAF Flight Safety Magazine; Dave Bussey; A.G. Calver; Denis Calvert; Squadron Leader Brian Carroll; Edwin Carter; Mick Cartwright; Derek Chilvers; Martin Chorlton; John Church; Roger Colebrook; AVM Peter S. Collins CB AFC BA; Mike Cooke; Bob Cossey; Ray Cossey; Alec B. Curtis; Squadron Leader Dick Doleman RAF; Tony Dossor; John Dunnell; Group Captain Ed Durham; Barry J. Dye; *Eastern Daily Press*; *East Anglian Daily Times*; J. Malcolm English; Kevin C. Farrow; Nigel Farrow; Daniel and Tony Fishlock; Mike Flowerday; Dave Freeman; D.E. Freeman; John Fuller, 432 (Woodbridge) Squadron ATC; Caroline Galpin; ACM Sir Joseph Gilbert; Ron Godbold; Tony and Brett Goodyear; Air Commodore Ken J. Goodwin CBE AFC; John Hale; A.L.S. 'Les' Hall; Joan Hammond; Ken Hayward; Peter Hayward; Ken Hazell; Group Captain Tim Hewlett; Mike Hillier; Group Captain Mike Hobson CBE; Del Holyland, Martin-Baker Aircraft Co. Ltd.; J.R. 'Robbie' Honnor; Group Captain W.B.G. Hopkins AFC; AVM John Howe CB CBE AFC; Mike Indge; Mick Jennings MBE; Squadron Leader Jimmy Jewell; Ken Johnson; Robert Johnson; Ronald Johnson; the late Roy Johnson; Tony Kemp; Brian Knight, Prospect Litho Ltd; Douglas Knights; Jim Lilley; Paul Lincoln; Squadron Leader Jack Love; Barry J. Madden; Steve Masterson; Nigel McTeer; Alec Michael; Vernon Miller; Captain Bruce Monk; Squadron Leader Gordon Moulds MBE; Captain Ted J. Nance; Pete W. Nash; Group Captain Hans Neubroch OBE; Air Marshal Sir John Nicholls KCB CBE DFC AFC; Flight Lieutenant R.E. Offord; Wing Commander George Parry DSO* DFC* OBE; Simon Parry; Tony Paxton; Gerald Pearson; Squadron Leader Henry Ploszek AFC; Bill Povilus; Pete Purdy; Richie Pymar; Wing Commander Alex Reed OBE; Richard Reeve; Jeremy Richards; Captain Mike Rigg; Ian H.R. Robins; Mike Rigg; Squadron Leader Derek Rothery; Ray Reed; Gary Revell; Graham Rollins; *Rolls-Royce Magazine*; Group Captain Dave C. Roome OBE MRAeS; Charles Ross; Squadron Leader Clive Rowley MBE; Adrian Savage; Group Captain Dave Seward AFC; Group Captain Mike J.F. Shaw CBE; Kelvin Sloper, City of Norwich Aviation Museum; Patrick and Lionel Snell; Steve Snelling; Laury Squibb; Jean Stangroom; Peter Symes; Geoff Syrett; Air Commodore M.J.E. Swiney; Flight Lieutenant Andy Thomas; Eric Thomas; Hugh Trevor, Lightning Preservation Group, Bruntingthorpe; Vic Yorath; Graham Vernon; S. Wade; John Ward; Sid Watkinson; John Watson; W.H. Welham; C.A. Wheatland; David Williams; Peter Winning; Andrew Woodroof; Group Captain P.T.G. Webb OBE DL; Arthur Wright; Ian Wright, 222 (Broadland) Squadron ATC; A. Yates.

CHAPTER 1

Flash of Fire – The First Fighters

'I first heard of the Lightning in 1953,' recalls Squadron Leader (later Group Captain) Dave Seward, 'when a wing commander from the Central Fighter Establishment visited No.1 Squadron at RAF Tangmere to give us a talk on fighter development. He discussed the problems with the Swift, the introduction of the Hunter and Javelin and then went on to describe the fighter of the future. At the time rumours were rife that we were going to get a jet-rocket fighter that took off on a trolley and landed on skids. To us this sounded too much like the Me 163 [a German Second World War rocket-powered interceptor] and we were not too enthusiastic. Also, this was the same time that the so-called 'moving runway' was in vogue. We reckoned that if you landed a bit too slow, the runway could be rotating too fast and you would end up through the windscreen. So, to get the real 'poop' from the horse's mouth for a change was eagerly awaited.'

The 'poop' that Squadron Leader Seward and others like him received centered on a radical and revolutionary new design by the English Electric Company. It was the result of Experimental Requirement 103, issued by the Ministry of Supply in May 1947, for a research aircraft capable of exploring transonic and low supersonic speeds of up to Mach 1.5. A year earlier, in 1946, the De Havilland Vampire was entering RAF service, and both Hawker and Supermarine were studying schemes for swept-wing jet fighters which would eventually emerge as the Hunter and Swift and which would be capable, just, of exceeding Mach 1 in a dive. At English Electric, chief engineer W.E.W. 'Teddy' Petter began sketching possible fully supersonic designs.

One of the immediate problems was finding a suitable engine, even though Britain had established her jet pedigree as far back as 1937, when Frank (later Sir Frank) Whittle had run the first gas-turbine aero-engine in this country. Jet fighter development accelerated in the Second World War, not least in Germany, where the Messerschmitt Me 262, powered by Jumo 004-0 jet engines, became operational on 3 October 1944. Britain's first operational jet fighter, the Gloster Meteor I, powered by centrifugal-flow engines, entered squadron service in July 1944. On 7 November 1945 a Meteor F.4 of the High Speed Flight established a new world air-speed record of 606mph. On 7 September 1946 the record increased to 616mph.

In 1947 America seriously challenged Britain's world lead in jet fighter design for the first time. Early American jet aircraft had not proved successful, but in June 1947 America captured the world speed record when the Lockheed P-80R Shooting Star raised the record to 623.74mph. The Douglas Skystreak raised it even further later that year, to 650.92mph. Jet aircraft at this time were all of conventional straight-winged design, but then the results of German wartime research into high-speed aerodynamics became available, and it was the American aviation and space industries which benefited most. German designers had explored ways of avoiding the problems of 'compressibility'. As an aircraft approaches the speed of sound, the air it displaces is compressed into a series

English Electric were helped greatly in the development of the P.1 by data provided by WG768, the Short S.B.5, a scaled down test-bed powered by a 3,500lb thrust Rolls-Royce Derwent jet engine and fitted with a non-retractable undercarriage, adjustable for centre of gravity variations. The S.B.5 first flew on 2 December 1952.

of high-pressure waves that stream back in a cone from the nose. As these hit the wing, they cause the airflow over that part of the aircraft to break up and cause added drag. They also create extreme buffeting, with harmful effects to the structure of the wing. The German designers discovered that if they swept back the wing, this delayed the onset of compressibility problems and allowed higher subsonic speeds to be attained.

On 14 October 1947 Captain Charles 'Chuck' Yeager in the Bell X-1 became the first man to break the sound barrier, when he attained a level speed of 670mph, or Mach 1.015, at a height of 42,000ft. America's F-86 Sabre, the first transonic, swept-wing jet fighter to see service in the West, had flown for the first time on 1 October 1947, and on 15 September 1948 an F-86A established a new world air-speed record of 670.98mph. By July 1953 the Sabre had increased the record speed to 715.75mph. On 29 October 1953 the F-100 Super Sabre, the world's first operational fighter capable of supersonic performance, established yet another new world air-speed record of 755.15mph. In the Soviet Union, the MiG-17, an updated version of the swept-wing MiG-15, also appeared in 1953 and was claimed to have exceeded Mach 1 in level flight three years before.

Britain could therefore be forgiven for the onset of despondency. She could also he accused of shooting herself in the foot. In February 1946, British technology was seriously jeopardized when, just as construction was about to start, the Miles M.52 supersonic research aircraft was disastrously cancelled; theoretically, this aircraft would have been capable of reaching 1,000mph at 36,000ft. By 1948 it was quite apparent that the lead in supersonic design had passed to America. John Derry in the De Havilland DH 108 made the first British supersonic flight on 9 September 1948, but only in a dive. Conceived in 1953, the delta-winged Avro 720, powered by an Armstrong Siddeley Viper engine and Armstrong Siddeley Screamer rocket unit, was theoretically capable of Mach 2 at 40,000ft. It was cancelled in 1957 just as the prototype neared completion. Although her Canberra and Hunter aircraft established speed records in 1953 (the latter raised the world speed record to 726.6mph on 7 September), it must have seemed that Britain had thrown away what could have been a world lead in supersonic research.

At Salmesbury around 1958 with Development Batch and early production F.1 Lightnings in final assembly. XG326 is behind the Second World War AEC bowser. (BAe)

However, Specification 103, which had called for a high-speed research aircraft, had already prompted both the Fairey and English Electric companies to initiate design studies. Fairey was to respond with the delta-winged FD.2 while at English Electric, Teddy Petter and his young, talented design team, started work on two prototypes and a third airframe for static test. In mid-1949 Specification F.23/49 was issued for a structural test specimen and two 7g research aircraft with guns and a sighting system 'to investigate the practicality of supersonic speed for military aircraft'. English Electric developed the P.1 supersonic day-fighter to meet it. The company had no direct research and experience to call upon. Indeed, English Electric's experience of aircraft production had been limited to producing Hampdens and Halifaxes in the Second World War and then Vampires after the war. But Petter's genius and the technical expertise of his team, already heavily engaged in bringing the EE.A1 jet bomber decision to reality as the Canberra, were ready to overcome all obstacles. They were helped greatly by data provided by the Short S.B.5. (WG768), a scaled down test-bed powered by a 3,500lb-thrust Rolls-Royce Derwent jet engine and fitted with a non-retractable undercarriage, adjustable for centre of gravity variations. The S.B.5 first flew on 2 December 1952. Various wing designs with a sweepback of 50, 60 and 69 degrees were tested, and a variable-incidence tailplane positioned either at the top of the fin or on the rear fuselage was also experimented with by Short Brothers. Further data was provided by the installation at the Warton factory of both water and transonic wind tunnels (the first in Britain), including equipment capable of operating at Mach 4 and Mach 6. Fifty-one models were tested and in excess of 4,600 runs were made in the various wind tunnels. Even so, to produce an operational front-line fighter capable not only of sustaining supersonic flight, but also of reaching Mach 2, was a challenge so daunting that in 1949 it was akin to trying to be the first to put a man on the moon.

A decision was taken to use two Armstrong Siddeley Sapphire AS-Sa5 axial-flow engines. These had a lower frontal area than the centrifugal-flow engines that powered the older Meteor and Vampire and were each capable of providing 7,200lb dry thrust

F.2s and T.4s nearing completion on the production line at Salmesbury. (*Aeroplane*)

with no re-heat. By this method, less fuel would be used than with a single large engine combined with afterburning. If the two engines were 'stacked' one above and behind the other, double the thrust of a single unit could be obtained, while the frontal area was increased by only 50 per cent. Most Soviet and American designers had tried to design a fighter capable of achieving supersonic speeds in level flight without the use of afterburners, but without success.

Even more radical were the wings, with 60 degrees of sweep to minimize wave drag; had the trailing edge been continuous they would have been of delta form like those of the FD.2. Petter rejected the delta wing, however, because it would not provide sufficient control during certain flight contingencies and the positive control provided by a tailplane would not then have been available. A deep notch was cut into the trailing edge of the shoulder wings at about 50 per cent of each half span, with the ailerons being carried along the outer transverse trailing edge to the tips. To avoid pitch-up problems, the sharply swept-back, all-moving tailplane was mounted below the level of the wing (beneath the lower tailpipe) on the slab-sided fuselage. Advanced avionics, powered controls and a very clever retraction of the main undercarriage wheels into the thin wings were other notable aspects of the design. The wings, despite having a thickness/chord ratio of only 50 per cent, gave a very reasonable fuel storage area and kept the fuselage free of fuel tanks – a feature, which would hamper the Lightning in later years. However, in 1947 the RAF wanted only a short-range, rapid climb interceptor. Fuel was not then the main consideration.

WG760, the first prototype P.1, was powered by two 7,500lb static thrust Sapphires fed through the single nose intake, which was bifurcated, internally to each engine. It had a delta fin with a rounded tip and an uncranked wing leading edge. To minimize wave drag, the top of the hood was virtually flush with the upper line of the fuselage. In 1950, Petter left English Electric to join Folland Aircraft, and responsibility for the design and subsequent development of the P.1 passed to F.W. (later Sir Freddie) Page.

The first indications that Britain had a world-beating supersonic design, which could catapult the RAF into the supersonic age, sparked understandable euphoria, as Squadron Leader Dave Seward confirms. '"It has an air intake right in the nose", the wing commander from the CFE said. "Wings swept so far back that the ailerons are on the wingtips and it has two engines – one on top of the other", he added. "Furthermore, it can climb to 36,000ft in under five minutes and it flies at one-and-a-half times the speed of sound." Then he said, "It's so secret, that you should forget what I've told you." Well, how could we forget such an aircraft when we were flying Meteor 8s, which could just

F.2s at the Lightning final
assembly line at Salmesbury in
March 1962. (*Aeroplane*)

about achieve Mach 0.82, almost out of control? The idea was to have a rocket pack fitted
underneath the fuselage to give extra thrust for acceleration and combat. Thankfully, the
rocket pack, which seemed to have a habit of blowing up no matter which firm made it,
was dispensed with and a ventral fuel tank was installed in its place.'

The P.1 prototype was finished in the spring of 1954 and was transferred by road
to the A&AEE, Boscombe Down, for its first flight on 4 August 1954 in the hands
of English Electric's chief test pilot, Wing Commander Roland P. 'Bee' Beamont.
Beamont reached Mach 0.85 on the first flight. On the third flight, on 11 August,
WG760 became the first British aircraft to exceed Mach 1 in level flight, but it was
not realized that this had been achieved until the following day when the aircraft's
speed was accurately computed! On 18 July 1955 P.1A WG763, the second prototype,
flew for the first time and that September it gave its first public demonstration when
it performed at the SBAC Display at Farnborough. The P.1A differed from the P.1 in
having a pair of 30mm Aden cannon in the nose and American-style toe brakes. In
the course of the development of the P.1 into the anticipated fighter, WG760 was redesignated P.1A, the fighter project becoming P.1B. WG763 was armed with a pair of
30mm Aden canon fitted in the upper nose decking, and flew with her heading edge
flaps fixed in place, as they had been found to be superfluous.

A decision was taken in 1954 to order three P.1B prototypes[1]. They would be
powered by 200-Series Rolls-Royce Avons with four-stage re-heat and have provision
for a Ferranti AI (Airborne Intercept) 23 (Airpass) radar and two De Havilland 'Blue
Jay' (later Firestreak) infrared homing missiles. This brought about a virtually complete
redesign of the aircraft, although the general aerodynamic layout and concept were
retained. The oval intake at the nose was changed to an annular design with a central
shock cone; the airbrakes were modified; plain instead of area-increasing flaps appeared
on the wing; and the cockpit canopy was raised. Handling trials revealed that a larger
fin area was desirable for better stability and this was increased later by 30 per cent.
The change to 200-Series Avons with re-heat nearly doubled the thrust available. An
order for a pre-production batch of twenty P.1Bs[2] plus three test airframes came soon
after, and was followed, in November 1956, by an order for nineteen production
aircraft, designated F.1, and a non-flying specimen. RAF plans for an all-weather heavy
interceptor (OR.329) capable of carrying two large radar-homing missiles (originally
called Red Dean, later 'Red Hebe') never reached fruition, and the RAF had to settle for
the lightweight Lightning armed with clear-weather IR-homing missiles.

XG336, one of the twenty P.1B pre-production batch, being towed out of the hangar at Salmesbury. (*Aeroplane*)

XA847, the first prototype P.1B, exceeded Mach 1 without re-heat on its maiden flight on 4 April 1957 from Warton with 'Bee' Beamont at the controls. Ironically that same day Duncan Sandys, the Minister of Defence, published the now infamous White Paper forecasting the end of manned combat aircraft (including a supersonic manned bomber) and their replacement by missiles! In part it said: 'In view of the good progress already made with surface-to-air missiles, the Government has come to the conclusion that the RAF is unlikely to have a requirement for fighter aircraft of types more advanced than the supersonic P.1 and work on such projects will stop.' The P.1 remained in being for the simple reason that supersonic interceptors were needed to protect the V-bomber force based in the United Kingdom. From now on, the role of Fighter Command was to be purely defensive.

In April 1958 the first deliveries of the pre-production P.1Bs began. The first (XG307) flew on 3 April 1958. On 23 October, the name 'Lightning' was bestowed on the P.1B at Farnborough. During the year the idea of installing a Napier Double-Scorpion rocket pack, as had been fitted to a Canberra to create a new world altitude record in 1957, was dropped. On 25 November 1958 XA847 became the first British aircraft ever to fly at Mach 2, bettering this achievement on 6 January 1959. The first P.1 production example flew on 30 October 1959. It had two Rolls-Royce Avon RA.24R 210 engines, each giving 11,250lb static thrust at maximum cold power, and 14,430lb static thrust in full re-heat. With an all-up weight of 34,000lb, the 28,000lb thrust of the engines provided a very good power/weight ratio. It had two 30mm Aden cannon in the upper front fuselage and could have two more fitted in the lower fuselage in lieu of the missile pack. It had the Ferranti AI 23 Airpass radar in the nose shock-cone and carried two Firestreak infrared missiles, one on each side of the fuselage.[3]

There were no dramatic problems during the development flying stage with the P.1 series. However, on 1 October 1959 test pilot John W.C. Squier was fortunate to escape death after ejecting from XL628, the prototype T.4 two-seat variant, which 'Bee' Beamont had first flown from Warton on 6 May. At 11.15am on the morning of 1 October, Squier took off from Warton and climbed to 35,000ft before accelerating to Mach 1.7 over the Irish Sea. His brief was to note engine data at every 0.1 Mach above Mach 1.0 to Mach 1.7, when he was to climb to 40,000ft, stabilize and make a 360-degree roll to starboard using maximum aileron with his feet off the rudder pedals. This manoeuvre had previously been accomplished in single-seat Lightnings, but it had never

On 18 July 1955 P.1A WG763, the second prototype, flew for the first time, and that September it gave its first public demonstration when it performed at the SBAC Display at Farnborough. (*Aeroplane*)

before been tried in the two-seat version. Squier reached Mach 1.7 and 20 miles due west of St Bees Head and he carried out the aileron turn. A high-speed roll immediately developed, and when Squier centralized the controls to halt it, XL628 yawed violently to starboard in a manoeuvre far fiercer than had previously been encountered during maximum aileron rolls in the single-seat Lightning. Squier knew that a structural failure had occurred and the aircraft was now totally uncontrollable, yawing violently right and left and pitching. He had to get out, fast. He reached up, noticing as he did so that the pilot tube was bent right across the air intake and grabbed the seat blind; and the seemingly slow-motion ejection sequence was put in motion. The canopy was whisked away into the void and the Martin-Baker seat fired him out of the doomed Lightning. As he exited, Squier took a blow to his right elbow from the SARAH (Search and Rescue Homing) battery, and both his legs from his knees downwards were badly bruised by the ascent. He tried to hold the blind to his face in the full force of the blast, which blew away his oxygen mask, but his arms were painfully wrenched away, almost out of their sockets. (Two compressed vertebrae were also diagnosed later.) Then the seat fell away but the parachute failed to deploy. Squier only became aware of this when he passed through cloud and could see that the sea was getting ominously close! Instantly, he pulled the manual override and at last the parachute deployed.

Squier plunged into the water and sank beneath the waves. He managed to inflate his life preserver and, as he soared to the surface, he became entangled in the shroud lines until he was able to disentangle himself and release the parachute. Fortunately, the dinghy in the PSP (Personal Survival Pack) had inflated and it now floated invitingly nearby. He managed to clamber aboard but it was full of seawater and in the absence of the bailer he had to use a shoe to scoop out the water. Then he rigged the SARAH homing beacon and its aerial, but, to his dismay, the apparatus failed to work – the high-tension battery, which was one week beyond its inspection date, was flat. For two hours Squier bobbed around on the sea before an amphibian approached. Squier managed to pull the pin on the two-star signal rocket, but it refused to fire and the aircraft failed to spot the tiny dinghy. Another hour passed and the aircraft returned, but again the signal rocket failed to work. Ironically, the third and final rocket worked perfectly, but by now the amphibian had departed.

Squier spent the rest of the day adrift on the sea and he must have begun to despair when darkness settled. He had still not been found the next morning when rain and bad visibility cloaked the horizon. However, he could make out what he thought must be the east coast of Ireland. (It was actually Wigtown Bay in western Scotland.) He tried paddling but all he succeeded in doing was to go around in circles. A piece of driftwood helped and he eventually reached a point about 200 yards from the shore. Finally, after passing ships hour after endless hour had seemingly ignored his whistles for help, Squier berthed alongside a tower in a small inlet and eventually he managed to reach the shore, from where he was able to stumble to the safety of a house. In the garden was a matron from an adjoining school who told Squier that she had seen the story concerning his disappearance in the newspapers. He had spent thirty-six hours on the surface of the sea. Squier was rushed to Stranraer Cottage Hospital where, the next day, four doctors from the Institute of Aviation Medicine at Farnborough, who diagnosed the two compressed vertebrae, examined him. His eyes and middle ears had also haemorrhaged and he became deaf after a week – fortunately only temporarily. Two weeks later, he was airlifted from West Freugh to Warton and was admitted to Preston Royal Infirmary, where he spent another month. The outcome of the investigation into the cause of the disaster found that the thickening of the forward part of the fuselage to accommodate the second seat had reduced the Lightning's stability, particularly with two Firestreaks attached. It would be eight months later before John Squier was able to fly again.

The Lightning entered service in December 1959 with the delivery to the AFDS (Air Fighting Development Squadron) at Coltishall of three pre-production P.1Bs. Prior to their arrival there were some concerns about the suitability of the Norfolk station to support Mach 2 aircraft. However, the runway had been extended to over 7,000 feet. The first three P.1Bs were followed in May-July 1960 by the first production F.1s for 74 'Tiger' Squadron, also at Coltishall. First to arrive was XM135, on 25 May. Squadron Leader John F.G. Howe, an assured thirty-year-old South African[4] who took command in February 1960, said at the time: 'We know that we can catch the bombers and, going on past experience, we know we can outfight any fighter equivalent to the USAF Century series. The performance of the aircraft, coupled with the ease with which it is flown, gives the pilots confidence, and the fact that it is felt to be the best fighter in operational service in the world today gives our Lightning pilots the highest possible morale.'

F.1s, though, were slow to arrive, and Lightning spares were almost non-existent. Although seven Lightnings had arrived by August, only one was operational. Then it was announced that the *Tigers* were to fly four Lightnings each day during Farnborough Week in September! However, this helped speed up deliveries and these enabled the squadron to begin work-up at Boscombe Down late that summer. Then the aircraft were back in the hangars at Coltishall again for much needed maintenance so that they could take part in Battle of Britain commemorations. Ground crews worked right around the clock, dealing with constant electrical failures and myriad other complex teething troubles to keep six to twelve Lightnings on the line at one time. 74 Squadron would not become fully operational until the following year. Progress was one step forward, two steps back. A few days after a three-day 'meet the press' event in February 1962, a serious Lightning fire hazard was discovered in the area between the ventral tanks and the No.1 engine and jet-pipe. As a temporary measure, the ventral tanks were removed for flight until the problem was solved by a manufacturer's modification. Finally, by the end of April, all 'Tiger' pilots had completed their conversion to fly the aircraft by both day and night.

Production of the twenty-eight improved F.1A version and twenty-one of its T.4 two-seat equivalent continued under the auspices of a new organization. In 1960 English Electric Aviation was merged with Bristol Aircraft, Vickers Armstrong (Aircraft) and Hunting Aircraft to create the British Aircraft Corporation (BAC). The F.1A had provision for a detachable in-flight refuelling probe under the port wing and improved windscreen rain dispersal. The other main difference was a UHF radio

WG760 being flown by English Electric's chief test pilot, Wing Commander Roland P. 'Bee' Beamont. The P.1A's leading edge chord-wise slot is very visible. WG760 flew for the first time at the A&AEE Boscombe Down on 4 August 1954 when it was also flown by 'Bee' Beamont, who reached Mach 0.85 on the first flight. (Charles E. Brown)

This head-on shot of WG760, the first prototype P.1, shows the pedigree of Petter's clean, aerodynamic design. WG760 was powered by two 7,500lb static thrust Sapphires fed through the single nose intake, which was bifurcated internally to each engine. On 11 August 1954 on only its third flight, P.1A WG760, flown by Wng Cdr Beamont, broke the sound barrier to become Britain's first truly supersonic jet, capable of exceeding Mach 1 in level flight. (*Aeroplane*)

in place of the F.1's VHF. It also benefited from a general cleaning-up of the electrics and layout (strakes were added). Later, all F.1s were modified to F.1A standard. The T.4 was basically a side-by-side two-seat version of the F.1A. It looked awkward and bulbous, but its performance was only very marginally down on that of the single-seaters. On the squadrons it was classed as a front-line aircraft. All squadrons had one T.4, and the LTF (Lightning Training Flight), soon to become 226 Operational Conversion Unit (OCU), had eight initially. The first F.1A (XM169) flew on 16 August 1960 (the first production T.4 having flown on 15 July) and the first examples were issued to the Wattisham wing. 56 Squadron began receiving the first ones late in 1960 and 'Treble One' Squadron began receiving theirs in early 1961.

In 1962 Lightning test pilot George P. Aird cheated death when he was forced to eject from P.1B XG332 near Hatfield on 13 September after an engine fire. Aird had just completed a re-heat test up to Mach 1.7 off the south coast of England at 36,000ft. All had gone well until during the return flight the test engine twice refused to relight. Aird's third attempt succeeded but fuel, which should have been vented, was retained in the rear fuselage by a blocked drain and eventually ignited via a small crack in the tailpipe. As Aird descended at 400 knots through 15,000ft, 15-20 miles northeast of Hatfield, a 'double re-heat' engine fire warning glowed on the instrument panel. He weaved from side to side but was unable to confirm the extent of the problem. With the Hatfield runway in sight he decided to attempt a landing, hoping that it was only the fire warning light that had malfunctioned. He decided not to jettison the large ventral fuel tank as it could seriously injure anyone on the ground. Unfortunately, Runway 24, which was nearer, was not in use and Aird had to make for Runway 06, which proved a shade too far for the Lightning to remain airborne. Just ten seconds from touchdown the tailplane actuator anchorage, weakened by the fire, failed completely, and XG332 pitched violently upward. Aird instinctively pushed the stick forward and was horribly surprised to find that, when he waggled it around between his legs, it appeared to be disconnected. Aird pulled the ejection seat face blind and was blasted out of the doomed Lightning. He landed in the middle of a large greenhouse by the St Albans road at Smallford. Although he suffered no lasting back injuries, both his legs were smashed.

The next stage of the Lightning's development was the introduction of the F.2, which externally resembled the F.1A and had the same radar and Avon 210 engines, but the latter with fully variable after-burning in place of the earlier four-stage system. It also incorporated a number of other refinements: a much improved cockpit layout, slightly better automatic flight-control system, all-weather navigational aids and liquid oxygen (LOX). XN723, the F.2 prototype, first flew on 11 July 1961 and it was delivered to AFDS at Binbrook in November 1962. A month later, 19 Squadron at Leconfield became the first operational squadron in the RAF to equip with the F.2. It was joined late in 1962 by 92 Squadron, which received its first Lightnings in April 1963, the Leconfield Wing becoming fully operational that summer. At the end of 1965 both squadrons became part of 2nd Tactical Air Force in RAF Germany, later becoming the Gütersloh wing.[5]

What was the performance like on these early aircraft? Dave Seward explains. 'If you look at the air intake of a Lightning, the radome forms a centre body, which offsets the effects of compressibility over the engines as the speed is increased into the supersonic range. Theoretically the Lightning could achieve Mach 2.4 or two-and-a-half times the speed of sound before the supersonic shock wave angled back into the air intake, which would cause the engines to stall and possibly flame out. This rarely occurred, however, because to achieve Mach 2.4 you would use an enormous amount of fuel and with the pointed fins, the 1, 1A, 2 and T.4 could lose directional control at very high Mach numbers if harsh control movements were attempted. So these early aircraft were restricted to Mach 1.7. To overcome the limitations of these early models, the F.3 was

P.1B XA847, the first of three P.1B prototypes, made its maiden flight on 4 April 1957 at Warton, piloted by Wng Cdr Beamont.

P.1B XA847 banking away.

P.1B XA853, the second of the three P.1B prototypes, was first flown on 5 September 1957.

P.1B XA853 mostly was used on gun trials and gas concentration tests until May 1963. (BAC)

F.1A XM171 first flew on 20 September 1960 and went to the A&AEE for type evaluation and handling trials. (BAC)

F.3 XP697, which flew for the first time on 18 July 1963. (BAC)

F.3 XP697, which became the F.6 prototype, flying for the first time on 17 April 1964.

F.3A XR754/M, which first flew on 8 July 1965 and joined 23 Squadron on 29 February 1968.

Right: P.1B XG332 was first flown on 29 May 1959 by J.W. 'Jimmy' Squier and was used by De Havilland's for Firestreak and Red Top trials. This aircraft was lost on 13 September 1962, when George P. Aird cheated death after he was forced to eject from XG332 just short of the Hatfield runway following an engine fire. Aird had just completed a re-heat test up to Mach 1 off the South Coast of England at 36,000ft.

Below: F.2 XN725 was first flown on 31 March 1962 and was later converted to the F.3 prototype.

Above: Warton test pilots, left to right: Don Knight, Desmond 'Dizzy' de Villiers, Peter Hillwood, Jimmy Dell and Roland Beamont. (BAe)

Left: Two-seat P.11 XL628, the first of two prototype T.4s, which first flew on 6 May 1959. (BAC)

Head-on view of XL628. Twenty two-seat T.4 aircraft were built.

T.4 (P.11) XL628 at Farnborough in September 1959, with nose markings of a stylized lightning flash in orange and script 'Lightning T.4' with a black spine. This aircraft was flown on 6 May 1959. (BAe)

On 1 October 1959 T.4 (P.11) XL628 developed a structural failure and had to be abandoned by test pilot Jimmy Squier over the Irish Sea. He was fortunate to escape death.

A Lightning getting airborne on full re-heat. The 1A's two Rolls-Royce Avons with re-heat produced 11,250lb of thrust 'dry', and around 14,000lb 'wet'. Fuel capacity with the 250-gallon ventral tank installed was 1,020 gallons (with 40 gallons unusable). All fuel shown on the two fuel gauges was 'usable'. Weight was around fourteen tons with full fuel load. Once the ventral tank was empty the power to weight ratio was better than 1lb of thrust to 1lb of weight. Fuel consumption at idle (31 per cent) was 156 gallons per hour per engine. At 100 per cent (maximum power) with re-heat, it was 3,119 gallons/hour per engine. Sortie time was normally around 45-50 minutes. With re-heat on, practice interceptions could be maintained for 20-25 minutes. For acceleration from a standing start to 60mph, most modern motorcycles will get there first! From 0-250 knots, the Lightning would be at 5,000ft before the motorcycle gets to maximum speed.

English Electric's Chief Test Pilot Wng Cdr 'Bee' Beamont piloting XR754. The aircraft went to the Handling Squadron/A&AEE at Boscombe Down on 3 December 1965 and was issued to 5 Squadron on 2 February 1967. That same year it was modified to F.6 at Warton and went on to serve with 23, 11 and 5 squadrons, flying for the last time on 24 June 1988. It as then used as BDR. (BAC)

Above: T.5 Prototype XM967, which began build on the T.4 production line but was transferred to BAC Filton for conversion to prototype T.5 and was first flown on 29 March 1962. In September that same year the aircraft was displayed at Farnborough. It never saw service, being used for flight-testing throughout its long career, which lasted until early 1974.

Right: Last-minute adjustments to the helmet of a suited up pilot getting ready to fly XG336/C of AFDS at RAF Coltishall. XG336 first flew on 25 August 1959. (via Tony Aldridge)

introduced in 1962. It had a larger, squared-off fin and bigger Avon 301 engines, each giving 12,690lb dry thrust and 16,360lb in re-heat. These aircraft were cleared to Mach 2. The F.3 had the upgraded AI 23b fire control system with greater range and better definition, together with a visual identification mode for interrogating targets [OR.946 with Mk.2 master reference gyro]. But, of course, you do not get anything for nothing, and the extra circuitry for the radar, plus a liquid oxygen system, meant that the gun had to be dispensed with – an unfortunate move which was to be felt later.'

The F.3 made provision for two jettisonable overwing tanks, but these were never fitted. It also introduced the Red Top (originally 'Blue Jay' Mk.4) missile, which was a development of Firestreak but which allowed a head-on attack to be made on supersonic targets.[6] XP693, the first prototype F.3, flew on 16 June 1962, and production models entered service with the RAF when XP695 was delivered to the Central Fighter Establishment at Binbrook in January 1964. 74 Squadron at Leuchars became the first front-line squadron to so equip, in April when it began replacing its F.1s, while 23 Squadron at the same station began replacing its Javelins with the F.3. Towards the end of the year both 56 and 111 Squadrons at Wattisham also began re-equipping with the F.3. Soon to join the F.3 in service was the T.5, a two-seat version of the F.3A.[7]

Lightnings were always been very tight on fuel, especially the F.3 and T.5, which had the more powerful engines and the small ventral tank. To overcome this, the F.6, essentially an F.3 but with modifications for extra range, was introduced. (Originally the F.6 was referred to as the F.3* or F.3A, or the interim Mk.6.) In addition to the 600-gallon ventral tank, provision was made for overwing 260-gallon ferry tanks, and it had an extra crank in the leading edge to give better control throughout the speed range. XP697, the F.6 prototype which flew for the first time on 17 April 1964, was, like the first production series F.6s, an early build F.3 in F.6 configuration. All had the flying characteristics of the new mark, but initially these were not fitted with the arrestor hook for runway cable engagements. (This modification, which entailed re-designing and strengthening the rear fuselage, was introduced later, in 1967, after it was found that the conventional arrestor barriers tended to ride over the Lightning cockpit and rupture the spine, often setting fire to the AVPIN [isopropylnitrate starter fuel]). The first of the sixty-two F.6 production models went to AFDS in November 1965, and shortly afterwards entered front-line service with 5 Squadron at Binbrook. In September 1966 74 Squadron at Leuchars began converting from the F.3 to the F.6, and in 1967 23 Squadron, also at Leuchars, followed suit. On 1 April 1967 11 Squadron at Leuchars began to equip with the F.6, and on 1 May 29 Squadron at Wattisham became the last Lightning squadron to form, when it equipped with the F.3. In August 1967 the final Lightning F.6 for the RAF came off the production line.[9]

By now, all UK front-line squadrons had either F.3s or F.6s, and the F.1As and T.4s were used in the OCU at Coltishall, together with F.3s and T.5s. It was then decided to convert all F.3s to F.6 standard, although in the end only enough aircraft were modified or produced to equip four squadrons (5, 11, 23 and 74). The remaining F.3s were eventually passed to the OCU, as they were an embarrassment to the squadrons due to their poor range endurance compared to the F.6. So the F.3, with its very short range, remained in service. It was decided, however, to rebuild thirty-one of the RAF Germany F.2s and give them the larger, 600-gallon ventral tank, large fin and cranked leading edge, while retaining the smaller Avon engines and the upper guns. These aircraft were redesignated F.2A. They were very popular with the pilots, and many reckoned that they were the most versatile of all the Lightnings.

Dave Seward concludes: 'In 1970, it was decided to fit two Aden cannon into the front of the ventral tank of the F.6s, reducing its fuel volume [by only 640lb] to 535 gallons [because some fuel was carried in a compartment formed in the gun pack]. The F.3, however, remained without the guns. [For peacetime policing sorties, guns can be used

XG336, which became the second P.1B delivered to the AFDS at RAF Coltishall on 19 January 1960, is seen here with a Javelin and a Hunter of the AFDS. XG336 did not remain with the AFDS for long, being loaned to 'A' Squadron A&AEE on 3 November 1960; it then returned to Warton on 23 January 1961 for test work. It last flew on 5 September 1968.

92 Squadron F.2s XN789/G, XN786/C, XN783, XN732 and XN735 getting airborne on full re-heat at Leconfield in 1963. 92 Squadron received its first Lightnings in April 1963 and joined 19 Squadron in the fully operational Leconfield Wing that summer. At the end of 1965 both squadrons became part of 2nd Tactical Air Force in RAF Germany, later becoming the Gütersloh wing. (via Tony Aldridge)

19 Squadron's F.2s ready to leave Yorkshire on 23 September 1965 for the flight to their new posting to Gütersloh in West Germany. Three months later, 92 Squadron's F.2s also left Leconfield for Geilenkirchen, to join them in RAF Germany. (John Hale)

19 Squadron F.2s on the pan at Gütersloh. (John Hale)

to fire warning shots to deter intruders, and in war the gun is the only weapon which is unaffected by electronic or decoy jamming. It is also a very useful thing to have in close combat].[9] We also fitted drop tanks to the Mk.6s to extend the range but, because the long undercarriage retracted outwards, putting them under the wing was impossible; so overwing tanks were installed. Only we British could defy the laws of gravity and prevent fuel from flowing downwards; the cases of non-feeding tanks were legion. Essentially they were a ferry tank, and, with them fitted, the aircraft was limited to subsonic speeds; but some squadrons put them on more less permanently in the quest for more flying hours.

'The aeroplane was superb to fly, a bitch to maintain and always short of fuel. In hindsight we probably wouldn't have wanted it any other way.'

1   XA847, XA853 and XA856.

2   XG307-313 and XG325-337.

3   The first Firestreak missile was successfully flight-tested at Larkhill on 17 January 1953, and the first air launch of a fully guided and controlled round took place at Aberporth, when a Firestreak fired from a Venom destroyed an unmanned radio-controlled Firefly. The first Mk.1 production versions entered service with FAA Sea Venom squadrons in 1958. The infrared guidance system consisted of a cassegrain IR telescope with 15-degree squint angle located behind an eight-faceted all-glass nose-cone. Cooling of the seeker head and onboard electronics was carried out by nitrogen in the launch aircraft. Target lock-on (rear only attack) was effected by two rings of sensors behind the main seeker head. The 50lb warhead was wrapped around the motor tube just forward of the fins.

4   The *Tigers'* second South African CO, A.G. 'Sailor' Malan, having been the first (August 1940-March 1941). Born in East London, John Howe went on to attend the Military College at Robert's Heights (subsequently Voortrekkerhoogte, now Thaba Tschwane) and in 1950 he joined the South African Air Force. In 1951 he flew as an F-51 pilot in 2 '*Cheetah*' Squadron SAAF in Korea, later becoming a flying instructor before coming to Britain and joining the RAF in 1954. His first job was instructing on Vampires, and in 1956 he moved over to the Hunter with 222 Squadron. That same year he did a four-month detachment for the Suez crisis, landing on the beach with Royal Marine Commandos to direct air strikes on the port. In 1959 he went on the day-fighter combat leader course. A short spell of instructing followed before he took over the *Tigers*.

5   Forty-four Lightnings were built as F.2s, thirty-one of them later being modified to F.2A standard with cranked and cambered wing leading edges, a large angular vertical tail; and a 610-gallon ventral tank which was part of the fuselage and thus could not be jettisoned, in place of the earlier 250-gallon jettisonable tank.

6   Originally designated the Firestreak Mk.IV, this collision-course missile, fitted with a new, more rounded seeker head, could lock onto the heat generated by the target aircraft's engines and also the friction hot spots created by its flight path. An improved rocket motor gave a top speed of Mach 3+ with an in-control range of 7 miles. The warhead carried 68lb of explosive. The first Red Top entered RAF service in 1964 with Lightning F.6s of 74 Squadron.

7   The T.5 prototype was produced by converting T.4 XM967, from which it differed externally in having a squared-top fin. Internally, longer cable ducting was used. Jimmy Dell first flew XM967 in its new T.5 configuration on 29 March 1962 at Filton, Bristol. XS417, the first production T.5, flew on 17 July 1964. Twenty-two production T.5 aircraft were built, the first entering service with 226 OCU at Coltishall in April 1965.

8   Inter-squadron rivalry being what it is, out of earshot 74 'Tiger' Squadron were referred to as the 'Ginger Toms', while it was said that when things get hot, 56 'chicken out' – a reference to its badge of the phoenix rising from the ashes! Treble One were universally known as the 'Tremblers', the 'Trembling First', or, if you really wanted to upset them, 'One, Double-One'. 92 Squadron were simply known as 'Ninety-Blue', a reference to their aircraft colour scheme.

9   Tony R. Paxton adds: 'The Lightning was designed as a high-level, fast response interceptor because that was the perceived threat at the time. As a result the aeroplane's guns pointed up by a few degrees, an angle which was exacerbated by the increased angle of attack if flying at a low air speed. The idea was that the Lightning would manoeuvre into a position astern of the target by using the information from the AI 23 onboard radar. The aircraft would then close into gun range keeping below the target's slipstream.

    'However, the actual threat during the service life of the Lightning was predominantly low level and if a low-level target had been engaged as previously described, the Lightning would have hit the ground or the sea long before achieving a gun firing position. The solution was a quite terrifying manoeuvre called the low-level guns attack. The complete intercept was carried out above the target and once astern; the Lightning closed the range maintaining 1,000 feet above and a track slightly to one side. The range continued to close until visual contact was almost lost because the target appeared to be disappearing beneath the Lightning. The technique then was to roll inverted, pull the gunsight through the target, and rapidly roll upright again. By this stage the aeroplane was in a quite steep dive with the gun sight behind the target, now pull the sight onto the "baddie", squeeze off a short burst and carry out whatever manoeuvre was necessary to avoid hitting the ground. Of course, the whole procedure relied upon the enemy holding a steady course throughout – which was highly unlikely. Even if he had I think the chances of success would have been minimal.'

CHAPTER 2

Firebirds, T-Birds, Tigers and Tremblers

Christmas came early for the Central Fighter Establishment in 1959. At the morning briefing at Warton on 23 December, Squadron Leader John Nicholls, an RAF liaison pilot and a member of the test-flying team, had been told that XG334 would be ready to fly to the AFDS at RAF Coltishall, Norfolk. The first of the twenty development batch aircraft for delivery to the RAF would be used for service handling trials. Aware that his Christmas present would perhaps be better delivered with him wearing a Father Christmas outfit, John Nicholls rang around to get one. A Santa suit was duly found and he took off with it for Coltishall. As he taxied in at the famous old Battle of Britain station, all and sundry who had gathered to welcome the momentous arrival could not fail to notice that the pilot was wearing a red hood round his shoulders, a huge white heard and a broad grin! John Nicholls then got a shock, as he recalls:

'I expected that the station commander, Group Captain Bird-Wilson, and a few others would be there, but as I taxied past I noticed this "area" of gold braid! Where had they all come from?! I quickly stuffed all the Father Christmas gear into my very early post-war flight suit, which I was wearing, and climbed out. All the top brass was there, from the AOC and his SASO to "Birdie" and others. Thankfully, nobody mentioned the Father Christmas outfit. I had a cup of coffee and waited for the Meteor 7 that was coming to take me back to Warton. However, one of them asked me how long I had been at Warton. I said, "About a year, Sir."

'"Where were you before that?" he enquired.

'I said, "Fighter Command HQ, Bentley Priory." (Where I had been Project Officer for the Lightning Simulator.)

'He winked and said, "Oh, you're a serving officer then?" Obviously, he had not noticed my rank tapes on the shoulder of my flying suit, which perhaps looked more like a rubber Mac!

'I'd done quite a lot of Lightning flying by that date. I'd been at Warton since May 1959 and had done about forty flights by then. I quickly discovered that flying the Lightning was hugely exhilarating. It was comparable to the F-104 which, as well as the F-100 and the F-86L, I had flown in the USA in 1958. The Lightning was a real kick up the behind, a terribly impressive aircraft for its day. There was never anything quite like it in that respect, as far as I was concerned, until I got a chance to fly the F-15.'

Later that month XG336 became the second P.1B delivered to the AFDS at Coltishall, and on 4 January 1960 the LCS (Lightning Conversion School) was formed at the station. Its job was to train Lightning pilots for the front-line squadrons in Fighter Command. At first, only the more experienced jet pilots with 1,000 flying hours or more were selected to fly the new aircraft, and some of these were retained as instructors before the qualifications were relaxed to include younger pilots on their first squadron tour. The initial training was accomplished with various systems aids

Line-up of 74 '*Tiger*' Squadron's F.1s at Coltishall, where the squadron was the first to equip with the Lightning in the summer of 1960. (BAC)

and a flight simulator, and because the LCU had no Lightnings of its own they were borrowed from AFDS and later 74 Squadron.

Flight Lieutenant Bruce Hopkins was the last of the original group to join the AFDS at Coltishall, at the beginning of February 1960. He recalls: 'The CO was Wing Commander David Simmonds, and Major Al Moore, an American on exchange, was the A Flight commander. The group also included Flight Lieutenant Peter Collins, an ex-Javelin pilot, and Flight Lieutenant Ken Goodwin and Flight Lieutenant Ron Harding, who were ex-Hunter men like myself. There were only three Development Batch Lightnings at this time.[1] Our role was to carry out trials to develop tactics and procedures for the aircraft and its weapon systems. We had Hunter 6s for target and chase work and a Meteor 7 for OR.946 instrumentation (later fitted to the Lightning F.2), which AFDS was trialling for the CFE. We also had two Javelin FAW.Mk.6 aircraft for target work. My first Lightning solo was in XG336 at Leconfield (the runway at Coltishall was being re-surfaced) on 16 May 1960. The Lightning was an awesome aircraft, totally different to the Hunter. For a Hunter pilot like me it was a long climb to the cockpit. On my first two trips I had difficulty in keeping the nose up high enough to get the right climb angle to climb at Mach 0.9 (400 knots to begin with). The performance was out of this world.

'On the early sorties we were chased by the Hunter, whose pilot would get airborne, then orbit at 10,000ft waiting for the Lightning to take off. It took the Lightning just 3½ minutes (with re-heat, under 2½ minutes) to reach 36,000ft, easily passing the Hunter in the climb! At height the Lightning pilot would watch the Hunter still climbing underneath. (The Lightning climb angle was 22 degrees without re-heat or 40 degrees with re-heat.) Once in position the Hunter, who was there to observe and to help out in an emergency, would chase the Lightning. As the Lightning accelerated to Mach 1.6 (our maximum cleared speed at that time because of the problems of directional stability) the Hunter got left behind, of course, and we would pick him up on the way back. We would then recover and land.

'We developed intercept techniques. Don't forget that the Lightning was the first RAF single-seat aircraft with intercept radar. We would film the radarscope pictures, and the navigators on the AFDS Javelins would advise us on the radar techniques. The radar handgrip controller had fourteen controls, so it took some time getting used to it. Radar profiles were practiced in the simulator. Another important consideration at this time was fuel. Every time we fired off into the blue in this aircraft, which had so little fuel, we became so fuel-conscious. How could we minimize the fuel use? As far as possible we did not use re-heat.

'Then we got five F.1s[2] for 74 Squadron – delivered to us at Leconfield. I flew XM135 on 13 June 1960. On 11 July I flew XM165 to Coltishall, where it became the first 74 Squadron aircraft, with the four other AFDS F.1s. When I arrived I was directed to the 74 Squadron flight line in this shiny, brand-new aircraft. After I had climbed down the ladder there was no "Thank you". Their only comment was, "Is it serviceable then?"'[3] There was little difference between the DBs [Development Batch aircraft] and the F.1s. They just cleaned up the cockpit a little. The first re-heat take-off was quite an experience. The performance was incredible. Reheat, though, was not necessary. The take-off performance was perfectly adequate, so we didn't use it as a rule.'

Early that July the conversion team at Coltishall had the task of converting 74 'Tiger' Squadron, the first front-line Lightning squadron. Pilots had to undertake a five-day aviation medicine course at RAF Upwood. On their return to Coltishall, a further seven days of lectures on such subjects as aircraft systems and emergency drills were followed by the simulator phase.

'At this point', recalls Ken Goodwin, 'I had nearly thirty hours on type; Squadron Leader John Robertson [who now commanded the team] had one or two and the remainder almost nil. However, we did have a set of those multi-coloured display boards, pilots' notes from English Electric and the confidence of the blind leading the blind. The conversion process consisted of lectures for a month. This was followed by a first solo (there were no two-seaters) which included a good brief before the instructor got airborne in a Hunter chase. Having wound on about 500 knots and timed a pass over the field nicely with the student's brakes off, the instructor kept the two aircraft in near proximity up to about 25,000ft. Thereafter, with much corner-cutting and help from Neatishead radar, we could join company again for the descent.

'I suppose the main objectives of the chase were firstly to tell the convertee if his nose-wheel was still down after selecting gear up – a fairly commonplace occurrence with new pilots being a little behind the rapid acceleration after take-off, thus allowing aerodynamic pressure to out-do the hydraulics. Secondly, to advise generally from close proximity (better psychologically than a remote ground station) on the unexpected or unfamiliar and, lastly, to offer an opinion on fire warnings – we had frequent spurious and spurious real warnings. Having done a good job with 74 – they flew a Diamond Nine with yours truly as No.9 and the solo aeros spot at the 1961 Paris Air Show – our little team and its boards went to Wattisham to convert 56 and 111 Squadrons.'[4]

Anthony 'Bugs' Bendell reported to the Air Fighting Development Squadron (AFDS) at RAF Coltishall in mid-July 1960: 'No.74 Squadron, the resident front-line squadron and the first to re-equip with the Lightning, was due to receive its aircraft in August. But the AFDS – the trials unit responsible for developing new fighter tactics and for the operational evaluation of armament – had already taken delivery of four Lightning F.1s. The Lightning presented a major challenge. It was the RAF's first supersonic, night/all-weather interceptor. In speed alone it doubled the performance of the Hunter. But more than that, with its combination of AI 23 (airborne interception radar) and Firestreak air-to-air guided weapons the Lightning had a genuine interception capability against high-performance bomber aircraft. The F.1 was also fitted with two 30mm Aden cannon, mounted at shoulder level aft of the cockpit. Alternative weapons packs, consisting of additional guns or unguided air-to-air rockets, could be fitted in place of Firestreaks. At that time opinion within Fighter Command was sharply divided as to the need for gun armament on modern fighters. Missile

Squadron Leader (later AVM) John F.G. Howe, a South African by birth, who had flown SAAF F-86 Sabres in the Korean War, (after a short spell of instructing) took command of the *Tigers*, the first operational squadron in Fighter Command to be equipped with the Lightning, in February 1960. (BAC)

aficionados claimed that only guided missiles would be effective in future air combat, while those who supported the gun – rightly, in my opinion – insisted that it was still the best short-range, multi-shot weapon available. But for the time being, the main thrust of the Lightning weapons' development was limited to the Firestreak ... With the introduction of the Lightning, air defence was at last being given an appropriate degree of priority. Many fighter experts thought that this was long overdue.

'At Coltishall I spent eleven hours in the simulator before flying my first Lightning sortie. There was no dual Lightning, so the first flight was also a first solo and thus it was very exciting. Even at idling power I had to ride the brakes to curb the acceleration. The main tyre pressures were a rock-hard 350lb psi but the long-stroke undercarriage smoothed out the bumps. In the Lightning F1, it was not necessary to use re-heat for take-off; even in cold power, nose-wheel lift-off at 150 knots occurred well within ten seconds of brake release. As one wag on 74 Squadron was later heard to comment, "I was with it all the way, until I released the brakes on take-off."

'As the first RAF station to be equipped with the Lightning, the morale at Coltishall was sky high, and the mess provided a lively social centre. The Norfolk Broads are very attractive, with many historic inns; few officers at Coltishall will ever forget the best pint of draught Worthington "E" in Norfolk, served at the Fruiterer's Arms, just off the market square in Norwich. It was a hard-drinking, high-living, fast life.

'In December 1960 56 Squadron received its Lightning aircraft. Treble One's first Lightning, F.1A (XM185) was delivered in March 1961. The F.1A's performance was similar to the aircraft at Coltishall, but it had several worthwhile refinements. Instead of two ten-channel VHF radios, the F.1A was fitted with the latest UHF radio with nineteen preset channels and with nearly 2,000 manually dialled frequencies available. Another valuable addition was a rain-removal system: hot air tapped from the engines could be blown in front of the windscreen to keep it clear of precipitation. The F.1 also had the necessary plumbing for flight refuelling, although refuelling probes were not fitted to our aircraft until February 1963.

Line-up of 74 'Tiger' Squadron at RAF Coltishall in 1961. (BAC)

'The black livery of our Hunters was inappropriate for the Lightning, so we had to redesign the squadron markings. There we several suggestions, but my proposal for a stylised bolt of black lightning outlined in yellow was eventually chosen for the fuselage. The boss decided that the motif on the fin, consisting of crossed sword and seaxes superimposed on a yellow Cross of Jerusalem, should be copied from the official squadron badge.

'The squadron's re-equipment was a long, slow business. Lightning aircraft were delivered at the rate of one a week, so it was mid-July 1961 before we reached our full complement of twelve aircraft. The equipment was not helped by the loss of XM185 on 28 June 1961. Following a services hydraulic failure, Pete Ginger was unable to lower the undercarriage and, since a wheels-up landing was definitely not recommended, he had no choice other than to bail out. The Mark 4BS seat was capable of safe ejection from ground level at 90 knots, but Pete wisely decided to climb to 8,000ft before making a copybook ejection. A few moments later, hanging in his parachute, he was pleased too that one of the chaps had come to see if he was OK. The pilot seemed to be cutting things a bit fine, though – in fact he was going to pass uncomfortably close. Pete then noticed that the passing aircraft had no cockpit canopy and no pilot – it was the aircraft he had just abandoned. After three more close encounters with XM185, Pete finally landed. His aircraft eventually crashed in a field near Lavenham. That evening a group of squadron pilots was having a drink in the Swan when they overheard one of the local farmhands shooting an incredible line about dropping tools and running to avoid this aircraft before it crashed on top of him. It seemed an unlikely tale, but it was enough to keep him in free beer for the rest of the evening. Some days later, the RAF salvage team dug up the ventral tank, which marked XM185's first contact with terra firma, to reveal the farmhand's hoe buried beneath it.'[5]

The Lightning first appeared on the aerobatic stage in 1960, when the *Tigers* of 74 Squadron, led by the CO Squadron Leader John F.G. Howe, introduced their routine of formation aerobatics. As from July only four aircraft were available and by the end of August the squadron had increased its Lightning complement to seven, but the *Tigers* were soon training hard for their new role, as John Howe recalls:

Right: 74 Squadron's F.1s led by Squadron Leader John Howe practising a Diamond Nine formation over Norfolk in 1961. A nine-ship formation was flown at Farnborough 1961, when the first public demonstration of nine Lightnings rolling in tight formation occurred. In 1962 the *Tigers* became the official Fighter Command aerobatic team. (BAC)

Below: XM165 was the first F.1 taken on charge at Coltishall, on 29 June 1960. (BAC)

'We started flying high-speed, low-level runs (just subsonic, at about 200ft) in formation, but this put the Lightning airframe under more than normal pressures. One day during that summer, 'Lefty' Wright was leading a box formation at Coltishall when the fin came off Jim Burns' aircraft. I watched from the tower as bits sprinkled to the ground. Jim now had no fin and no radio either, so I told 'Lefty' to close in and try to tell Jim of the problem. Should Jim now eject or land? The weather was perfect and the wind straight down the runway so he was cleared to land. He did and without any problems. Thereafter he was always known as 'Finless Jim'.[6] Unfortunately the C-in-C now ruled out high-speed, low-level runs in formation so we flew high-speed, low-level in battle formation (spread out).'

Incidents still occurred, however. On another occasion Flight Lieutenant Tim Nelson's drag chute failed to deploy on landing. Mindful on the restrictions on braking, he put the Lightning into full afterburner to go around again. Just as he rotated, the chute deployed and it was immediately engulfed by the re-heat. As every Lightning pilot knew, landing without a brake chute was a hazardous undertaking that often would result in the brakes being burned out, but this time Coltishall's long runway and the close support of the Fire Section carried the day and Nelson was able to land safely.[7]

The *Tigers* performed before the public for the first time at Duxford on 14 August, at Little Rissington on the 28th and at Stradishall on the 31st. By the end of August, John Howe, for instance, had just eight hours on Lightnings in his logbook! Beginning on 5 September he led his formation of four in fly-pasts at the Farnborough Air Show each day, except one when the weather was too bad, and the team finished the month with a Battle of Britain display at Coltishall on the 16th. Before each display or rehearsal, the CO would brief the pilots who were to fly in the formation and explain the programme. For example, when the four-aircraft display was given:

'Tiger Black, four aircraft to do formation aerobatics over the airfield. R/T checks will be on Four Romeo, India and Four Quebec, followed by a drill start-up. Taxi at 100-yard intervals and line up on the runway in echelon. We'll use 80 per cent rpm holding on the brakes and roll at three-second intervals for maximum re-heat take-off. Aim to use the same pull-up point for an 80-degree climb. I'll call cancelling re-heat and use 82 per cent rpm to give us 300 knots at 6,000ft, join up in box. The display will start with the fly-past in "Swan" with wheels and flaps down. We shall clean up the aircraft in front of the crowd to move into the rest or the display. No.4 remember to call "Clear!" for the change into line astern and Nos 2 and 3 guard against dropping low in the very steep turn. Rejoin in box for the run in and two-way break; we shall fly synchronized circuits leading to the ten-second stream landing. Any questions?'

With such a radically new and complex aircraft as the Lightning, there was a corresponding change in the technique of formation flying: the physical and mental strains imposed on pilots flying high-speed aircraft in close formation are intense. With a power/weight ratio of roughly 1:1 there was an immense reserve of power, and the team leader had to use it with discretion, bearing in mind that the rest of the formation must from time to time use more power to maintain their position. Although the Lightning was a Mach 2 aircraft, aerobatics in close formation, only five or six feet apart, could be flown at 450mph – about one-third of the speed which the Lightning would achieve in level flight on an operational mission. Like the Hunter, the Lightning was an extremely manoeuvrable aircraft, and despite its great size and weight was capable of astonishing low-speed turns, even when the re-heat of the two Avon turbojets was not being used. The tight turning qualities of the Lightning permitted a display to be given in a small area of sky, so that the public could have no difficulty in keeping the formation in view.

The two engines of the Lightning caused greater jet wash than the single engine of the Hunter, and in formations the aircraft had to be stepped down to a slightly greater extent to avoid interference. The rapid rate of rotation in a turn meant that the pilot at the rear had to fly a slightly longer flight-path to avoid the jet wash and still hold his place. In a tight turn the Lightning was put onto its side, the power stepped up and the nose pulled back to increase lift; and the aircraft would go round smoothly.

At higher speeds an aircraft like the Lightning is surrounded by an envelope of disturbance which must be avoided by other aircraft in the formation. The 60-degree swept wing of the Lightning made it a little more difficult for the pilot to maintain accurate formation than the Hunter, because he could not see his own wingtips. Accordingly, when flying in echelon, he lined up on the trailing edge of the aileron of the adjacent aircraft. Judgement of lateral separation comes only from experience, and constant practice is necessary before pilots can hold their aircraft in a tight and accurate formation. Each man lines up a point on his wing leading edge with a point on the fuselage of the next aircraft and after lengthy practice can accurately estimate his distance. The leader has no fixed point on which to fly. He concentrates on placing his aircraft in the best possible position to let the crowd see the show, timing to a split second each stage of the flight, and the rest of the team watch him constantly and are alert for his radio instructions ('Pulling up for wing-over starboard. Pulling more g. Taking off bank and relaxing back-pressure. Pulling up for roll to port and rolling – NOW!').

1960 proved an auspicious year for 74 Squadron in more ways than one. When John Howe discovered that an old friend from the Korean War, Lieutenant Colonel Ed Rackham, was commanding the 79th Tactical Fighter Squadron – the *Tigers* – at Woodbridge, they got together to form the first of the now famous 'Tiger meets'. The *Tigers* finished their first year as the Lightning aerobatic display team with a fly-by over all the fighter stations in East Anglia on 23 December.

In the new year, 1961, the *Tigers* received more Lightnings – enough for a Diamond Nine formation, a solo aerobatic display pilot and spares – and work-up began in earnest for the Paris Air Show scheduled for 3 and 4 June. By the end of April all of the 74 Squadron pilots were operational on the Lightning and cleared to fly both by night and day. During that summer operational training had to be combined with displays and publicity events, as the RAF was eager to introduce the new aircraft to the public. John Howe's team of *Tigers* was a mixture of youth and experience. Flight Lieutenant Maurice J. Williams (30) and Flight Lieutenant Alan W.A. 'Lefty' Wright (30) were the two flight commanders. The two deputy flight commanders were Flight Lieutenant 'Finless Jim' Burns (26) and Flight Lieutenant Jeremy J.R. Cohu (24). The son of an air vice-marshal, Cohu had converted to Lightnings in 1960 after flying Hunters in 74 Squadron at Horsham St Faith. The rest of the team comprised Flight Lieutenants Tim Nelson (25) (the adjutant), George P. Black (29), Edward J. Nance (25), Jeremy E. Brown (25), Martin Bee (23) and Michael J. Dodd (26). The Flying Officers were David Maxwell Jones (27), Jacques W. Kleynhans (33), Peter J. Phillips (24), T. Vaughan Radford (23), an admirer of Picasso, Graham Sutherland and Mike S. Cooke, who had converted to the Lightning in June 1960. Kleynhans, like his CO, was a native of South Africa. Sutherland's ability to paint abstracts in oils was put to good use between flights, painting the squadron crest on the main hangar.

The solo slot was flown by Flight Lieutenant Ken Goodwin of the LCU, whom John Howe rated as one of the most fantastic low-level acrobatic pilots he'd ever seen. The *Tigers* performed wing-overs with nine F.1As, the largest number ever seen publicly together and rolls with four. Between times Ken Goodwin, having detached himself at the end of the nine-man demonstration, put in solo aerobatics, which included Derry turns and low inversions. It was all a stunning success. Back home again, the *Tigers* displayed at Farnborough in September. *Flight* reported:

'Nothing in the show exuded more sheer power than the three-second interval stream take-off by the nine Lightnings of 74 Squadron, beating down the runway in a sustained blast of brown dust and stomach-shaking noise. As the rear machines were taking off, the leaders were climbing an invisible, vertical wall over Laffans Plain. All were airborne in 35 seconds. [After the sixteen blue Hunters of 92 Squadron] the Lightnings were on stage, smoking in towards the airfield in arrowhead formation, changing to Diamond nine and including wing-overs and [in tight formation] a roll in their programme. A split into three echelons preceded the final run-in and break for landing.'

More displays followed, on Battle of Britain day at Biggin Hill and Coltishall and at Cranwell on 21 October. Two days later, at Leconfield, they performed for the Queen Mother, and on the 24th John Howe brought his team back to Coltishall to bring the curtain down on a highly successful season. Persuaded to land first he was surprised, then delighted, to see the other eleven Lightnings fly over him in 'H-Howe' formation!

In December 1961 John Howe left to take up a new post at Fighter Command HQ at Bentley Priory, and on the 12th Squadron Leader Peter G. Botterill assumed command of 74 Squadron. He did not get to fly a Lightning, however, until 26 March 1962, because the early Lightnings had all been grounded pending modification and all pilots had to use the flight simulator before being permitted to fly a Lightning again. By early May sufficient Lightnings were modified, and that same month an advanced party left Norfolk for Scandinavia to demonstrate the Lightning at the trade fair and at other locations. (The *Tigers'* visit paved the way for eight Draakens from two wings of the Swedish Air Force based at Norrköping and Uppsala to visit Coltishall on a five-day exchange in 1961). On their return the *Tigers* began work on their full display routine, because 92 Squadron's Hunters began converting to the Lightning and the *Tigers* became the only official Fighter Command acrobatic team. Work-up began for a full aerobatic display with five Lightnings at Upavon on 16 June.[8] At Farnborough the team brought down the curtain with an unforgettable diamond fly-past of seven Lightnings and sixteen Hunters.

Beginning in December 1960 the Lightning F.1A, which was fitted with a port-mounted probe for in-flight refuelling, was issued to 56 and 111 Squadrons at Wattisham.[9] In 1961 a joint RAF/USAF exercise was held to demonstrate the compatibility of the Valiant tanker with American fighters and fighter-bombers, and of the American KB-50J tanker with Valiant, Vulcan, Victor and Javelin receivers. Although the Lightning F.1As did not participate, the valuable close co-operation between the two nations did have benefits for the Lightning force the following year, as Squadron Leader Dave Seward, OC 56 Squadron, recalls:

'Now, when the F.1A first entered service, each squadron was given various development tasks to perform. On 56 Squadron we were ordered in December 1961 to develop air-to-air refuelling techniques for the Lightning force using Vickers Valiant tankers. The timetable directed that during January-July 1962 we would work up six pilots in the AAR role, and in July send two Lightnings to Cyprus with tanker support. Full squadron deployment to Cyprus was scheduled for October 1962.

'This sounded OK, but over the period August-December 1961 we experienced odd, unpleasant happenings with the Lightning. You would be flying along in cruise power when the re-heat fire warning lights would illuminate without having re-heat selected. As the only method of extinguishing re-heat fires was to select re-heat and shut down the engine, it was rather thought-provoking if both re-heat lights were on without being in re-heat, and the only alternative seemed to be to become a glider! Some pilots shut an engine down, and in some cases the fire indication went out. To their cost, others hoped it was a spurious warning. We lost one of the AFDS (Air Fighting Development Squadron) aircraft when the back end burned off and in another incident, all was revealed when an aircraft landed with the re-heat area on fire. The cause was traced to hydraulic pipes (which were aluminium rather than high-tensile steel) chafing inside the fuselage, causing the hydraulic fluid to pour back along the inside of the rear fuselage and swirl around the back of the jet pipes where it caught fire in the re-heat area.

74 'Tiger' Squadron pilots step out for the camera. *From left to right:* Squadron Leader John Howe, CO; Jerry Cohu; 'Lefty' Wright; Ted Nance; and Mike Cooke. (AVM John Howe Coll.)

A ground crewman guides F.1A XM171/R of 56 Squadron back to its hardstand outside Wattisham's No.3 hangar with the aid of illuminated 'wands'. This Lightning first flew on 20 September 1960 and went to the A&AEE for type evaluation and handling trials. It joined 56 Squadron on 28 February 1961. The aircraft was re-coded 'A' when the squadron adopted the *'Firebird'* colour scheme in March 1963. (MoD)

'Thus in January 1962 it was decided to replace and re-route the hydraulic system in all aircraft, and at Wattisham 56 Squadron and 111 Squadron [and 74 Squadron at Coltishall were modified. It was going to be a four-week job for the lot, six weeks at the outside; so plans were made to have the air-to-air refuelling ground school in January and start flying in February. Unfortunately, the hydraulic modification was not completed in four weeks, but dragged on for sixteen weeks. However, Fighter Command was adamant that two Lightnings had to be at Akrotiri, Cyprus, in July and that the squadron would be there by October!

'It was purely fortuitous that at Wattisham we had a social relationship with the American 55th Tactical Fighter Squadron, 20th Tactical Fighter Wing, at RAF Wethersfield. Over drinks one Friday I mentioned our problems to their commanding officer. I remarked that the flight refuelling system on their F-100F Super Sabres, although being on the opposite side (starboard) to the Lightning (port), was basically similar, and what a good idea it would be if we learned our flight refuelling on the F-100. Things must have been desperate, because on the following Wednesday we had permission from both Fighter Command and HQ USAFE for six pilots from 56 Squadron to fly flight-refuelling sorties in the F-100 using the KB-50J Superfortress tankers [of the 420th Air Refuelling Squadron]. Although the KB-50 flew at 180-200 knots indicated, and probes on the Lightning were angled to squarely hit a Valiant basket, the refuelling went remarkably well. Front Aldburgh to the Humber we did dry, then 'wet' proddings. The USAF would have a KB-50 on station off Aldburgh flying a racetrack pattern and would listen out on a particular frequency. When a chap needed fuel he would call using his call sign and 'book in' and the fuel was then attributed to the squadron. In the half hour to go before the KB-50 had to dump excess fuel, refuelling during this time was free. They'd all come in then because the squadron would not get charged for the fuel.

'Two of us were up one day on PIs and I heard this guy say that he had half an hour to go and was throwing away the fuel. We gave the call sign for Wethersfield, which was "Trout, Three-Five and Three-Six". "Roger, you're clear in astern," he replied. He asked, "What type of aircraft?" We said [untruthfully] "Foxtrot 100"! He said, "Roger". We flew in, lowered the flaps and took on the fuel from the KB-50. Thinking about it afterwards, we knew we were taking on JP4 and our Avons were not tuned for AVTUR, but we kept that to ourselves (our engineers were worried about the lubrication of the fuel pumps, but we had no problems). We each received six tanking sorties in the F-100 (needless to say, the Americans all had trips in the T.4 Lightning), before starting our tanking with Valiants on 13 June.

'The method we used, as recommended by both English Electric and the USAF, was to position the Lightning about 30 yards behind the Valiant and synchronize speeds, with the Valiant at about 250 knots indicated, at 30,000 or 36,000ft. We then set the No. 1 throttle at about 94 [per cent] and set up an overtake speed of about 5 knots, using the No. 2 throttle to vary the speed. You lined up with the basket and edged forward, not looking at the basket, which is going up and down about 3ft, but getting what is called a 'sight picture' of the Valiant and flying steadily in. As the basket passes the nose of the Lightning it is 'trapped' and if your line-up has been good, your probe goes into the centre of the basket and you make a good contact. You then move forward into a close formation line astern, keeping a slight bow in the hose and when contact and positioning is confirmed by the tanker, he passes the fuel to on. Fly too low and the hose becomes taut and the probe could break. (You could also break the probe by being too far left or right.) You could also break a probe having too high an overtake speed and thus hit the basket too hard. On the other hand, if you are too cautious and hit the basket slow with too low an overtake, you will get a soft contact and end up being sprayed with fuel or, in extreme circumstances, have your engines flame out with fuel pouring into the intake.

F.1A XM179 (right) and XM178 (left) of 56 Squadron taking off from Wattisham in 1963. 56 Squadron converted to the Lightning F.1 at Wattisham, Suffolk, in December 1960, and it was the first squadron to receive the F.1A, the full complement being received by March 1961. XM179 was lost in a collision near the station on 6 June 1963. (BAe)

'A trick in getting at least the vertical position right was to fly in with the fin tip just "burbling" along the bottom of the Valiant's jet efflux – a technique that we were to regret somewhat later. Still, all went well and the schedule was met. We simulated the trip to Cyprus by going twice around the UK and got the first two aircraft (myself and John Mitchell, attached from AFDS) to Cyprus on time, flight refuelling to Akrotiri on 23 July (Exercise *Tambour*).'

The second detachment, *Forthright One*, involving six other 56 Squadron pilots, went ahead on 6 October 1962, as Flight Lieutenant Bob Offord recalls:

'We went in pairs, three tankers per pair, and I flew XM153. Jerry Cohu and I flew at Mach 1.7 until Crete, where we carried out our seventh and last refuelling. In Cyprus the Turkish inhabitants took one look at our red aircraft and thought, "Hooray, here comes the Turkish air force!" We spent about eight weeks in Cyprus, carrying out low-level PIs, one against one and the odd Canberra at 60,000ft from Akrotiri's four resident squadrons. We'd pull up to 36,000ft and zoom up to in excess of 50,000ft. The radar stations at Cape Gata and Mount Olympus also aided us. We could not do low-level work in the UK but the Mediterranean is much calmer than the North Sea and the radars could better see. The AI 23 was good for its day but at high level it was difficult to see the Lightning beyond 25 miles on radar and even worse at low level, where it was down to just five or six miles because of the sea returns. Most days we worked in the mornings and swam in the afternoons. These were the best days of Lightning operations. We returned to the UK in April, and then spent the summer exercising and tanking, part of it at Coltishall for three to four weeks while Wattisham's runways were repaired.'

In February 1962, meanwhile, Flight Lieutenant 'Bugs' Bendell finally got his chance to work up a solo Lightning display.

'Les Swart of 56 Squadron and Ken Goodwin of the Lightning Conversion Squadron, who had provided demonstrations in 1961, had moved on. No. 74 Squadron was still providing the formation aerobatic team, but the solo Lightning slot was now vacant. I always believed that solo demonstration flying required thorough professionalism. Any fool could beat up an airfield in a high-performance aircraft, but it needed

56 Squadron F.1A
taking off on full
re-heat from RAF
Wattisham. (BAC)

practice and precise judgment to put together an impressive demonstration ... It was easy to impress people with the Lightning but the show had to be repeatable. Maurice Williams, a potential Lightning display pilot on 74 Squadron, once lost control while attempting a Derry turn at 1,500ft over the airfield and flicked into a flat spin. Maurice immediately engaged re-heat – there was usually a three-second delay before they lit up – and more by luck than good judgment Maurice just managed to recover control before hitting the ground. The aircraft was so low, the flames from the re-heats set fire to the grass on the airfield.

'In June I was one member of a three-man board of inquiry into a fire incident on an aircraft [XM176] flown by Squadron Leader John Rogers – OC, 56 Squadron. The Lightning's fire and overheat warnings were displayed on a standard warning panel, which also triggered klaxon bells and flashing red attention-getters. There was never any question of missing a fire warning; in fact, the pilot's first action was usually to cancel the klaxon bells before dealing with the emergency. Unfortunately, the Lightning had gained a reputation for fire warnings, both real and spurious. The fire sensors, running through the engine bays and jet pipe areas, would detect any local increase in temperature, caused either by fire or simply by a hot gas leak. When the source of heat was removed, the warning light would extinguish and the system would automatically reset. Attempts to find the cause of warning often disturbed the engines and, in the process, destroyed the evidence. But in John Rogers' incident [on 14 February 1961] the fire had re-ignited in dispersal, indicating a genuine fire rather than an illusive hot gas leak. An expert investigator from the accident investigation branch at RAE Farnborough eventually proved that excess fuel trapped on top of the ventral tank had been sucked back through fuselage drain-holes on the hot jet pipe, causing an intense but fortunately brief fire. This positive finding did little to restore confidence in the Lightning's warning system, and we continued to experience fire warnings, often for no apparent reason.

'September [1962] was a busy month. To mark the anniversary of the Battle of Britain I flew displays at Biggin Hill and Wyton. Then on 18 September I did a show at Wattisham for the first half of a Royal College of Defence Studies visit. The weather was poor, with a thick layer of haze reducing the horizontal visibility to less than a mile. But, as is so often the case in fog, the vertical visibility was better and I managed to do a complete display. The spectators were hard-pressed to keep sight of the Lightning. I landed from a high visual circuit, much to the chagrin of a pair of 41 Squadron Javelins that had been obliged to land off a GCA approach.

F.1A XM179 of 56 Squadron pulls in to refuel from a Valiant tanker. 56 Squadron began perfecting the art of air-to-air refuelling in early 1962, training first on USAFE F-100Ds with KC-97s as tankers, before tanking from Valiants.

'Two days later I was scheduled to repeat the performance for the remainder of the course and a visiting group of officers from the RAF College of Air Warfare. No problems with weather on this occasion – there had been a complete change of air mass and it was a much colder day. I usually concluded my show with a high-speed run in front of the crowd. With both engines at maximum re-heat, the Lightning's silent approach, followed by a thunderous departure with flames issuing from the jet pipes, all made for an impressive finale. There was just one small problem. In the F.1A, re-heat ignition could not be guaranteed at speeds above 350 knots, although once they were lit the re-heats were stable throughout the speed range. Because of this I always started my high-speed run from a high wing-over, engaging re-heat at about 300 knots. When the burners lit up I would dive for the runway and level out fifty feet or so above the ground. The Lightning accelerated extremely rapidly. It was not possible to monitor the instruments closely at an altitude of fifty feet, but my speed abeam the tower was usually about 600 knots. On this particular day, because of the low ambient air temperature, the engines were more efficient than usual and the local speed of sound was relatively low. The aircraft was moving very fast as I went past the tower. I thought Air Traffic Control were joking when they called on the R/T to say that they no longer needed air conditioning. But after landing the boss met me at the aircraft and told me to report immediately to OC Ops – with my hat on I was in deep trouble. Apparently my high-speed run had caused extensive damage to the tower and surrounding buildings.

'Wing Commander Bill Howard's office was in a single-storey prefabricated building alongside the tower. It appeared undamaged from the outside, but that was deceptive. Actually, the roof had been lifted a fraction and the walls had been nudged sideways. All the internal doors were hanging askew, and the pictures hung away from the walls rather than on them. The office was lit by neon tubes, normally suspended from the

F.1A XM183/N and XM178/H of 56 Squadron about to begin in-flight refuelling from a Vickers Valiant. The loss of the Valiant force in 1965 left the RAF with no tanking facilities, so the USAF made available three KC-135s over a six- to nine-month period for much-needed in-flight refuelling practice.

ceiling on chains, but now all the chains had jumped off their hooks and the lights dangled on the ends of their electric flex. I had to part these pillars of light to get in. Bill was sitting behind his desk, covered in white dust, a ghost of his former self. The only blue thing about him was his hat, which had been in a desk drawer when I flew over.

'He looked up as I came in, and, with a perfectly straight face, said with a nasal twang "I suppose you think that's funny!" I had to admit that I did. But apologies were in order; and he suggested I start with local control. The tower was a shambles, at least six huge double-plate-glass windows had been shattered and there was a stiff breeze blowing across the controller's desk. The staff, who were busy sweeping up, were taking it all in good spirits.

'Next I went to apologize to the duty met. man, whom I found sitting huddled on a stool in one corner of the Met office. The room looked as dusty and dilapidated as Bill Howard's office. The Met man appeared to be suffering from battle fatigue.

'"I served throughout the war;" he said, "and I have never been so frightened in all my life. And what about my barograph?" He pointed to the sensitive pressure instrument that traces a record of the barometric pressure on a rotating drum. The drum was still rotating but the pen was bent up against the top stop.

'In sympathetic tones I suggested that the Queen would probably buy him a new one.

'"Maybe," he snapped, "but she won't buy me a new raincoat."

'The coat in question had been hanging on the back of the door; but now it was pinned in place by a large splinter of glass.

'I apologised profusely and returned to the safety of the squadron crew room.

'It was not long before another message came from on high. I was to change into best blue and be "on the mat" in the station commander's office, immediately if not sooner. This was getting serious – the station commander, Group Captain Simmonds, was my old boss from the AFDS. I had always got on quite well with him before, but this promised to be a rather one-sided interview.

'And so it proved. After a stiff haranguing which seemed to go on for ever, he ordered me to report to the Air Ministry the following day – the implication being that I would be immediately posted. He finished by demanding. "What do you think about that?"

The F.1A was fitted with a port-mounted probe for in-flight refuelling, and it fell to 56 Squadron to pioneer this technique in the Lightning squadrons. Squadron Leader Dave Seward (seen here in XM179, taking on fuel from Valiant XD816 during in-flight refuelling trials prior to Exercise '*Tambour*' to Akrotiri on 23 July 1962) and his pilots began perfecting the art of air-to-air refuelling in 1962, training first on USAF F-100Ds with Boeing KC-97s as tankers, before air-refuelling in earnest with Valiant tankers. (via Dave Seward)

Now a staff tour in London was just about the worst fate I could imagine, and frankly I thought it was uncalled for. So I let fly, pointing out all the reasons for it being unfair.

David Simmonds burst out laughing and explained that I was being called forward for briefing prior to an exchange tour with the USAF at Nellis Air Force Base in Nevada.

'That evening in the bar they told me how the high-speed run had appeared from the ground. The pilots who had been watching from outside the squadron knew that something was amiss when they saw the grass on the airfield being flattened behind my aircraft. A high-ranking army officer had been heard to comment, as he dusted glass splinters from his uniform and surveyed his badly cut toe-caps, "I will say this, when the Air Force put on a show they don't spare any expense."

'In addition to the damage sustained by the tower, two other prefabricated buildings alongside were rendered unfit for habitation. Overnight I became something of a celebrity among the local schoolboys, who would point me out, "That's Bugs – he's the guy that broke all those windows ..."'

On 5 February 1963 'Bugs' Bendell went to Buckingham Palace for an investiture, and was presented with the AFC by Her Majesty Queen Elizabeth the Queen Mother. Later that month the squadron started flight-refuelling training on the Valiant tanker.

'For me, air refuelling was a unique experience. In simple formation flying the pilot must at all times avoid the other aircraft, but with flight refuelling he deliberately makes contact. I flew one sortie on the Valiant, which was all useful experience for my forthcoming tour in the States, but the bulk of the training was reserved for the other members of the squadron who were due to deploy to Cyprus.

'In March I flew tactical checks with the pilots on "B" Flight. The Squadron's first two-seat Lightning T.4 had been delivered in October, and had since been involved in acceptance checks. My last flight on Treble One was a dual low-level aerobatic demonstration for the benefit of Alan Garside, who had volunteered to take over the solo aerobatic slot. Some months later Alan was tragically killed during a display.

'My tour on Treble One had lasted twenty-seven months; during that time I had accumulated barely 270 hard-won hours on the Lightning. On any other aircraft this would have accounted for little, but Lightning flying was special. The experience I gained on Treble One would stand me in good stead throughout the rest of my flying career.

The *Firebirds*, led by their CO Squadron Leader Dave Seward, line up for the camera at Wattisham. In 1963 56 Squadron – the *Firebirds* – became the second of the official Fighter Command Lightning aerobatic display teams. The team's name was derived from the squadron's 'Phoenix rising from the ashes' emblem. Behind the Boss's left shoulder is Flight Lieutenant 'Jimmy' Jewell. Third from left is Flt Lt Brian Allchin. Second from right is Flt Lt Henry Ploszek; behind Dave Seward's right shoulder is Terry Thompson, RCAF. Fourth from left is Flt Lt John Curry, a flight commander. Far right is Flt Lt Tim Mermagen. (via Dave Seward)

'Meanwhile, a new Lightning acrobatic team, from 56 Squadron, had been selected for the 1963 season. Squadron Leader David Seward, the 32-year-old CO, had first got wind of his squadron's new role in mid-October 1962, as their second detachment in Cyprus came to a close.

'We began to pick up rumours that 74 Squadron were starting air-to-air refuelling and 56 Squadron were to become the next RAF formation acrobatic team. This was indeed confirmed a week later. The first thing was to get ourselves a name. We chose Firebirds because of the 56 Squadron badge, the phoenix rising from the ashes, and we devised a paint scheme. We painted the spine and fin red and we rounded this off with the leading edges of the wings and tail-planes red also.

'We started the leaders doing individual aerobatics and in choosing the leaders and deputy leaders I went purely on seniority in the squadron. In other words, I was the formation leader; the "A" Flight Commander, 27-year-old Flight Lieutenant John M. Curry, led the rear formation; the "B" Flight Commander, Flight Lieutenant Jeremy Cohu, was my deputy leader; and the deputy "B" Flight Commander was the deputy rear formation leader. Four of us had experience in formation aerobatics. [Curry had flown in the 229 OCU acrobatic team before March 1960 saw him with Treble One Squadron at Wattisham, flying with the 'Black Arrows', while Cohu (and Mike Cooke) had of course flown with the 'Tigers' acrobatic team before joining 56 Squadron in October 1962.] I had dabbled in the 1950s in Meteors and on T-33s, Sabres, F-102s and F-106s whilst on an exchange tour in America, but not really seriously. As

The still smouldering crater left by the impact of F.1A XM179/J on 6 June 1963. The pilot, Flight Lieutenant Mike Cooke, had hit F.1A XM171/A flown by Flt Lt Mo Moore, during the practice bomb burst over Wattisham. Moore managed to get XM171 down safely at Wattisham but minus both his Firestreak missiles, which were dislodged in the collision and fell harmlessly in the RAF married quarters area. Mike Cooke ejected, but the dynamics were outside the Mk.4 seat's design envelope and though he survived, he suffered almost total paralysis as a result of the accident. His flying career was finished at the age of only 23. (Brian Allchin)

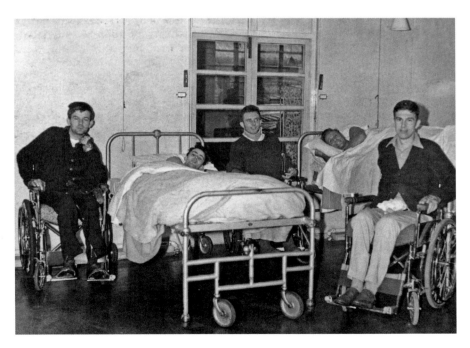

Mike Cooke (far left) with fellow patients at Stoke Mandeville Hospital, Buckinghamshire, following his terrible accident. (Mike Cooke Coll.)

F.1A XM172/B in the new *Firebird* scheme in formation with F.1A XM216/P of 111 Squadron and Gloster Javelin FAW.9R XH984/T of 41 Squadron over Suffolk on 21 October 1963. (Peter M. Warren)

luck happened, all the leadership choices fitted in. We also had one or two queens who fancied themselves, but who really had no experience. We had fifteen pilots on the Squadron. So that was ten in the team plus an airborne reserve. The solo man ['Noddy' MacEwen] made twelve and the commentator/manager [Flight Lieutenant Robert F. 'Bob' Offord, a QFI who had flown Meteors and Sabres with 66 Squadron before converting to the Lightning] only left two on the squadron as spares.'

Apart from those already mentioned, the other pilots were all equally first-rate Lightning men. Flight Lieutenant Henry R. Ploszek (27), the No. 3, had flown Hunters before converting to the Lightning, and had been with 56 Squadron since September 1960. His father had been a major in the Polish Air Force, and joined the RAF in the UK in 1940, serving as an engineer officer during the war. After the war he joined the RAF, retiring as a wing commander. Ploszek and his mother came to Britain in 1946. (In the 1980s, Henry, now a squadron leader in his early fifties, managed the world famous *Red Arrows* team for several seasons and he also flew the team's spare aircraft, Red 10.) The rest of the squadron comprised Flight Lieutenants Robert J. Manning (26), Timothy F.H. Mermagen (25), Terry R. Thompson RCAF (31), Ernie E. Jones (30), Malcolm J. 'Mo' Moore (30), Peter M. 'Jimmy' Jewell (29) and Richard Cloke (24). Wing Commander Bernard H. Howard (39) was team manager, and Flight Lieutenant Brian J. Cheater (25) was the adjutant.

The real work of building up the team began on 1 March 1963. Dave Seward continues: 'The only guidance we were given was that the main formation was to be a nine-ship, and for the display we were to provide continuous aerobatics so that something was going on in front of the crowd all the time. There were to be no gaps. We decided, therefore, that we would start the show with a stream take-off and the very steep climb. As we joined up in formation, a solo Lightning would perform solo aerobatics, clearing as we came round in a Diamond Nine to do the odd roll and loop before splitting into two formations of five. We had a tenth man airborne to link up with the rear formation after the first bomb-burst away from the nine. We then would do manoeuvres in two separate fives, with the solo man interspersing with bomb bursts and join-ups when a gap appeared. [In a bomb burst the aircraft break formation sharply and fan outwards.] We also devised a means of making smoke. The Lightning had fuel in the flaps. We isolated the port flap tank, ran a copper pipe from the tank along the inside port spar strake on the fuselage (the starboard strake carried all the electrical wiring looms and the left-hand one was a dummy strake to balance it up) to

F.1A XM173 of 56 Squadron with Super Sabre 55-2821 of the 48th TFW at Lakenheath, Bentwaters, on 23 May 1964. (Tom Trower)

a small nozzle above the bottom jet pipe. Then an electric pump was connected to the gun trigger. We filled the flap tank with diesel fuel, selected 'guns', pulled the trigger and we had instant smoke. Now, we did all this ourselves by self-help, at very little cost, but I got a telling off from Fighter Command engineers for being too 'enthusiastic'.

'So there we were: a name and a paint-job and smoke on demand, and four of us reasonably proficient in aerobatics. We then worked up in pairs doing steep turns and wing-overs, then loops and rolls, progressing to five-ship formation changes doing all the various aerobatic manoeuvres and formation changes. This was "arrow formation" and we called this "Fork". We used to do these various changes during a roll, loop, or wing-over. We then worked up into the full nine doing rolls, loops and wing-overs. Unfortunately, we then hit a snag. The tail fin-tips started to work loose. The aerobatics were blamed and we were banned from doing rolls or loops in the 'big nine' formation, so we had to step our line astern position down lower. I was suspicious from the start, as my aircraft, which had always been the lead ship, was one of the ones to have a loose fin tip. By coincidence, it was the one which had done the most flight refuelling in the Valiants' jet efflux. But despite our protestations, the powers that were would not lift the ban on aerobatting the nine ship so we were restricted to level turns and formation changes with the nine formation before splitting into the two five-ship formations. We then did semi-synchronized manoeuvres with the two fives and the solo man, ending up with the lead five bomb-bursting down, and the other five bomb-bursting up through the smoke. We then joined up in a big 'vic' formation, with the airborne reserve and the solo man in as well for a simultaneous 'vic' peel off and rapid landing, followed by a formation taxi in.'

At first all practice had been carried out at an altitude which would have given pilots enough time for recovery if any snags were encountered. After the 'threes' had achieved a reasonable degree of skill, Squadron Leader Seward had added two *other* aircraft to fly 'fives'. Soon after this he was confident enough of his pilots' ability to ask for clearance to operate down to 1,500ft. This was granted, and a short while later was followed by another clearance down to 500ft and finally clearance was approved down to just 200ft, one of the lowest clearances ever given to an RAF acrobatic team.

On the morning of 13 May 1963, Geoffrey Norris of the RAF *Flying Review* was privileged to fly a forty-minute sortie with the *Firebirds* in T.4 XM989, as the team

Left: Jimmy Jewell taking a well-earned breather! (BAC)

Below: F.1A XM182/P of 56 Squadron, which it joined on 13 March 1961, a month after it first flew on 6 February. (BAC)

began their work-up to show standard. He wrote: 'With Flight Lieutenant Bob Offord at the controls, we took off as number six behind a section of five. This may have been only a practice sortie, but all the excitement of a real show was there. The six aircraft taxied along the perimeter track, staggered with alternate aircraft left and right. At the end of the runway we lined up in position, our aircraft almost struggling to go as the brakes held it against full throttle.

'The Section Leader was Flight Lieutenant John Curry. When we were all set he announced that he was rolling, and his aircraft accelerated rapidly down the runway at Wattisham. At three-second intervals the others followed. By the time it was our turn to go, the runway had almost disappeared in a haze of swirling fumes, and just before Offord released our brakes, Curry's Lightning suddenly leaped skywards like a runaway rocket at the other end of the runway. This steep, afterburner take-off had become an accepted part of Lightning aerobatics, and the Firebirds have proved they can do it as well as any others. It certainly is most exciting to watch; it is breath-taking to actually do it.

'As soon as we had started rushing the acceleration was patently obvious. Then Offord cut in the afterburners and there is only one word for it – we simply *belted* down the runway. Glued firmly to the back of my ejection seat, I watched the ground flash past and, at regular intervals, the aircraft ahead of us shot upwards. Then we were airborne with our wheels up. For a few seconds Offord held the aircraft level at about 30 feet to let the speed build up.

'By roughly three-quarters of the way down the runway we had 250 knots showing. Then Offord pulled the stick back smartly into his stomach. The ground disappeared as if by magic, and I sank into my seat as the sudden upwards turn gave us 3½g – not much by modern standards, but quite something at such an early and critical part of the take-off. But perhaps the biggest sensation of this dramatic take-off technique is the frightening loss of apparent speed. One second you are roaring down the runway with trees and hangars blurring in the distance and the next you are almost on your back in the rear cockpit, looking straight up at the clouds with seemingly no speed whatsoever. A reassuring glance at the air speed indicator showed, however, that we still had 230 knots and the Lightning, which, with full afterburner, has almost as much thrust as its weight, could maintain this attitude and speed for a long time. Still with the afterburners on, we trailed the five aircraft ahead, which were already forming up. As we broke through the clouds, Curry in the leading Lightning eased off the climb and announced that he was coming out of afterburner. There was a short breathing space while we looked for a clear area in which to practice and then, over a large break in the clouds below, we started. Curry calmly announced rolls, wingovers and loops and the formation changes while the team followed. As we brought up the rear in the T.4, making all the manoeuvres with the team, the sky and the ground ceased to mean up or down. Our reference point became the five aircraft ahead and the Suffolk countryside and the horizon whirled over and around us unceasingly as the section of five flew smoothly through their practice. At no point were we straight and level for more than a second. The accelerometer showed peaks of up to 4g and most of the time we were between 2 and 3g. Our speed remained fairly constant at 350 knots.

'Keeping station within the *Firebirds* as we were, one could appreciate their faultless station keeping and the smoothness of their manoeuvres. It was almost like putting a work of art under a microscope and still finding it flawless. Watching the team in action like this it was difficult to realize that, only a few months previously, hardly any of the pilots had experience of formation aerobatics. That they have achieved a standard of perfection is a tribute not only no the general calibre of the average RAF pilot today, but to the work of Squadron Leader David Seward.

'Although the *Firebirds* display is, in every way, a team effort, right through from pilots to the equally essential and highly skilled ground crew, there is little doubt that

Dave Seward is the man who can make or break a show. One of the great assets of the Lightning for formation aerobatics – apart of course, from its excellent handling characteristics – is the great amount of power which pilots can call on if necessary. This means that the pilot on the outside of a turn should have no difficulty in keeping his station. This excess power does, however, pose problems for Seward. He must concentrate on flying a course which pilots in all parts of the large formation behind him can follow. If he allows too much power to build up in a turn he could well cause embarrassment to a pilot on the outside of the formation.

'We stayed with Curry's section at practice for twenty minutes. Although Offord had not flown as close to the formation as the other aircraft were close to each other (the view from the T.4 is a little restricted for close formation aerobatics) he had to concentrate closely on the movements of the aircraft ahead of us. Obviously, the pilots who were literally flying only a few feet apart were concentrating even harder. Back on the ground I asked several of them whether they found this concentration tiring. They did not seem to take their task as anything particularly out of the ordinary. "You have to concentrate pretty hard anyway when you are flying a Lightning" one said. This applies whether you are flying formation aeros or making a radar interception.

'But one thing is certain. Although the pilots might say that their job is not particularly out of the ordinary, by the end of this summer many people in various parts of Europe will have had an opportunity to judge for themselves how "out of the ordinary" their show is. My guess is than the *Firebirds* will he adjudged one of the best yet.'

'However', continues Dave Seward, 'before we really got going, "Noddy" MacEwen, the solo man, was posted and promoted, so Flying Officer Alan Garside, the 111 Squadron solo aeros man, joined us. [In April 1963, Flight Lieutenant Brian C. Allchin (25) joined 56 Squadron. 'Alch' had flown Hunters in 92 Squadron and in the *Blue Diamonds* aerobatic team in 1961 and 1962.] Everyone then became involved after we had a mid-air collision.'

The collision occurred during a formation horizontal bomb burst over Wattisham airfield on 6 June. 'The day before', recalls Mike Cooke, the No.3, (left of centre in the five-vic formation, in F.1A XM179, behind Gerry Cohu), 'Squadron Leader Seward had given us a "pleasant ear-bashing" to smarten up the horizontal bomb burst because of the "slack" bomb burst at the end of the sequence. We did a practice. On one roll I must have been low because I saw rather a lot of trees near the airfield at Wattisham. We were then coming in, each Lightning 6-7ft apart as usual and Gerry Cohu ordered "Bomb Burst, Bomb Burst ... GO!" "Mo" Moore, the No.5 and No.4 went straight away. One second later it was my turn and that of the No.2. I made a very sharp turn and at the same time I pulled the stick to make it "slicker". You then didn't normally look too far over to the left. We were about to reassemble and I looked ahead for the leader, took off the left bank, coming out of the left turn to go right.

'Suddenly, I felt a bump. [His port wing had touched the under fuselage of XM171, "Mo" Moore's Lightning, knocking the starboard Firestreak missile off. Moore managed to land safely at Wattisham.] Immediately the aircraft carried on rolling to the right, despite full left aileron and full left rudder. I couldn't stop it. I remember that the height was 500-700ft AGL. In a few milliseconds I realized I'd have to eject. At that height I could eject onto the ground, so I had reflex – "Go for the handle!" I used my left hand to pull it. Glancing at the ASI I saw that it was around 400-500 knots and rising. I pulled. It seemed an age before something happened. The canopy went. I waited for the "nip" in the back of the neck (previously I had done two training ejections in a static ramp), but it did not happen.

'The next thing I remember was that I was coming down in the parachute and into a green field. I could not move my arms or my legs. I couldn't breath either. Because of

F.1A XM182/P was one of the first two Lightnings to visit Akrotiri, in July 1962, during early flight refuelling reinforcement trials, and later served with 226 OCU, Binbrook TFF and 23 Squadron. Finally, in July 1974, XM182 was flown to RAF Gütersloh for surface decoy duty. (BAC)

Firebirds in formation. (BAC)

Treble One Squadron began receiving F.1A aircraft on 6 March 1961, taking delivery of XM185, XM215/C, the nearest aircraft, on 2 August 1961 and XM216, the last F.1A built, later that month. XM190/G, which arrived on 111 Squadron on 20 June 1961, later joined 226 OCU. It crashed into the sea off Cromer, Norfolk, on 15 March 1966. Captain Al Peterson USAF ejected safely. XM188/F later served with 226 OCU and was written off in a crash at Coltishall on 21 June 1968.

Flight Lieutenant 'Bugs' Bendell, 111 Squadron solo display pilot, in F.1A XM188/F taxies in at RAF Wattisham. (Peter Symes)

the whiplash effect caused by a malfunction in the ejection seat sequence, the parachute had opened at too high a speed (called a hangman's deployment). The whiplash effect had broken my neck (actually, my fifth and sixth vertebrae had been severed), although I did not know this until a few days later. (A "hangman's deployment" is so-called because we breathe though the diaphragm and when someone is hanged on the scaffold the noose breaks the neck and breathing stops. This is what had happened to me when the parachute had deployed.)

'I came to on the ground. I still had my facemask on. I could not breathe too well. I thought that this was because I was lying on my breathing apparatus. Two labourers came over. I said, "Mask off, Mask off!" They said, "He's still alive" and answered back. Overhead, another Lightning circled, pin-pointing my position presumably. A crash crew arrived with an ambulance and a very uncomfortable ride ensued. I was taken to hospital in Ipswich and later that day I was helicoptered to Stoke Mandeville.

'Dr Grossman oversaw my treatment. He was a German Jew who had fled to Britain in 1937 and had become world-renowned in the treatment of spinal injuries at Stoke Mandeville. His technique was to permit the patient good, basic nursing to avoid potentially dangerous bladder and kidney failures later and so prolong the patient's life span. (At one time, the normal prognosis for spinal injury patients was only ten years.) I had a tracheotomy to improve my breathing and my head was put in traction for three months after a harness was bolted to my skull. The first night I couldn't move and I was more occupied with coping with the present effects of my accident than thinking about what the future now held. Stoke Mandeville was something of a culture shock after RAF station quarters. The wooden huts had nicotine-stained ceilings and it was so cramped, you could touch the patient's bed next to you on both sides. The food wasn't at all good. Everyone, though, was in the same boat. Recovery, if you do recover, comes after six weeks. At the time of my accident my wife Patsy was five months pregnant and she was understandably very upset. All told, I spent seventeen weeks in bed. Gradually, my arms got a little movement. My first day's outing on 23 October coincided with the birth, at RAF Bicester, of our son, Simon.'[10]

Flight Lieutenant Peter Symes, recently arrived at Wattisham from Cranwell remembers: 'After 56 was given the aerobatic commitment it was fascinating to see them gradually working up into shape. When they began to display at lower level over the airfield, almost everybody used to stop to watch. Eventually we became accustomed to their routine, and they just became a noise in the background. However, on 6 June 1963, in my office on the upper floor of SHQ facing the back of the hangars, I noticed an unusual WHOOMPH as the formation did its horizontal bomb burst head on to the hangar line. Glancing out of the window I saw an airman outside the guardroom looking to the sky above SHQ in obvious amazement, and I noticed something glinting as it tumbled down into the Airmen's Married Quarters. Realising that something had gone wrong, I dashed up onto the roof in time to see a mushroom cloud of smoke starting to drift downwind – then a Lightning starting to orbit at low level. Shortly afterwards the wife of the Disci Sergeant came into SHQ to see her husband. She was in a very distressed state. XM179 had thundered into a field of peas only about 50 yards from the narrow road on which she had been driving towards the station and it had seemed to be heading straight for her.'

Dave Seward, who had been filming the formation from the ground, now had tough decisions to make: 'Sad though it was, I had a job to do and suddenly, you have to fight back the tears, harden it and get on with the job. Not a pleasant thing. You've got to tell the relatives. The station commander asked me what I was going to do. I said, "We carry on." It was the only way. This was one of the times when you had to make a hard decision. You're not the most popular guy. Then again, you're not running a popularity poll. We had a Queen's birthday flypast the next day and not only that but we were scheduled to

This night-time re-heat run by 74 Squadron's XM145/Q is one of the most dramatic photos ever taken. (BAe)

A seven-ship formation of 74 Squadron's F.6s early in 1967. The *Tigers* were the first squadron to receive the full production standard aircraft. Nearest aircraft is XS921/M, which first flew on 17 November 1966 and joined 74 Squadron on 21 December 1966. This aircraft later joined 11 Squadron and it crashed on 19 September 1985 about thirty miles off Flamborough Head due to control restriction. The pilot, Flight Lieutenant Craig Penrice, suffered leg injuries during the ejection. (MoD)

Right: F.1A XM187/D of 111 Squadron in a dive. The aircraft first flew on 20 March 1961 and joined Treble One Squadron on 24 April. It had a short service life, being relegated to ground instructional airframe duty after its undercarriage collapse during a landing accident at Wattisham on 19 November 1963. The pilot, Flight Lieutenant M.R. Smith, suffered a compression fracture of the spine. XM187 finished its service life at Coningsby where it was used for fire practice.

Below: Ground crew attach a Firestreak missile to a F.1 of 74 Squadron at Coltishall in 1961. With Firestreak, the kill radius from the Lightning's base for a hostile aircraft flying at a speed of Mach 1.5 at an altitude of 45,000ft was 300nm. With air-to-air rockets it was 390nm. With rockets or Firestreak the kill radius against a hostile aircraft at Mach 0.9 at 36,000ft was 480nm. Against a hostile at 350 knots at 20,000ft the kill radius was 475nm with rockets or Firestreak. According to the sales brochure, from Lightning take-off a Mach 1.5 intruder at 45,000ft could be destroyed in 6.2 minutes with rockets, or in 8 minutes using Firestreak. By the same token, an intruder at 36,000ft could be destroyed in 3.3 minutes and a 350 knots intruder at 20,000ft in 2.1 minutes. (BAC)

lead it. I'll give Mo Moore his due. I said, "This accident has shaken you up boy. What are you going to do?" (I counselled him and told him he had done nothing wrong). He said, "I'll carry on". We needed all the aircraft so Edwin Carter and his engineers changed the missile pack on Mo Moore's aircraft and hammered the dents out and put it in the air.'

Although the *Firebirds* gave most of their displays with synchronized aerobatics from two sections of four or five aircraft, each show that summer of 1963 was opened by the full formation of nine with, sometimes, an extra solo performance thrown in. On 18 July 1963 Flying Officer Alan Garside was killed when he became disorientated in cloud during an aerobatic presentation at RAF Wittering, and so Sam Lucas, the 111 Squadron solo aerobatic pilot, took Garside's place in the *Firebirds* for the rest of the season. Seward recalls that, 'Lucas was an "ad libber" who would get "bored" with his show and throw in some unannounced routines. On one occasion I saw him enter the fog at Biggin Hill inverted and I never expected him to come out alive, but he did!'

On 12 June the *Firebirds* flew to France to perform at the Paris Air Show at Le Bourget. The *Flight* correspondent wrote, 'The programme at Le Bourget proved that Dave Seward was fully aware of the showmanship part of his job as he was of his airmanship. The French crowd was treated to a dazzling display of colour and spectacle, but, above all, one of precision, which began as soon as the pilots strapped themselves into their cockpits. If there was to be a full take-off of ten Lightnings, the onlooker would be treated to the sight of ten canopies closing as one on Squadron Leader Seward's orders. Next, the immaculately white-overalled ground crew would march smartly forward in line abreast as the aircraft prepared to move off. This move was not just "bull". Each airman was there to marshal one of the Lightnings from its line-up position and to give it a last-minute visual check. The aircraft moved off in two sections of five and, again on their Squadron Leader's command, each aircraft in each section of five would check its brakes at precisely the same instant after it had rolled a few feet. The effect was almost that of a gracious bow towards the crowd. 56 Squadron's pre-take-off manoeuvres were, certainly, a fitting prelude to the precision which was to follow in the air.'

Unbeknown to the *Flight* correspondent, things did not go as smoothly as hoped, as Dave Seward explains: 'We were pushed for time (the Greek Air Force had already been diverted for overstepping their slot). We only had something like twelve minutes from take-off to landing. (Normally, we timed ourselves from the time the first aircraft [mine] started to roll.) The French said that our start time was as soon as I taxied out.' Dave Seward was also the man who faced the last-minute decision on what type of show was to be given: 'Despite met. reports it is sometimes impossible to know exactly what flying conditions are like until you are in the air. Basically, we planned for three different types of show to meet all eventualities. If the clouds were above 4,000ft we would give the complete show. We had another display which we could use if the ceiling was lower and a final bad weather show with which we operated within a radius of two miles with a 500ft ceiling. For Paris we would do a loop in a 5,000ft cloud base. However, it was a murky day and so I had sent Bob Manning, the spare, up to see what the cloud base was. He said, "No clouds below 6,000ft." I told John Curry, "OK, we'll do the full show." Up we went – straight into cloud at 2,500ft! We did the whole loop in cloud using the attitude indicator (a nasty little instrument with no 'aircraft' mounted on the artificial horizon)[11] and came out at 2,500ft. It was a 'dodgy' time but we all stuck together – I'll say that for the team. So then the rest of the display was the flat show. Afterwards, I asked Manning why the hell he had told me there was no cloud below 6,000ft and he said, "Well Boss, you've been practising the loop for so long now, that I thought you wouldn't want to miss it!" After we came down we went into the BAC tent. [Air Marshal Sir Desmond] "Zulu" Morris, the C-in-C Fighter Command, had a face as black as thunder. I could see him looking at me and saying, "What about that loop?" He was not that happy anyway that a front-line squadron had been taken out of the line for aerobatting. (It did not make economic sense using a front-line squadron like us when you're trying to maintain a watching brief in a Cold War situation.) I explained to him that we'd been given the wrong weather forecast and that was it. He was just starting to get to the awkward question when Bill Bedford suddenly dropped the P.1127 Kestrel right outside the judges' tent! The crash took me off the hook and with other things now on his mind, Zulu Morris never mentioned it again!'

Geoffrey Norris' prediction that the *Firebirds* would be adjudged one of the best yet was proved true and they became the last squadron formation aerobatic team to display. The following September a team of five yellow-painted Gnat T.1 trainers from 4 Flying Training School led by Flight Lieutenant Lee Jones performed at Farnborough 1964. The *Yellowjacks'* success led, in 1965, to the world-renowned *Red Arrows,* whose first public performance was at Biggin Hill in May that year. The rest, of course, is history.

1 XG334, XG335 and XG336. On 5 March Harding of the CFE was forced to abandon XG334, which John Nicholls had delivered on 23 December, after hydraulic failure. On selecting the undercarriage down for landing, the port leg would not lower beyond 30 degrees. Harding initiated the emergency system without success, and after a series of slow fly-bys over the airfield to allow engineering staff to access the situation as best they could, XG334 was abandoned off the Norfolk coast near Wells-next-the-Sea. It was only the second Lightning loss so far recorded. Harding ejected safely but suffered spinal injuries and was picked up by helicopter from the sea.

2 XM135, XM136, XM137, XM138 and XM165, which was delivered by Wing Commander Roly Beamont, late in the afternoon of 29 June 1960.

3 Squadron Leader John Howe, who after a short spell of instructing had taken over 74 Squadron in February 1960, first flew this aircraft on 14 July.

4 By 22 July 1960 all of the 74 Squadron pilots had completed conversion training. In addition, Wing Commander Evans, OC Flying, had flown at least one sortie.

5 *Never In Anger.*

6 On 26 April 1963 Burns was forced to abandon XM142 B after hydraulic power loss, off the Norfolk coast, whilst on an air test following a 400-hour servicing. He ejected safely, missing 33,000-volt electricity cables by just 30 yards as he landed.

7 *RAF Coltishall Fighter Station: A Station History* by Mick Jennings MBE. (Old Forge 2007).

8 *RAF Coltishall Fighter Station: A Station History* by Mick Jennings MBE. (Old Forge 2007).

9 Fighter Command first introduced the in-flight refuelling technique in June 1960, when 23 and 64 squadrons, operating the Javelin FAW.Mk.9, began receiver training. In August, a 23 Squadron Javelin was flown to Akrotiri non-stop, refuelled and escorted by Valiant BK.1 tankers.

10 Mike Cooke's RAF career was finished; he was just 26 years old at the time. Incredibly, he did not qualify for compensation (under Section 10 of the Crown Proceedings Act of 1947, he could not sue the MoD), nor a pension; he had not been in the RAF long enough. Without a trace of bitterness, he says: 'The RAF is there to fight wars, not look after the injured.' The RAF Benevolent Fund also was unable to help the pilot, who was now a paraplegic. However, Sir James Martin at Martin-Baker had told Patsy Cooke that if there was anything Mike needed he could have it. In 1968 Martin-Baker provided money to enable the Cooke's to buy a Citroen Safari and to have it specially adapted for his use. Mike used it for twelve years and Martin-Baker then provided another £10,000 for him to replace it with a Nissan Prairie.

11 Tony Paxton adds: 'The Lightning was designed as a high-level, often supersonic fighter. The pressure instruments, that is those flight instruments operated by changes in the atmospheric pressure surrounding the aircraft, were subject to varying degrees of "pressure error". By far the greatest error was with the altimeter, which underfed by a significant amount at subsonic speeds, but was accurate once the aeroplane was flying faster than Mach 1. The rule of thumb to correct for pressure error to the pressure altimeter was that the instrument under-read by the Mach No. 2 x 100 feet. Therefore if flying at Mach 0.7 at 500 feet above the sea the altimeter would read zero! The rule of thumb was valid up to Mach 0.8 and then the error rapidly increased until just before Mach 1.0 it was 1,250 feet; as the aircraft accelerated through the "sound barrier" the altimeter would suddenly wind up 1,250 feet to read accurately. The error could be quite disconcerting at night or in marginal weather conditions. If one were flying at 450 knots (Mac 0.75 at sea level) to fly at 300 feet above the sea the altimeter would be showing 99,750 feet having wound down 250 feet below zero, and believe me there is a strong psychological baffler to flying around with that sort of indication.'

CHAPTER 3

Ab Initio

The LCU had moved to Middleton St George in August 1961 and become the Lightning Conversion Squadron (LCS). Group Captain Freddie Rothwell was Station Commander, Wing Commander Charles Laughton OC Ops and Squadron Leader Ken J. Goodwin Commander of the LCS. The LCS were without aircraft until December 1961 when their first T.4 came, only to leave almost as quickly as it had arrived. It returned six months later after a major rework of the hydraulic pipes in No.1 engine bay. The LCS continued to borrow Lightnings, now mainly from 56 and Treble One Squadrons. Usually, only a single aircraft for a few days at a time could be spared, but nevertheless the LCS was responsible for the successful conversion of several squadrons to Lightnings. Not until 27 June 1962 did the LCS receive its own aircraft, when T.4 XM970 was delivered to Middleton St George and was coded 'G'. By the end of July the number of T.4s had risen to four. One of the LCS's first students was AVM 'Tubby' Clayton, AOC 12 Group, who was sent solo after only five dual rides. By the end of October the LCS had eight T.4s on strength. On 12 December 1962 XM993 ran off the runway at Middleton St George after landing while returning from Chivenor and turned over. Fortunately, Al Turley of the LCS and his student, Wing Commander G.M. Gibbs, escaped before the aircraft caught fire and burned out.

On 1 June 1963 the LCS was re-titled 226 OCU (Operational Conversion Unit) and shortly afterwards it received seven ex-74 Squadron F.1s, via 60 MU (Maintenance Unit), where they had been overhauled. In August, the OCU introduced a red and white livery which was based on the St George's Cross and reflected the unit's 'shadow' identity, which was adopted during the many Fighter Command exercises that would follow and in time of crisis.

Ken Goodwin was posted to Bangkok in October 1963. That same month, Squadron Leader Dave Seward arrived from 56 Squadron to be the Chief Ground Instructor in the ground school. 'Already', he recalls, 'Geoff Steggall and Roly Jackson from the EQS had developed an effective organization. I was sent to Coltishall in February 1964 to set up the OCU there prior to their move in April. [Middleton St George had been sold, for just £340,000, to become Teesside Airport, and on 13 April 226 OCU and its fourteen Lightnings flew to their new home at Coltishall.] 74 Squadron had moved to Leuchars and we had Coltishall to ourselves, save for the search and rescue helicopters. Setting up the OCU at Coltishall went very smoothly and the station personnel, from the CO, Group Captain Roger Topp, down were all very enthusiastic to receive the new unit.[1]

The plan was to provide the OCU with three squadrons. No.1 would be responsible for *ab initio* conversion to the Lightning, the course length being around seventy hours, split between the T.4 and solo hours on the F.1A. No.2 would give basic radar training on the AI 23 (and AI 23B for pilots going to F.2 and F.2A squadrons in RAF Germany), while No.3 would provide advanced radar training on the AI

23B for students joining UK F.3 and F.6 squadrons and Cyprus. Occasionally it would operate Interceptor Weapons Instructor (IWI) courses for the RAF Germany Lightning squadrons and be responsible for advanced weapons training, including the AI 23B/Red Top missile system. (Later, No.3 Squadron operated only T.5s, and what little solo flying there was on this final part of the course was completed in the two-seat aircraft.) During 1964, Les Davis, OC 3 Squadron, was away with the front-line squadrons and OC 2 Squadron had not yet converted, so the OCU operated essentially a two-squadron organization. Students were a mixture of ex-Hunter and Javelin pilots, including Flying Officer (later ACM Sir) Bill Wratten, Paul 'Humpty' Holmes, Al Morgan and Gerry Crumbie and various staff officers.

The OCU was not without incident, as Dave Seward recalls: 'An accident on 11 September 1964 involved a bail out by Squadron Leader Terry Bond, the Unit Test Pilot. He was flying a F.1 on a post-Minor air test when he could not get the starboard undercarriage leg fully down, as it had suffered a serious hydraulic failure. The secondary system also failed, and, after a series of low, slow flypasts, it was obvious that there had been a sequence valve malfunction and the gear was stuck partially (almost halfway) down on both sides. It was therefore decided that he would eject. A runway landing was considered, but advice was that the aircraft could cartwheel. Terry Bond ejected as near to the coast as possible to ensure the aircraft went into the sea, but he hoped to keep his feet dry. In the event, he landed about twenty yards off the shore just south of Bacton with the helicopter virtually waiting for him. I had worked out his ejection area using met. winds to 10,000ft, and he was quite annoyed that I'd played it just too close. He was unhurt and quickly returned to flying status.

There was one other accident, which was really an incident, that was very well handled by the student, Ian MacFadyen. He had a nose wheel stuck in the up position and landed on the runway keeping the nose up until the last moment, causing only minimal damage to the aircraft.

In 1965 the OCU began to expand to its full strength, and during this period we received the first *ab initio* students straight from Training Command. On the first of these courses were John Ward, Dickie Duckett (who would later lead the *Red Arrows)* and Doug Aylward, who all did exceptionally well on the Lightning.'[2]

In mid-1965, Wing Commander Mick Swiney took over as chief instructor and OC Flying Wing. On 20 April XS419, the OCU's first T.5, arrived. By now the F.1s were being replaced with F.1As from 56 and 111 Squadrons. By the late 1960s the OCU had forty-two Lightnings on its inventory, divided fairly evenly between the three versions, to which eight F.3s were added in June 1970. Some of the F.1As were now periodically operated as targets, in much the same way as the Target Facility Flight (TFF) Lightnings, with the AI 23 radar replaced with a Luneberg Lens to create a larger radar 'signature'.

Along the way there were a few accidents at 226 OCU at Coltishall. In 1966 three Lightnings were lost. On 15 March Captain Al Peterson USAF safely ejected from XM190 after an ECU fire, and the F.1A crashed into the North Sea off Cromer. On 1 June Flying Officer Geoff Fish, who was on his first T.5 solo in XS453, suffered an undercarriage failure on the down-wind leg in the circuit. At the end of runway zero-five Wing Commander Mick Swiney was waiting to start his instrument rating test with Don Oakden in a T.4.; Swiney recalls:

'Fish flew by the tower at 500ft and we could all see that the young South African was in trouble. He was told by Pete Van Gucci, the DOCFW (Deputy Officer Commanding Flying Wing), to re-cycle the undercarriage. I decided we could go up and see what was what. We formated close behind his tail and could see quite clearly that there was a "hugger's muddle". The sequencing of the oleos and the undercarriage doors had gone wrong. A "D" door had closed prior to the undercarriage leg being retracted.

T.4s of the Lightning Conversion Squadron (LCS) at RAF Middleton St George for the Battle of Britain Day Air Show, 14 September 1963. XM972 first flew on 29 April 1961 and XM971 joined the LCS in July 1962. (Tom Trower)

T.4s of the Lightning Conversion Squadron (LCS) at RAF Middleton St George for the Battle of Britain Day Air Show, 14 September 1963. Left is XM971, which first flew on 23 June 1961 and joined the LCS on 23 July 1962. Centre is XM996, which first flew on 13 April 1962 and joined the LCS on 8 January 1963. XM996 went to 226 OCU on 6 March 1969 and was SOC on 2 July 1974. (Tom Trower)

T.4 XM969 at the 1965 RAF Waddington Open Day. This aircraft first flew on 28 March 1961 and had joined 226 OCU in June 1963. (Tom Trower)

It was quite clear that he was not going to get that aircraft down on the ground. Fish would have to eject. We stayed with him the whole time. SAR were alerted and positioned over the sea off Happisburgh. Fish seemed very calm, although his fuel was now running out. Flight Lieutenant Jimmy Jewell in the tower had the presence of mind to tell Fish to check that his straps were done up tightly – they weren't as it happened. He had failed to insert one of the harness lugs properly during strapping-in prior to start-up. Coolly, Fish undid and then reconnected them. By now his No.1 engine had flamed out, and he had to go now while he still had a modicum of control provided by the No.2 engine. At about 3,000ft he ejected perfectly. His 'chute opened, as it should have. From my cockpit it all seemed to happen in slow motion. Then, to our great alarm, the Lightning started to head back towards land! Essentially, though, it nosed into the sea. Fish was picked up so quickly he hardly got his feet wet.'

A few weeks earlier, on 6 May, XM213 had crashed on take-off from Coltishall. Squadron Leader Paul Hobley, CGI, who was unhurt, was flying the F.1A. 'As CGI', recalls Flight Lieutenant Alex Reed, his flight commander who authorized the flight, 'Paul could only fly on a "grace and favour" basis. SCT (Staff Conversion Training), though, was required. I was coming back from lunch through the hangar. By then I knew there had been an accident. Paul had done a normal take-off, but he took the gear up too quickly and sat it down on its ventral tank. Guys who saw it said they saw a great stream of flame going down the runway and off onto the grass, thirty yards short of a brick building. He was very lucky to walk away. Paul just looked at me. "Sorry Alex, I just f—ed it!" was all he said

'"Don't worry", I said, "but for the grace of God ..."'

On 24 October 1966 Flying Officer Roger J. Colebrook of 226 OCU, who at that time was undergoing conversion as a 'First Tourist', was flying T.4 XM968 for his first solo on type. Whilst climbing at 450 knots with full cold power set, FIRE 1 illuminated as the aircraft was passing through 6,000 feet. Full fire drill was taken during the turn back towards base, but the light remained on until the ventral was jettisoned into the sea one mile off shore. Colebrook recovered to Coltishall, and he attempted to join downwind but was too fast. A wide single-engine circuit was made, followed by a precautionary landing. The brake parachute was slow to deploy and the No.2 engine was shut down on the runway. The T.4 was steered onto the ORP (Operational Readiness Pan) and stopped; the brakes were then released to prevent them welding on. The pilot's reactions to the emergency were copybook and he was awarded a 'good show' in the December issue of the Flight Safety Review.[3]

T.4s of 226 OCU at RAF Coltishall in June 1965, when Coltishall began to expand to its full strength and received the first *ab initio* students straight from Training Command. On 2 January 1967 XM971 was abandoned in flight after the radome collapsed and debris entered the air intake. The Lightning crashed nearby at Tunstead. Squadron Leader Terry Carlton and Flight Lieutenant Tony Gross ejected and landed safely. (EDP)

F.6 XR763/G of 23 Squadron from RAF Leuchars at RAF Coltishall on Battle of Britain Day, 14 September 1968. This Lightning first flew on 15 October 1965 as an interim F.6, and joined 5 Squadron on 11 February 1966. After conversion to full F.6 standard it joined 23 Squadron on 1 November 1967. It went to 11 Squadron on 30 June 1970. (Tom Trower)

T.5 XS420 joined 226 OCU on 29 April 1965. On the night of 31 January 1973 Captain Gary Catren, a USAF exchange officer attached to 226 OCU, with student pilot Flight Lieutenant George Smith, attempted a take-off for an SCT sortie in XS420 from Runway 04 at Coltishall, but the lower re-heat failed to ignite. XS420 took the barrier with it into the overshoot, but the T-bird fortunately dug in before it crashed into a railway line and both pilots walked away unhurt. XS420 flew for the last time in May 1983.

Roger Colebrook recalls: 'I was well aware that all was not well, as my total fuel remaining was decreasing at an alarming rate on the fuel gauges. I was not aware that it was being pumped overboard by the aircraft system, owing to the fact that the seal that was designed to keep the fuel in was not carrying out its design function. I landed with about 400lb total fuel remaining, having been airborne for only ten minutes! As I climbed out on to the ORP after shutting down, fuel continued to run out of the ventral fitting, much to the consternation of the fire crew as the wheel brakes were red-hot. If I had carried out a missed approach, the aircraft would have run out of fuel and become a total loss on that occasion! As this was my first solo, my instructor, Flight Lieutenant M.J. Graydon,[4] was in the control tower. He debriefed me after the flight and commented that the observers in the control tower had seen what they thought was smoke coming from the underside of the aircraft, as I passed downwind. They decided, however, not to tell me at the time, in case I panicked!

'Following my debrief I made myself a coffee in the crew room and recounted my dice with death to others on the course, who wanted to know what had happened. While this was going on, several different instructors came in and engaged me in rather forced conversation, or peered in the door at me before returning to their previous duties. Later, I discovered that a heated debate was going on in the operations room as to whether my nerve had gone and that my next flight should be with an instructor, or whether I was considered sane enough to fly an aircraft solo immediately to complete my first solo exercises. The various instructors had been sent to make an appraisal and report back to the flight commander! I am pleased to say that I was considered normal and launched off a short while later on my second First Solo!

'The debate as to whether I needed to fly with an instructor or solo almost led to a second incident when I got airborne on my next flight. Whichever way the decision went, I was to fly in a T.4. Initially, the line engineers were told that an aircraft was to be prepared for a dual flight. This necessitated the activation of the right-hand seat, where the instructor sat. Harness straps were made ready for their occupant and, critically, the liquid oxygen for that seat had to be turned on. Subsequently, after it had been decided that I should fly solo again, the line engineers were given new instructions. The right-hand seat was now to be de-activated! As a result, a harness-restraint apron was fitted to the right-hand seat, to ensure that loose straps and connectors did not flail about during manoeuvres and, critically, the liquid-oxygen supply to that seat was now turned off! Shortly after commencing my take-off run, as I hurtled down the runway in afterburner, the centralised warning system activated to alert me to a problem. This was exactly the same system that had alerted me in the fire on my first solo. Although it covered all critical aircraft system failures, it used exactly the same audio alert to draw the pilot's attention to the panel, where an appropriate caption illuminated to advise the pilot of the particular failure he had experienced.

'After my experience on the previous flight, my adrenaline level was probably higher than normal as I roared down the runway and when the alarm bells sounded, I found I had instinctively cancelled the afterburners as I glanced down at the system warning panel. I suppose I had expected to see another fire warning; however, the "OXY 2" light was illuminated. Realizing my mistake, I pushed the throttles back through the afterburner gate and continued with my take-off, lifting off quite a bit further down the runway than normal.

'I expect the line engineers were only notified of the change to "solo" configuration at the last minute and, consequently, the line pressure in the instructor's oxygen system had started to leak away when the system was turned off. The time at which the system activated the low pressure warning, (OXY 2), just happened to coincide with my take-off and could have resulted in an aborted take-off, or an excursion into the Safeland Barrier, due to my inexperience.

'Despite my parlous introduction to the Lightning, I enjoyed every minute on the aeroplane. So much so that, when I was posted to Central Flying School to become an instructor at the end of my tour, I protested that I wanted to stay in the air defence role. In doing so, I presumed I would be posted to another Lightning squadron, as this was the only air defence aircraft in service with the RAF at the time. Unbeknown to me, a decision had been taken to decommission HMS *Eagle*, the Royal Navy's secondary aircraft carrier. Consequently, its complement of Phantom FG.1s was in the process of being transferred to the RAF for the formation of an air defence squadron, with a secondary role of fleet defence. The intention was to back up the Royal Navy's only air defence Phantom squadron on HMS *Ark Royal*. The Air Member for Personnel accepted my request for a change of posting and I found myself posted to 43 Squadron, operating the Phantom FG1 from RAF Leuchars, in Fife. Having protested once I did not feel I could object to this new posting. I accepted my fate and became a WIWOLA! (Wish I Was On Lightnings Again)'[5]

Flight Lieutenant Alex Reed recalled another occasion, on 2 January 1967, when he was coming back from lunch ('these things always seemed to happen after lunch!'), he bumped into Squadron Leader Terry Carlton, OC No.2 Squadron. Reed recalls, 'I was surprised because I knew he should be airborne. He said, looking across the airfield at a plume of smoke, "that's my aircraft!"' Carleton had been on a dual radar sortie in XM971 with his student, Flight Lieutenant Tony Gross, when, on the climb-out shortly after take-off, there was a very expensive noise internally and an immediate loss of power. (The radome had come loose and the engines had ingested the debris.) Assuming control, Carlton throttled back and commenced a recovery to Coltishall. On a high downwind leg, he applied throttle to check his descent, but found that he had no power. Gross ejected first, Carlton going at about 800ft and the aircraft crashing at Tunstead. A Whirlwind helicopter from the SAR Flight of 202 Squadron on the base recovered both pilots, each of whom suffered minor spinal injuries.'

Carlton was involved in another incident, on 12 September, returning from working up on Red Section in a four-ship formation. Alex Reed was flying No.3: 'We carried out an echelon starboard break into the circuit and Terry called "Downward for the formation". As he came round on finals at the far end there was a "twinkle, twinkle,

T.5 XS422, which first flew on 24 March 1965 and joined 226 OCU at Coltishall on 1 June that same year. It joined 111 Squadron on 15 August 1969 and continued to operate in first-line service until its last flight (with ETPS) on 13 August 1987. It is currently at Stennis Airport, Hancock County in Mississippi.

226 OCU Lightnings in formation. T.5 XS419, which first flew on 18 December 1964, was the first to arrive on the OCU, on 20 April 1965. It was damaged shortly afterwards when it hit a landing light, but was repaired, and later it served with the LTF at Binbrook. T.4 XM997 first flew on 22 May 1962 and was originally delivered to the LCS at RAF Middleton St George on 14 January 1963. F.1A XM216 first flew on 28 July 1961 and joined 111 Squadron on 29 August that same year. It joined the OCU on 15 January 1965 but sustained Cat.4 damage on 26 April, when a defective starter exhaust ignited residual fluids. After repair at Warton, it was returned to the OCU in September 1966 and was operated until 10 July 1974, when it was flown to Gütersloh for use as a surface decoy. (BAC)

T.4 XM968 of 226 OCU at Coltishall. It was abandoned on 24 February 1977 near Gütersloh, after total hydraulic failure led to loss of control. Squadron Leader Mike Lawrance, 92 Squadron, and Sqdn Ldr Christopher 'Hoppy' Glanville-White, Harrier Squadron CO, ejected safely.

T.5 XS419 of 226 OCU at Coltishall.

T.4 XM997, which first flew on 22 May 1962 and joined the LCS at Middleton St George on 14 January 1963. (BAC)

F.3 XP696 of 2T Squadron, 226 OCU at RAF Coltishall. This aircraft first flew on 2 July 1963 and it joined the CFE at Binbrook on 16 January 1964. XP696 took part in Red Top trials at Boscombe Down from 16 February 1966 to 5 June 1967, before modification to full F.3 standard at Warton. It joined 226 OCU in August 1972 at Coltishall, where in 1974 it was painted in a white fin and spine scheme adopted by display champion pilot Flight Lieutenant Pete Chapman, who was noted for his spectacular aerobatic performances. (BAe)

boom"! Obviously, an aircraft had crashed! Terry saw this as well and as we had all broken and fanned out bethought his No.4 must have crashed. Terry called, "Check in!" and we all did. I was just coming off the runway as the crash vehicles were heading for the column of smoke, 200 yards off the runway. Well, we were all here. Puzzled, we wondered, "Where did that come from?"'

Flight Lieutenant Jock Sneddon, a Wattisham TTF pilot, had experienced a cockpit fire in XM136. Sneddon ejected safely and he landed at Scottow, close to RAF Coltishall. The F.1, which had begun its career with 74 Squadron at Coltishall, seemed to know its way home because the wreckage landed on the airfield boundary!

During the afternoon of 7 March 1967 there occurred another incident at Coltishall, the first in a series to plague the T.5 Flight Lieutenant Mike Graydon and his instructor, Flight Lieutenant Bob Offord. They were at the end of a Rad-ex in XS454 and alighted on Runway 22, when suddenly, despite three greens showing on the instrument panel, the main undercarriage collapsed! The nose wheel, however, stayed down. Bob Offord recalls: 'The drag chute hit, then the wheels went. Because the levers were on his side, I told Mike Graydon to shut down the engine and open the canopy. We had no control. It just went straight in and then veered off to the right and stopped. I said, "Get out!" and I went over the side. I didn't know at this stage what had happened. You can imagine the looks we got!'

Peter Hayward, a technician at 226 OCU, explains: 'The landing gear failures affected only the T.5. The leg(s) would fold towards the end of the landing run when the aircraft was rolling relatively slowly. So, apart from the pilots' injured pride and a somewhat scraped wingtip, little damage was done. Many investigations were carried out and many theories put forward. One theory was that the pilots were inadvertently operating the "gear up" lever instead of the brake chute lever – on the T.5 the two levers were quite close to each other. This was immediately rejected by the pilots, who pointed out that with the aircraft on the ground with weight on the landing gear, the gear select lever is locked in the down position and a positive override action is required before it can be selected "up".

'The theory that pilots were inadvertently operating the landing gear lever led to an unexpected bonus for the ground crews. "Joy trips" for technicians in the right-hand seat of a Lightning were highly desirable, but, because of the training commitment at Coltishall, were rare occurrences. When the above theory was first mooted, the decision was taken that whenever a T.5 had to be flown solo (test flight, conversion pilot's first solo etc.), the right-hand seat would be occupied by a ground technician so that the brake chute could be deployed by him from the lever in the right-hand side of the cockpit. There was no shortage of volunteers.

'On some flights the opportunity arose for a member of those technicians to join the 1,000mph Club. I achieved it during a flight with Flight Lieutenant Henry Ploszek. Two other flights I had as a passenger are indelibly recorded in my mind. One of these was a low-level PI with Flight Lieutenant "Oscar" Wild. Low-level PIs consisted of flying at 50 to 250ft above the sea and intercepting "enemy" aircraft (usually another Lightning). Interceptions were carried out under instructions from ground control and using the information supplied by the aircraft's AI 23B radar. This meant that the pilot had his eyes glued inside the radar visor and the aircraft was flying on autopilot in the altitude hold mode. Now, this may sound perfectly normal. But if you are a passenger sitting in the right-hand seat and have got nothing to look at other than the whitecaps of waves or North Sea rigs and shipping flashing past below you at close range, and perhaps if you do not share the pilot's blind faith in the technology that is supposed to prevent you flying into the sea, then a feeling of being in the wrong place can overcome you.

'Similarly, a formation let-down with a USAF exchange pilot at the controls led to a feeling of wishing I was back in the crew room enjoying a cup of coffee and a cigarette. There were perhaps four aircraft in the let-down. Above the clouds in the bright

T.4s XM994 and XM996 of 226 OCU at Coltishall over Norfolk in November 1969. XM994 first flew on 12 March 1962 and was issued to 19 Squadron at Leconfield on 6 November 1962. After being used to help conversion of both 19 and 92 Squadrons to Lightnings, XM994 was transferred to 226 OCU at Coltishall on 27 June 1963, where it served until 8 May 1974. The aircraft was scrapped in 1977. XM996 first flew on 13 April 1962 and was issued to the LCS at Middleton St George on 29 January 1963. It operated with 226 OCU from 1 June 1963 until June 1974, when it was withdrawn from use, and was finally scrapped after being used for fire practice at Manston. (Dick Bell)

T.5 XV328/Z of 29 Squadron. This T-bird first flew on 22 December 1966 and was issued to 29 Squadron in March 1967. It was badly damaged in October 1969 while on detachment at Coltishall. Repaired, it re-joined 29 Squadron in February 1970. XV328 subsequently went on to serve with 5 and 11 Squadrons and the LTF at Binbrook. In June 1968 it was one of several Lightnings purchased by Arnold Glass and based at Cranfield. (Dick Bell)

T-5s XS452 and XS449 of 226 OCU taxi past the tower at Coltishall in May 1969. XS452 first flew on 30 June 1965 and joined 226 OCU on 20 September that year. XS449, which first flew on 30 April 1965, joined the OCU on 15 July 1965. The T-Bird was scrapped in 1987. XS452 continued to operate from 'Colt' until February 1971 when, after overhaul at 60 MU, it was allocated to Treble One Squadron, being SOC in June 1988. On 9 March 1999, now registered ZU-BBD, XS452 became the first of four of Mike Beachy Head's Lightnings in his growing family of jets in the Thunder City operation in Cape Town International Airport. Thunder City's three other flyable Lightnings are T.5 ZU-BEX (XS451), and F.6s ZU-BEY (XP693) and ZU-BEW (XR773). (Dick Bell)

On 24 September 1974 XM172, the first F.1A in RAF service, was placed on display outside the main gate area at RAF Coltishall in the markings of 145 Squadron. The aircraft was formally unveiled six days later, ironically the last day of Lightning operations from Coltishall. In April and May 1989 the aircraft underwent a total repaint, and the markings of 145 Squadron were replaced by those of the OCU. In 1989 XM172 was put up for disposal but remained as the Coltishall gate guardian until 2000, when XM172 moved to Booker airfield in Berkshire with the hope that one day it would be displayed on a roundabout at Farnborough. This never happened and a private collector in Cumbria now owns the airframe.

T.5 XS417/Z of 23 Squadron at RAF Leuchars in July 1973. XS417 was the first production T.5 to fly, on 17 July 1964. It was used for forty-seven flights in development flying, and was first issued to 226 OCU at Coltishall on 25 May 1965. XS417 then joined 23 Squadron in February 1966 where it was coded 'Z'. Between October 1970 and April 1971 XS417 was loaned back to the OCU. After a spell with 56 Squadron in 1975, 'Z' went on to serve with the LTF, 11 Squadron and finally, from March 1983, the LTF.

Group Captain Mike Hobson, RAF Coltishall Station Commander 3 June 1966-3 January 1969, at the controls of a Lightning. As it was the main operator of two-seat Lightnings, 226 OCU's T.4s and T.5s were in great demand to qualify people to be members of the 'Ten Ton Club', complete with scroll and special tie. On 29 February 1968 nineteen-year-old Pilot Officer Vivian Whyer WAAF, a flight control officer at Coltishall, became the 1,000th member of the Ten Ton Club, when Group Captain Hobson flew her at 1,000mph plus in T.4 XM970. Because only one engine would go to re-heat, Mike had to put the nose down over the North Sea to reach the magic 1,000mph! (Group Captain Hobson Collection)

sunlight everything looked easy and was most enjoyable, but then we entered cloud and remained in formation. The separation from the other aircraft was maybe ten or fifteen feet and the only visual contact I had with them was the flash of the anti-collision lights on the wingtips. Then the lights would disappear again in the gloom. It was like driving in thick fog with candles for headlights. The relief, when we finally broke cloud, was immense. It was after this flight that I realized why pilots are called "steely-eyed".

'BAC sent a team of specialists to assist the RAF. Test equipment was installed on a single T.5, and even a movie camera was mounted in the airframe to take a film of the behaviour of the landing gear during the landing. However, as is often the case when you want something to happen, it never does, and no incidents occurred on the test aircraft. So, nothing was proved conclusively, and it was decided that stray voltages induced into the wiring to the landing gear control unit were the most likely cause of the problem and that the routing of the wiring would be modified. This involved approximately two days' work on each side aircraft, and the Coltishall T.5 fleet (which included four T.55s belonging to the RSAF) was completed in the record time of three weeks.'

Coltishall's association with Norwich stretches back to the Battle of Britain in 1940, the days of Douglas Bader and Bob Stanford-Tuck. A most notable event in the station's calendar in 1967, therefore, was the Freedom of Norwich flypast on 6 April, held to mark twenty-seven years of RAF association with the fine city. Group Captain Mike Hobson selected Wing Commander Mick Swiney to lead the formation flypast. This would comprise no fewer that twenty-seven aircraft (made up of twenty-four Lightnings and three Spitfires from the Battle of Britain Memorial Flight), the largest Lightning formation ever to take-off from and recover to its parent station, as Mick Swiney recalls.

'No other station could produce so many Lightnings from their own resources. I had forty-two. Also, I had enough instructors to fly them in boxes without turning a hair, so I decided we would fly in boxes of four, all in line astern, behind the three Spitfires. Flight Lieutenant Gil Pink (37), a Canberra PR.7 navigator and an old acquaintance from my Laarbruch days, was on a ground tour at Coltishall and he helped plan the route and calculate the precise timings needed. A brilliant navigator, he also loved flying. He flew two recces with me in the T.4. Our first practice was with twenty-four Lightnings on 3 April, and on the auspicious day the weather intervened and I took just a token box across the city to coincide with the parade outside city hall, together with three Spitfires. On 27 April I led sixteen Lightnings in formation for the AOC's parade. In the meantime, 23 May was chosen to re-stage the mass flypast over Norwich and this time I was able to mount the whole show. We could not get twenty-seven aircraft onto the runway at once, so I led twelve Lightnings off in three boxes and Squadron Leader Brian Farrer, OC 3 Squadron, with twelve in the second lot, would fall in behind. I led Red, Blue and Green boxes off, did a wide, right-handed circuit, turned in over the coast and ran up the runway at 1,000ft. Brian Farrer's formation took off and pulled in behind. I did not want our entire formation to snake, so, to avoid any changes in direction, we had a long run in point. (I got one of the SAR Whirlwinds to drop a smoke float at a precise point in the sea.) Ahead of us were two Spitfires (a third developed engine trouble after take-off and had to return so Flight Lieutenant Alex Reed, the 'whipper-in', replaced it to make up the magic twenty-seven). We lined up and led all twenty-five Lightnings straight to Norwich, aiming for the cathedral spire. The Spitfires flew at 180 knots, the Lightnings at 360 knots. I am happy to say that it was a DCO [Duty Carried Out] exercise. I sent Brian Farrer's lot in to land first, as they were slightly thirstier aircraft.'[6]

In October 1967 Wing Commander George P. Black AFC arrived at Coltishall to take over command of 226 OCU/145 Squadron and the added responsibilities of CFI/ Wing Commander Flying. Having already accumulated 1,000 hours on the Lightning, he was given a brief conversion course consisting of one dual and three solo sorties to initiate him in his new post! Being the main operator of two-seat Lightnings, 226

OCU's T.4s and T.5s were in great demand in 1963-74 to fly VIPs and other notables at speeds greater than 1,000mph. This would qualify them to be members of the Thousand Miles Per Hour Club, otherwise known as the 'Ten-Ton Club', complete with scroll and special tie. On 26 August 1963 226 OCU had made it possible for Diana Barnato-Walker, a famous flyer and wartime Air Transport Auxiliary pilot, to become the first British woman to achieve the distinction when she was accompanied by Squadron Leader Ken Goodwin the CO in XM996. Diana clocked Mach 1.65 (1,262mph) which for a short time was an unofficial women's speed record, beating that of Jacqueline Cochrane of America and Jacqueline Auriol of France.

It was also around this time that a Guinness toucan bird, stolen from a pub in Newcastle, was flown to 1,000mph membership and became a jealously guarded trophy held for short periods variously by 19 and 92 Squadrons and the LCS. Amid all the publicity, Guinness threw a celebration party at the Park Royal Hotel in London, but the festivities were brought to an abrupt end after the Park Royal tower clock disappeared.

By 1968, appropriately the RAF's fiftieth anniversary year, the club's membership now included well over 900 members, from royal personages such as King Hussein of Jordan and the Shah of Iran, to people of more humble origins. On 27 February Mr Hastings, a member of the Norwich Observer Corps, became the 999th member of the club when Group Captain Mike Hobson flew him at 1,066mph! 1968 being a leap year, the station commander considered it appropriate that a woman should be the 1,000th member to achieve the distinction of membership to the Ten-Ton Club. Nineteen-year old Pilot Officer Vivian Whyer WAAF, a flight-control officer at Coltishall was the lucky candidate, on 29 February. (The three safety equipment workers responsible for packing their parachutes were all women.) 'However', recalls Mike Hobson, 'the weather was appalling and all flying was cancelled, but the press and the TV were there in force so we couldn't really back down. It was all right to take off and I could always land elsewhere if necessary, so off we went in the T.4 (XM970). Only problem was, once Neatishead said that the high-speed run could begin, I could only get one engine to re-heat, so to reach the magic 1,000mph, I had to put the nose down over the North Sea!'

Colonel Akbar Khan, chief of staff to the C-in-C of the Royal Afghan Air Force, who had just presented the RAF with a Hawker Hind as a fiftieth anniversary present,[7] became a member of the Ten-Ton Club on 12 June 1968 when he flew in XM974 with Mike Hobson. 226 OCU also flew Colonel Cesar Rohon, the Ecuadorian Chief of Staff, as Mike Hobson recalls: 'He duly received his tie but he did not receive his certificate. An opportunity to correct this came late in 1969. I was now DD Ops at MoD and was one of the team sent to Ecuador with BAC when it looked like the Ecuadorians were going to buy Lightnings. I sent Rohon's certificate to the Air Attaché in Quito, only to be told that he had been kidnapped! About five days later he was found dumped by the side of the road and a few days after that, he was placed under arrest. He never did get his certificate!'

Meanwhile, in 1968 Fighter Command had made way for Strike Command, and at Coltishall twenty Lightnings (in four boxes of four, plus reserves) were required for the fiftieth anniversary flypast at Abingdon on 1 April. Fuel requirements for the flypast dictated flying from RAF Wyton so most of the Coltishall Wing was deployed there for almost two weeks. Wing Commander George Black recalls:

'I led the formation in a T.5 and behind the Lightnings were four boxes of four Hunters led by Wing Commander Nigel Price, 229 OCU. The exciting bit was the join-up, and on one of the rehearsals the Hunter Wing overcooked the join-up and came in at a very interesting angle. I graciously let them have the lead! On the very last day we could not get all the way around the route safely and chose to come back to Coltishall; we really had to land at Wyton. But we had tremendous confidence in the aircraft and the systems, so we devised a somewhat unusual plan for the recovery. Once we had completed the flypast a

T.5 XS423, which first flew on 31 March 1965 and was delivered to 226 OCU on 1 June 1965. In September 1966 the aircraft was loaned to 29 Squadron, and it returned to the OCU in March 1967. It suffered an undercarriage collapse on landing at Coltishall on 17 January 1968, but it was repaired and continued to be used operationally until its final flight (with the RAF Binbrook ASSF) on 11 September 1974. (Dick Bell)

On 21 June 1968 Squadron Leader Arthur Tyldesley of 226 OCU taxied in with no brakes, and F.1A XM188/F buried itself into the side of No.1 Hangar. Both engines jammed at about 80 per cent power, and a Rolls-Royce technician scrambled underneath to the engine bay and eventually managed to stop the engine. Tyldesley climbed out of the cockpit onto the roof of the hangar offices. (RAF Coltishall)

T.5 XS459 of 226 OCU taxing past the control tower at RAF Coltishall in July 1968. This aircraft first flew on 18 December 1965 and joined the OCU at RAF Coltishall on 13 April 1966. It later joined 29 Squadron on 29 February 1972, and in 1975 it joined 56 Squadron. (Group Captain Mike Hobson)

code word was given and we all shut down one engine! Once overhead Coltishall every single engine was re-lit without a problem and we did two flypasts at Coltishall before landing. It was shortly after this that we had to produce twelve aircraft for the demise of Fighter Command.[8] The flypast was not so spectacular as we were involved in Abingdon and we also had aircraft in the Queen's Birthday Flypast.

'Another significant incident during my reign was on 21 June 1968, when Squadron Leader Arthur Tyldesley taxied in with no brakes and buried the aircraft in the side of No.1 Hangar. Both engines jammed at about 80 per cent and the Rolls-Royce rep. did a splendid job going underneath to the engine bay and eventually managing to stop the engine. It was a horrific sight as the intake sucked in the bricks and mortar (and much of Bob Lightfoot's and Nick Galpin's desks), chewed them up and then hurled stones and gravel at ATC; there was a brown column of dust about 200ft high. Arthur Tyldesley climbed out of the cockpit onto the roof of the hangar offices and was an amusing sight running around as though his hair was on fire.

'Our recent formation flying proficiency was remembered, and I was persuaded to put up a Diamond Sixteen, which had never been flown by Lightnings before, in the September Battle of Britain Open Day at Coltishall.'

First, a rehearsal was flown and then, at the beginning of Battle of Britain Week, Monday 9 September, the formation flew over the city hall. All this activity placed a great strain on the ground crews, as Peter Hayward recalls: 'Preparations were pretty hectic. This was always a joint effort between the two flights of 226 OCU. (One flight alone did not possess sixteen aircraft.) It was often said that to get one Lightning serviceable for a flight was a pretty remarkable achievement, but to get thirty-two Avons started in quick succession (the most infernal noise imaginable) and see sixteen aircraft off without any major problems bordered on a miracle!' Problems, however, did arise on the Saturday during the Battle of Britain Day show, but it had nothing to do with the Lightnings, as George Black explains: 'We had twelve to fourteen aircraft landing, following the convention of the time landing left-right-left etc., when a Hunter landed and called, "No brakes!" The pilot somehow "threaded the needle beautifully", took the lead from me and went straight into the barrier in front of me. An unfortunate end to what had been a great occasion. It was a year of interesting flypasts that interrupted the OCU training but ensured that everyone on the OCU worked extremely hard, and, as a result, we even managed to get the courses out on time.'

On 19 September 1970 the Battle of Britain airshow ended in disaster at RAF Coltishall with the loss of XM990. The T.4, which was crewed by Flight Lieutenants

T.5 XS459 of
226 OCU at RAF
Coltishall. XS459 is
now on display at
Wellesley Aviation at
Narborough, Norfolk.
(Tom Trower)

John Sims and Brian Fuller of 226 OCU, was being used as a reserve for the diamond-sixteen formation display and was called into the centre of the box. However, Squadron Leader Eric Hopkins' Lightning with a locked brake blocked the Coltishall runway and the formation had to be diverted to Wattisham. On the return later that evening XM990 lost aileron control when a bolt dropped out,[9] and the aircraft began corkscrewing and losing height with every revolution. To people on the airfield it seemed that the single Lightning was treating them to an impromptu air display! Both pilots were able to hold the wing up, but landing was not possible and they were forced to eject. Sims went first, at 1,500ft and 220 knots. Fuller, who had to time his ejection on the next upward corkscrew, followed at 1,000ft. The aircraft had time to complete only one-and-a-half more turns before it crashed into a small wood bordering the A140 Norwich–South Walsham road near the village of Little Plumstead. Part of the tail unit was hurled across the road, inches in front of a car driven by 28-year old Michael Howard who, with two friends, was returning from an unsuccessful fishing trip. Standing by his car a few minutes after the crash, Mr Howard recounted:

'Suddenly there was a hell of a screech and a shrieking noise. I glanced up to the trees on the right-hand side of the road – they were almost overhanging the road – when I saw a white flash going into the top of the trees. The plane hit a big oak tree and burst into a mass of flames right in front of my eyes. The tailpiece crashed right across the road a few feet in front of me. The next thing I knew I was right in a mass of flames from the trees where the rest of the plane was burning. It was all over in a flash. Then we were OK. I thought that the whole road was a ball of flames as we drove through it. We were all in one piece and the car was all right.'

Another local who recalls the crash is Mike Baxter, whose interest was stimulated by the Lightning crashing two miles from his home and only 600 yards from his brother-in-law's bungalow. 'He thought his time had come when he saw the jet heading straight for him until it veered away on its last corkscrew and hit the trees. Apart from this connection, it was only later during the Manx Grand Prix on the Isle of Man racing motorcycles that I found out that my friend Tony Martin was stationed at Coltishall and worked on the Lightnings with 226 OCU. He even declined a flight in a T.4. He reckoned it was too risky and this from a man who has finished fourth in the MGP on a TZ350 Yamaha!

'I got the whole story years later from a RAF engineer at Coltishall while working for Air UK at Norwich. He was detailed to retrieve the ejection seats, PSP and canopy from the crash site. Local people hurried to assist the crew. One [Flight Lieutenant John Sims] had parachuted into a wood. He was located in a small clearing, having removed his helmet and lifejacket and complaining of pains to the back of his neck. His parachute

T.5 XS418 during a sortie from RAF Coltishall on 25 September 1974. This aircraft had joined the OCU on 7 May 1965, and on 23 August 1968 had crashed at Stradishall when the undercarriage retracted on landing. Flight Lieutenant Henry Ploszek and SAC Lewis were unhurt. (Dick Jeeves/EDP)

was hanging about ten feet up a tree. He was concerned about the other crewman and also about where the Lightning had crashed. He said he had had only seconds before the crash to eject and asked them to tell his wife he was OK. As he was speaking, the other crewman [Flight Lieutenant Brian Fuller] came into the clearing looking for him and upon seeing each other they both looked greatly relieved. The Coltishall SAR Whirlwind soon arrived and took them to hospital, one of them on a stretcher. [Sims had a scuffed neck while Fuller had just harness bruising]. The crash site was cordoned off for nearly a week while the RAF examined the wreckage before it was removed, along with tons of topsoil: even today you can see the depression. The inquiry, following the crew's evidence, concentrated on the controls and control surfaces. Helped by the lack of a major fire, it was found that one of the aileron linkages had not been securely fitted and had vibrated out with the aileron movement causing loss of control. Fortunately, the crash of XM990 did not result in any loss of life or any great damage to property.'

Meanwhile, the Royal Saudi Air Force had contracted to buy newer marks of Lightning to replace their earlier marks[10] and in 1969 226 OCU was given the Saudi training commitment, with four Saudi T.55s (two more were purchased by Kuwait) being attached to No.3 Squadron. *Magic Palm*, the second phase of the Saudi delivery programme, had begun in 1968, the year that Kuwait also took delivery of the Lightning. The F.53 was first used in action by the RSAF on ground strikes against border positions in Yemen late in 1969. Kuwait operated the Lightning for seven years, before replacing them with the French Mirage. At Coltishall, the RSAF course was almost double the RAF course. To quote the Koran, 'The lightning all but blinds them'. George Black recalls one memorable incident which involved a Saudi student who somehow managed to align his compass 180 degrees out, and instead of heading out over the North Sea, ended up over London at 36,000ft – much to the consternation of Air Traffic Control. Another aircraft had to be sent up to get him back.

Flight Lieutenant Bob Offord, who completed three years as an instructor on 3 Squadron, 226 OCU, in 1969, the year he retired from the RAF, recalls the Saudi pilots: 'During my time, 1968-69, I flew Captain Ahmed Behery,[11] Captain Bakry, Prince Turki bin Nasser,[12] Major Essa Ghimlas,[13] Major Hamdullah, Captain Aziz and Prince Bandar

Faisal, one of the King's sons. Bandar arrived at Coltishall in a Lamborghini, crashed it and bought another. Not to replace it, mind, for when the first one was repaired, he kept both. The Saudis were loaded and well paid, but to them, flying was a hobby rather than a career. Some of them came from Cranwell. Some had flown F-86s. Most of them were quite good, some pretty good, three we would like to have had in our squadron. I went out to Saudi Arabia in 1969 and continued training for Airwork Services. The runways there were longer. Dhahran, for instance, was a former USAF SAC base.'

'For a young Air Traffic Controller in the early 1970s', recalls Flight Lieutenant Dick Doleman, 'there was no finer place to be than the Lightning OCU at Coltishall. You did not have to be a pilot to enjoy the aura or potency of this magnificent beast, and I never tired of watching it. The Lightning seemed to attract or develop pilots of a certain character. For me this character was epitomized by the leadership team that came together about a third of the way through my tour. A finer bunch of larger-than-life characters you couldn't wish to meet. Group Captain Joe Gilbert (station commander); Wing Commander Dave Seward (OC OPs Wing); Wing Commander Paul Hobley (OC 2(T) Squadron), an ex-Junior "Mr Midlands"; and Wing Commander Murdo MacDermid (OC 65(F) Squadron) – the "gang of four"! They were all immensely likeable people with totally different but complimentary characters and a great pleasure to work for and with.

'The instructors on the OCU were an equally impressive and unforgettable bunch of personalities. These included "Furz" Lloyd; Pete "Chappie" Chapman, whose spectacular solo display was never bettered; and "Oscar" Wild, whose premise that a fighter circuit meant no levelling of the wings before the threshold resulted in some spectacular approaches and one-wheel touchdowns. Sometimes, it was rumoured that to achieve the objective required the judicious use of burner in the finals turn! Others were "Taff" Butcher, Rick Peacock-Edwards, "Thumbs" Gosling, Duk Webb, "Jimmy" Jewell, Dave "Quingle" Hampton,[14] "Jonx" Kendrick, Ian Sanford (later killed in mid-air between Gnats while instructing at Valley), Rick Groombridge, John Spencer, Bob Turbin, "Jack" Frost, Dicky Duckett, Trevor "McDoogle-Boogle" McDonald-Bennett and Rory Downes, to name just a few.

'Coltishall was a very busy OCU, and like all OCUs each conversion course was a mixed bag of both experience and rank. The description of a Lightning as an "aluminium tube with a frightened teenager strapped inside" was not altogether strictly correct as it could sometimes contain a frightened group captain! From a controller's viewpoint, work at Coltishall was always interesting and very often demanding. Student inexperience, weather, aircraft speed and shortage of fuel often combined to make for some very "interesting" moments; adrenaline was never in short supply. Considering the prodigious fuel consumption of the Lightning and the limits to which it was operated, it has always surprised me that we never lost an aircraft due to lack of fuel. However, it was mighty close on many occasions and flameouts on the ground were not unheard of. As Captain Ed Crump, a USAF exchange officer and Vietnam veteran succinctly summarized: "With that kind of endurance, I don't call take-off, I call PAN!"[15] Another tribute to the OCU at Coltishall is that, so far as I am aware, there was never a fatality, and the aircraft attrition rate was surprisingly low compared to my experience at other fighter bases operating more modern types of aircraft.

'There were so many memorable controlling incidents that it is very hard to pick out the outstanding moments. Some memories, however, seem more vivid. Rory Downes (2(T) Squadron) launched on a very foggy Friday. It was his last day in RAF service and he needed the flight to achieve the coveted 1,000 hours on type. No pressure to fly of course! Unfortunately, his exodus spurred the otherwise dormant opposition (65(F) Squadron) into instant action and a mass launch. A pair on the runway baulked Rory's minimum fuel instrument recovery. With only fuel for a visual circuit, he completed this in the fog using only vertical visibility to position himself onto finals. An ambition only just achieved in more sense than one.

'A further incident occurred around one of the AOC's [AM Sir Ivor Broom] inspections early in my tour. As part of the occasion, it had been decided to fly a Diamond Nine [led by Wing Commander John McLeod, who had taken over as OC OPs Wing and Chief Instructor (although not a QFI) in October 1969] and a solo aerobatic display. Unfortunately, the weather once again had its part to play. Before the planned take-off, we had been tracking a truly large thunderstorm on radar which was heading directly for the airfield. Despite our best advice, it was decided to launch. The arrival of the formation and the thunderstorm coincided perfectly and chaos soon ensued. The radar was now completely weather cluttered and unable to help. The frequency became frenetic with all kinds of join-up calls being made as the broken formation tried to re-establish contact. In the middle of this chaos, the solo display pilot ran in fast at low level, hotly pursued by one of the formation who assumed he had found part of his section. The subsequent manoeuvre seemed to take him completely by surprise! The first landing on the by now flooded runway resulted in aquaplaning and the aircraft overrunning and entering the barrier [safety net at the end of the runway]. The wind had now changed direction as the storm passed overhead, necessitating landing in the opposite direction. Calls of "Land over me" from the pilot in the barrier went unheeded as the various elements diverted off to Marham, including one aircraft having declared "Mayday". I'm not sure whether the AOC was impressed or not!'

Brian Carroll recalls the initial impact that operating a Lightning in realistic operational conditions had on one trainee pilot who was about to start his conversion flying at the OCU at RAF Coltishall.[16] 'The unit in question was the LXV Fighter Squadron (*Vi et Armis*), whose prime role was to carry out conversion training for pilots just out of Hunter flying at Chivenor. At that time we operated the T.4 trainer along with the F.1s and F.1As. We were also tasked as a front-line squadron. As such, we were subject to alerts and TACEVALs (Tactical Evaluation Exercises) in just the same way as the full-time front-line squadrons. To set the scene, the time was late 1971 and we had recently received a new intake of pilots. They had completed their initial ground school programme of lectures and were reasonably conversant with the Lightning's systems and operating procedures. They had also started flight simulator sorties and all had been airborne on Exercise I. This was by way of being an 'Instructor's Benefit' sortie, during which the full potential of the aircraft was demonstrated! All manoeuvres, needless to say, were within the approved flight envelope.

'We were just into the third week of October when a TACEVAL was called at 03.00 hours. The weather was cold and wet with steady rain that had been falling all of the previous day and was to continue for the next forty-eight hours. Cloud was extensive, the lowest as I recall being around 800 to 1,000ft and going all the way to 30,000ft without a break – just the weather that fighter pilots dream about (well maybe on a bad day). Within a very short time, the squadron was a hive of activity. The ground crews were working at a feverish pitch, pre-flight inspections were being completed as rapidly as possible and aircraft were then positioned in their pre-determined slots, ready for the pilots to mount up. Weather and exercise briefings for the aircrews were all well under way, emergency and other procedures were all covered and we then awaited the first call from the operating authority to start the ball rolling. Meanwhile, the new course of students was being kept busy with routine jobs in operations and the coffee bar. Operating, as we did, a number of two-seaters, it was decided that we would fly as many of the new course students as possible in the right-hand seats to let them see what operating a Lightning as a weapons system was all about. They had, of course, no knowledge at this time of the radar, so it was left to each instructor to attempt to brief on that aspect during the sortie.

F.1A XM171 and XM215 of 226 OCU. XM215 originally served with 111 Squadron before joining the OCU and later served with Binbrook TFF.

'Word finally came through to bring a number of crews to cockpit readiness. I had been allocated a T.4 and so had a student with me. I had already carried out my own pre-flight inspection, so we were able to climb straight into the cockpit. Strapping in took but a few moments, helmets were plugged into the telebrief, ground power was on line, radio frequency selected, flight instruments erected, weapons checked and we were all ready to start engines as soon as scramble instructions were received. We had only been strapped in a few minutes when instructions came to scramble. "Eagle 04 (my call sign) vector 120, make flight level 220, contact when airborne on Stud 7, SCRAMBLE."

'Three minutes later we entered the active runway, applying full power and accelerating as only the Lightning could. The rain was still falling and the runway lights blurred as we raced into the darkness – now airborne, gear retracted, radar scanning, a hard turn onto our designated heading of 120 degrees and into a standard climb out as we changed frequency to Stud 7. Now snug and warm in what I called my "airborne office" (it was nice to be out of the rain), I explained briefly what the radar picture was showing, though I doubt that my passenger was able to make much of the orange scene displayed. Less than two minutes had passed since we entered the runway when we levelled off at 22,000ft.

'Our target was said to be at 25,000ft some forty miles away and crossing our track from right to left. To this day I do not think that my student actually saw the contact on the radar even though I talked the attack right through to the kill. We were, of course, in thick cloud, so never made contact with the hostile intruder. As I broke away from this interception, new instructions were passed from ground control to take another target. This one was at a high level and closing fast. Reheats were engaged and a rapid climb made to 36,000ft, speed was increased to Mach 1.3 and weapons rearmed. As we closed from astern I pulled the aircraft into a steep climb in an attempt to scan the target on radar. A good contact was achieved and the target was splashed (killed) at 47,000ft.

'Back to cruise power and a gentle descent to 35,000ft, briefly enjoying a clear sky above, well spattered with stars but no moon. The night was really very dark. I was beginning to think we would now be allowed to recover to base when another target was allocated. (They did actually ask whether we had sufficient fuel for one more – we did!). This next one was at low level, apparently bent on attacking our base, so a rapid descent was required. Back on the power to idle/fast idle, air brakes extended and with gravity on our side, we were soon plunging into the cloud layer at 30,000ft – levelling shortly after at 2,000ft to start the search for our third target. We were vectored towards the intruder and finally caught him at 500ft, still some fifteen miles from the coast. This had to be a "guns" kill as I had used the available missiles on the first two interceptions. Closing in with a degree of care, I finally made visual contact at around 200 yards – success number three. We were now cleared to recover to base.

'Briefly back to 3,000ft to intercept the Instrument Landing System (ILS), we were cleared into the approach pattern. We were now getting low on fuel and had to make the first approach count. Rain was still falling as we broke out of the overcast at around 800ft. The runway lights, a welcome sight as always, came into view and fifty minutes after rolling we touched down. Taxying back to dispersal I asked the student what he had thought of the sortie. He was remarkably quiet for some time. Eventually, as we were walking back to the operations building, he looked at me, shook his head and said there was no way he could ever do a sortie like that. From take-off to recovery he reckoned not have caught up with what was going on, even though I told him as much as I could, bearing in mind the fact that my work load was high and I had little time to chat. I did make the point that he would not undertake a mission of that nature for quite some time to come, but it would give him some food for thought as he progressed though the course. Some months later, he successfully completed the conversion and weapons course and finally arrived on his first operational squadron. That sortie did, I think, make quite a significant "first impression".'

In November 1971 Wing Commander John McLeod left for HQ 11 Group and was succeeded by Wing Commander Dave Seward, who filled the posts of Chief Instructor and OC Ops. For operational reasons it was decided to declare the Lightning F.1A element of the OCU to SACEUR (NATO) as an operational squadron. No.1, with F.1A and T.4 aircraft, now became a front-line squadron, taking the 'numberplate' of 65 Squadron. No.3 was absorbed by 2(T) to become a full training squadron and postgraduate course using F.3s (and F.6 systems) and T.5s. Wing Commander Murdo MacDermid became OC 65 Squadron, which was declared to NATO as such with its war base at Coltishall. OC 2 Squadron, Wing Commander Paul Hobley, became known as OC 2(T) Squadron and in war either would operate from Coltishall, or disperse its aircraft and personnel to support other front-line squadrons.

'We therefore had,' recalls Wing Commander Dave Seward, 'an OCU with a wing commander chief instructor, who was also OC Ops Wing RAF Coltishall and two wing commander squadron commanders, one of which had a front-line number plane. Personally, I have always thought this to be distinctly unfortunate as it really split the thing into two. Before this, we were one identifiable unit with a single reserve squadron number, which engendered a true unit spirit. If it were imperative that No.1 Squadron should become 65 Squadron, I felt that 2(T) Squadron should have retained the reserve number plate of 145 Squadron. Then at least we would have had parity in squadron identification, but just one squadron number plate for the whole OCU would have been preferable. In the event, the running of the unit required careful handling and demanded the utmost co-operation of the three wing commanders in carrying out the OCU training task as well as maintaining operational efficiency to front-line squadron standards.

'I started my refresher conversion course on No.67 Course in January 1972. I had hoped to refresh on the full long course with both squadrons, but in the event it was decided that I should be in post by the end of April 1972 when Coltishall's runway was to be complete.[17] For me the course was reduced to three months, half with each squadron. Thus, for four months the OCU was dispersed. 65 Squadron went to Honington, Suffolk, and then back to Norfolk, to Marham and No.2 (T) to Binbrook. The Battle of Britain Flight went to Wattisham. Due to an attempted takeover bid by Ken Goodwin to retain the historic aircraft at Wattisham, I was dispatched there for most of the detachment to ensure that it returned to Coltishall. I therefore managed to get some hours on the Lightning in those four months, but had a veritable feast on the Hurricanes and Spitfires. 226 OCU returned to Coltishall on 1 September 1972, much to the surprise of some new homeowners in the area who had purchased their property believing that all flying had ceased. We had a few months of complaints and visits to local councils and organizations plus several parties visiting the station to see for themselves, but by Christmas all was relatively serene.'[18]

In December that same year one aircraft-mad enthusiast received an early Christmas present. Brian Stiff was a young man with an ambition in the 1960s. Like hundreds of others, he wanted to fly in a Lightning. His story began in the 1960s, when, as a teenager living near RAF Coltishall, he began to develop an interest in the Lightning as it entered service with 74 Squadron. Throughout the 1960s he spent hours watching the aircraft movements from the perimeter fence, determined that one day he would fly in a Lightning. A job promotion meant moving to North Wales, where his determination to achieve his ambition became even stronger. In the autumn 1969 he wrote to the commanding officer at RAF Coltishall, seeking his permission for a flight. Of course, he could not sanction his request, but he did invite Brian to tour the facilities at Coltishall. He did and he flew the Lightning simulator. Fired with an even greater desire to fulfil his dream of flying in a Lightning, Brian hit on the idea of approaching the editors of the Chester and Liverpool newspapers to ask if they would be interested in publishing his story if he ever achieved his ambition. To his delight both editors agreed, so with their blessing he wrote to Headquarters Strike Command seeking approval for a flight in a Lightning. Brian was ecstatic when on 29 May 1970 he received a letter from Strike Command informing him that he would be offered a flight in the not too distant future. It was not until the autumn of 1972 that he heard again from Strike Command, when he was given details of what his schedule would be prior to flying from RAF Coltishall. Brian Stiff recalls.[19]

'Firstly, I would visit RAF Cosford where I would undergo a stringent medical. From there I would go to RAF North Luffenham for a decompression test and two days of instruction on aspects of the Lightning's functions and survival training. On 7 December 1972 my dream became a reality when I flew in Lightning XS413 on a sortie with 2T Squadron. After my most memorable experience I wrote the following story for the press:

'A long line of blunt nosed, gleaming Lightning Jet aircraft faced me as I stepped from the crew room onto the tarmac of RAF Coltishall, Norfolk. I was about to have my first flight in this 1,500mph RAF fighter – a rare privilege for a civilian. Having already undergone a stringent medical decompression test, lectures on safety and survival and a fully clothed dip in a swimming pool to see how I coped with survival equipment, I was passed fit to fly. Fully briefed, I was to accompany Liverpool-born Flight Lieutenant Christopher Coville on a routine patrol. At 27 he is an Instructor on No.2 (Training) Squadron at RAF Coltishall, having had experience of flying other types of jet fighter.

'We reach our aircraft and I climb up the ten-foot ladder, slide down into the tiny cockpit. Outside there is feverish activity as our ground crew prepare for 'firing up' the two mighty Avon Jets which can catapult the Lightning up to an altitude of 9 miles in 60 seconds. In the cockpit I fumble with the countless straps which anchor every part of my body to the seat ... on with the helmet, clamp on the oxygen mask, remove pins 1,2,3 and 4 – ejector seat primed. Beside me, Chris is already working hard – No.1 engine running ... No.2 engine running. The cockpit canopy clicks shut. We begin to taxi. Line up on runway 22. A final methodical check of the masses of instruments and dials.

'"Clear for take-off," rasps a voice in our earphones. Engines run to 85%.

"Rolling ... Rolling ... GO!" calls Chris.

'"Brakes off. Reheat on." A terrific thump in the kidneys as the 33,000lb of thrust blasts us along the runway. Airborne at 200mph. The undercarriage slams home. The

Lightning shudders. We streak over the perimeter at 350mph, bank left and bore up into the clear blue sky. My arms and legs are pinned down by the force. I can just about move my head. We level out at 35,000 feet. The speed reaches 700mph, the acceleration gradually decreases and I am able to move my limbs again. Below, the North Sea and to the right the Dutch coast. We are cruising "on station."

'The headphones crackle, "OK, you fly it, Brian."

'I take the controls. Still shaken by the rapid take-off and climb, I am content to fly a straight and level course, enough for me to feel, however, just how responsive the Lightning is.

'Suddenly, a new voice breaks through the routine chatter. It's from the Ground Control Interception station, part of the radar stations networked over the UK, warning us of an unidentified aircraft approaching from the north east, about to penetrate British airspace. Chris grabs back the controls. Am I about to witness an "international incident?" With data provided from the ground, Chris pushes buttons, flicks switches. The aircraft with its two air to air missiles slung beneath the wings, is ready to strike.

'Again the phenomenal thrust as the re-heat cuts in. MACH I – smoothly through the sound barrier. Guided by a voice from the GCI station, we swing northwest. I'm riveted to my seat, barely able to open my eyes, head forced between my shoulders. MACH 1.4, MACH 1.5, 1.6 – that's 1200mph (Liverpool to London in 10 minutes!)

'"Tally Ho!" yells Chris as the target appears on our radar.

'Fifty miles away and closing at a combined speed of 2000mph. Another numbing turn as we climb onto an attack vector. Chris makes a split second speed and fuel calculation (at these speeds the engines consume 50 gallons a minute).

'"Missiles gone!" – Well, that could have been the situation had this been a genuine interception, but not on this routine training exercise. Reheat off, throttle back and there's our target, a sister aircraft from Coltishall still four miles away. We turn for base. The nose dips toward the North Sea. We lose height gradually. An air traffic control station remote from Coltishall guides our initial approach. Ten miles out, the home station's own precision radar controller takes over and talks us down until we sight the runway. Panel lights indicate wheels down and locked. A slight jolt as we touch down at 201mph.

'Out comes the brake chute and we are home. We had been airborne 35 minutes and the metal beast had devoured enough fuel to drive a mini around the equator. The aircraft had reached a speed of 1,200mph, considerably less than its maximum and I had been initiated into the "Ten Ton Club," exclusive to those who have handled the controls of a Lightning at speeds in excess of 1000mph.'

'1973' continues Wing Commander Dave Seward, 'was an exceptionally busy year. We had a very vigorous TACEVAL and incidentally won the TACEVAL Trophy.[20] On 27 July we had a Royal visit by His Royal Highness the Prince Philip, Duke of Edinburgh, which was very successful, and training continued at an intensive rate. In addition to the long and short Lightning conversions and refreshers, we ran the Interceptor Weapons Instructor (IWI) courses. During my period of office, we had three accidents. Two were bail-outs and one an aborted take-off. The first bail-out [14 December 1972] was due to the break up of an engine when [T.4 XM974] the target aircraft was acting as a high-speed, low-level target for the IWI (Intercept Weapons Instructors) course. In order to maintain 650 knots, re-heat was engaged and shortly afterwards the engines rapidly exited the rear end of the aircraft in a plume of thick black smoke. The crew, an instructor and a student who had finished his course and was awaiting posting [Squadron Leader John Spencer and Flying Officer Geoff Evans respectively] both ejected.'

At 1,000ft near Happisburgh and flying at 600 knots XM974 developed an ECU/re-heat fire. Spencer pulled up to 9-10,000ft and put out distress calls. At 270 knots and one minute after the critical emergency, Evans ejected first, followed by Spencer. Both men were picked up after eighty-five minutes (thirty of them in the dinghy) by helicopter. By then Spencer, who was wearing too small a girth of immersion suit and totally inadequate insulation, was hypothermic. Evans, on the other hand, in his Bunny suit and Mk.10 coverall, was reported to be warm and dry.

'It is possible' continues Seward, 'that somehow medical records may have been inexplicably switched because the student, looking exceedingly healthy, was kept in hospital and the instructor, with his head sagging to one side, was returned to duty. I seem to recall that he was posted to RAF Germany as a flight commander and was very rapidly sorted out in Wegburg [RAF Hospital in Germany]. He also went on to complete a very distinguished career and achieved air rank.

'The aborted take-off was a singularly unfortunate occurrence. The F.6 used flap for take-off in order to give more positive lift off during the take-off roll. It is interesting that take-off in order to give more positive lift off during the take-off roll. It is interesting that, due to not having inter-connected flaps, the F.2A did flap-less take-offs without any difficulty. Higher authority decided that all re-heat take-offs by F.3s and T.5s would also be with flaps down. This was a very uncomfortable manoeuvre and was considered by the OCU to be unnecessary. We were overruled. The case [31 January 1973] involved an instructor, [Captain Gary Catren] a USAF exchange officer, on an SCT [Stall Continuation Training] sortie in a T.5 [XS420] with a student [Flight Lieutenant George Smith] as ballast. During the re-heat take-off at night the lower re-heat failed to ignite and, with flap down, the resultant force of the upper re-heat did not allow the nose-wheel to be raised. The whole affair was settled when the instructor uttered an expletive, which the student interpreted as "*Chute* George", and he promptly deployed the drag-chute. Although it rapidly burnt off, the deployed chute scuppered any chance of take-off and the aircraft took the barrier with it into the overshoot. Of course the instructor took the blame, and when I tried to take the matter up with the Wing Commander Training at HQ 11 Group, he had already progressed to better fields; but I seem to recall that flaps were no longer used for re-heat take-offs in F.3s and T5s.

'The second bail-out occurred [on 5 June 1973] when the student [Wing Commander Chris Bruce of 74 Squadron, in a solo sortie in T.4 XM988] pitched up when carrying out a hard diving turn from supersonic to subsonic. He hit the transonic cobbles and lost control, causing a violent pitch up, which became uncontrollable. [Bruce, who was just twenty-three minutes into his flight, called "Mayday" during the descent, the Lightning spinning to the left, nose down and out of control.] At just above 10,000ft he ejected using the SPH [Seat Pan Handle] and landed in the North Sea, suffering from a few cuts and bruises. After forty-five minutes in the water (which was 10 degrees C) he became hypothermic, but after being picked up by helicopter and once back at Coltishall a hot bath restored matters. Bruce was unhurt and continued with his distinguished career as a senior officer.)

'By the end of July 1974 the writing was on the wall for the Lightning OCU; the F.1s and T.4s were disposed of to various airfields as decoys, crash, rescue, etc and I flew my last Lightning sortie on 29 August. Jaguars were now at Coltishall and those Lightnings to be retained were flown to Binbrook, where the LTF continued to serve the remaining Lightning squadrons.

'I found the task of running 226 OCU during the period 1972-1974 to be challenging and extremely satisfying. I am sure that we had a first-class team at Coltishall and produced for the squadrons a very high calibre pilot. Most of these young men went on to give excellent service and many distinguished themselves in their future careers.'

In September 1974, 226 OCU was disbanded and many of its Lighting F.1As and T.4s were withdrawn from service and scrapped.

1 Group Captain Roger Topp continued in the post until 3 June 1966, when Grp Cpt. Mike Hobson took over.

2 Douglas Aylward who was from Darlington went to Durham School and had planned a career as a vet, but, attracted by the adventure and challenge of flying, he applied to join the Royal Air Force and was accepted in December 1961.

3 Inspection of the aircraft revealed that a small fire had occurred on the starboard side of No.1 engine in zone 2. The fire was caused by engine oil which had leaked from a defective joint coupling on the overboard vent pipe for the No.1 engine wheelcase breather. The accumulation of oil spilled into the No.1 engine hatch during the climb and ignited when it came into contact with the jet pipe. Because of the concealed position of the seal normal servicing procedures did not reveal the defect. When the aircraft rejoined the circuit it was seen to be streaming fuel from the underside of the aircraft. This was caused by the ventral tank/aircraft fuel connection seal remaining fouled in the self-sealing coupling after the ventral was jettisoned. Fuel vented overboard only 12 inches from the scene of the fire thus considerably increasing the hazard to the aircraft. The seal was probably displaced during assembly of the ventral tank to the aircraft and would have eventually caused a ventral feed failure. This is a well-known defect as a result of poor design. Steps are being taken to introduce a modification to position the seal correctly during assembly.

4 Later ACM Sir Michael Graydon GCB CBE ADC FRAeS, Chief of Air Staff

5 Sadly, the Phantom, with Spey engines, was a pig to fly! With a radar operator in the back, the workload was laughably low for the pilot, who became little more than an aerial chauffeur! (There were no radar controls in the front cockpit) Worst of all. I clashed with my superiors over the unrealistic training, peacetime mentality and poor operational standards achieved. I decided to exercise my option to leave the service, at my eight-year option point and became a civilian.

6 'Sadly, Gil Pink, who had got me to the right place at the right time, was killed on 22 June when the SAR Whirlwind he was riding in on a training exercise lost a rotor blade and crashed into the sea, killing everyone on board.

7 The Hind is now displayed at the RAF Museum, Hendon.

8 At the disbandment parade at Bentley Priory on 25 April, the fly-past was by Lightnings of 5, 23, 29 and 111 squadrons and 226 OCU.

9 The week prior to the Battle of Britain Open Day, XM990 was undergoing checks to solve control problems which added to the already high workload the maintenance engineers were under preparing over sixteen Lightnings for the flying display. After an air test and practicing the formation, XM990 had been declared 'ready'.

10 Saudi Arabia ordered thirty-four of the F.53 export variant (twelve were also ordered by Kuwait) and aircraft 53-666, the first Lightning for the Royal Saudi Air Force, flew on 1 December 1966, the first delivery taking place in December 1967. The first Saudi pilot to convert to the Lightning was Lieutenant A. Thunneyan, whom Mick Swiney checked out on a standardization sortie at the conclusion of his conversion phase on 9 June 1967. In an effort to stop Yemeni incursions, the delivery of the Saudi Lightnings was preceded, in June 1966, by the arrival in that country of five ex-RAF F.2s (designated F.52), two ex-RAF T.4s and ex-RAF pilots to fly them. The programme, codenamed *Magic Carpet*, also included Hunters and Thunderbird surface-to-air missiles (SAMs).

11 Later, General and Commander of the RSAF.

12 Later, Brigadier General, Deputy Defence Minister.

13 Killed in an F.52 whilst practising single-engine approaches to Khamis Mushayt on 28 November 1968.

14 Squadron Leader Dave 'Quingle' Hampton was killed on 7 April 1975 during an AI exercise in Cyprus.

15 Ed was killed flying his own home-built aircraft in 1975, aged 34, when he hit a tree at Seeley Lake, Montana.

16 Writing in *Lightning Review*, March 1993 and September 1994.

17 This involved digging out the existing runway to 12ft and replacing it.

18 Before the move, on 6 September, 226 OCU lost a T.5 flying from Binbrook when Squadron Leader Tim Gauvain took Lieutenant R. Verbist of the Belgian Air Force on a familiarization trip in XS455. Fifteen minutes after take off, near Spurn Head, Gauvain was alerted by both hydraulic captions illuminating on his instrument panel. The T.5 had suffered a double hydraulic failure! Four minutes later, Gauvain sent a 'Mayday' and said he and his Belgian passenger were both ejecting. Gauvain landed in a cornfield, suffering four crush fractures. Verbist landed hard near houses and twisted his right knee. The aircraft crashed in the North Sea off Withensea.

19 'TEN TON TARGET – My Ambition To Fly At 1,000mph in a Lightning' by Brian E. Stiff, writing in *Lightning Review*, September 1992.

20 Despite all the problems, RAF Coltishall also won the 1973 Stainforth Trophy for the 'most efficient station and flying efficiency'.

CHAPTER 4

Tanking

When in January 1965 92 Squadron's turn to fly a detachment to Cyprus came, the requirement unfortunately coincided with the withdrawal from service of all Valiants after dangerous metal fatigue had been discovered in their airframes in August of the previous year. Flight Lieutenant Alex Reed, one of the four pilots in 92 Squadron at Leconfield who would still fly the trip, explains how it was carried out, now that the Valiants were unavailable:

'We were going to "puddle-jump" our way to Cyprus, four of us, in two pairs. We took off from Leconfield on 9 January (I flew XN792), made our first stopover at Geilenkirchen in West Germany before going on to Istres in southern France, then crossed the Mediterranean to load at Decimomannu, Sardinia, before stopping the night at Luqa on Malta. Next day we rook off for El Adem in Libya, the last stop before Akrotiri. We thought before we went that this sounded a pretty good trip, and it was. We had a ball. At each stop we did a quick run in and break and we all received glowing tributes!

'While on the detachment on Cyprus, we flew PIs or "Profit Sorties" against Canberras of 360 Squadron. Unlike in Britain we had the added benefit of the radar station on Mount Olympus to help us. We would be scrambled off, go out and find the target, "fire" two missiles and then, after the targets were "splashed", we would break off and cream our way back to Akrotiri. Back on the airfield again we would go straight unto the ORP, ready to scramble again. This was the most exciting operational flying I did! I averaged twenty-three minutes per sortie (we did four sorties each). We were flying the Lightning to its maximum operational capability. Mind you, it was under optimum conditions, but tough work in the hot sun. Then Squadron Leader Les Hargreaves, our CO, decided we would do low-level interceptions at night. Les said, "I'll lead the first pair. We don't want to push it." (Low-level PIs on a black night using AI 23 left a lot to be desired.) Les added that we would have the target at 1,000ft so we'd have plenty of room. It was pitch black. He came back, looked at us and said, "Right, we'll put the target at 1,500!" The rest of us heaved a big sigh of relief.'

It was in Cyprus that Brian Carroll had his first encounter with the Lightning, as he recalls:

'One's actual thoughts at the time of flying the Lightning for the first time are now difficult to re-crystallize. Nevertheless, I intend to try and cast my mind back to those heady days when I first flew the better part of eighteen tons of highly polished metal, projected by 32,600lb of thrust. My first encounter with the Lightning was at a time when I was flying the Gloster Javelin Mk.9, also nicknamed the "harmonious dragmaster" (an aircraft designed to prove that drag can overcome thrust), in 1963-65 at Nicosia and then Akrotiri in Cyprus. A UK-based Lightning squadron had arrived there for a month's detachment and was sited just a few yards from our dispersal,

Royal Navy Sea Vixen refuelling F.1A XM189/E of Treble One Squadron on 28 May 1963. (Cobham PLC)

so we were very much aware of the noise, if nothing else. One particularly clear memory from those days was, "What an ugly aircraft. I wouldn't wish to fly one of those". I hasten to add that my opinion changed totally once I got my hands on one but that was not to be for another three years, until March of 1968. Well, even that is not totally correct. I did have a passenger ride in a T.5 on 9 July 1965 and another in December of the same year. I think that it would be true to say that one has a terrific loyalty to whichever aircraft one is currently flying and, in spite of somewhat derogatory remarks that have been made about the Javelin, it was a great aircraft to fly.'[1]

Meanwhile, the conversion of Victor B.1 bombers to K.1A in-flight refuelling tankers was speeded up. The first to fly was XH620, on 28 April 1965. 55 Squadron, which had become non-operational as a Medium Bomber Force Squadron at Honington on 1 March, moved to Marham on 24 May 1965 to operate in the in-flight refuelling role. The Squadron's first two Victor K.1A two-point tankers[2] arrived the following day and two more[3] arrived at the end of May. (These interim, two-point tankers severely limited long-range operations, as they were unable to permit Victor-Victor refuelling operations and would be withdrawn and be replaced with three-point tankers at a later date.) 55 Squadron's full complement of six Victors would not be reached until October but, like the 7th Cavalry, the Americans again came to the rescue. Arrangements had already been made with the USAF for the use of three KC-135s over a six- to nine-month period so that much-needed in-flight refuelling practice could commence immediately. Two SAC KC-135s from the 919th Squadron, to be stationed at Upper Heyford, would begin in-flight refuelling with 23, 56, 74 and 111 Squadrons' Lightnings in the UK while another, from the 611th ARS, to be based at Adana, Turkey, would operate with 29 Squadron's Javelin FAW.9s at Akrotiri.

Operation *Billy Boy*, as it was called, began on 5 April with 1½-hour sorties with 23 and 74 Squadrons' Lightnings, refuelling with 3,000lb of fuel each sortie. Pilots discovered that the KC-135's rigid refuelling boom, to which was attached a seven-foot flexible hose and drogue, called for a much different receiver technique to that used on the hose and reel-equipped Valiant. Flight Lieutenant Bob Offord, now on 23 Squadron, who did his first 'bracket' with a KC-135 on 5 April, recalls: 'This caused us no end of problems because we were not set up. On 7 April I became the first pilot in the squadron to break a probe, which cost me a barrel of beer! However, my probe breaking was the first of many. [Of the twenty-two conversion and twenty-five continuation training sorties flown, the loss of probes on 15 per cent of these sorties

F.6 XS919, which first flew on 28 September 1966 and was used for over-wing tank trials before squadron service in 1967. XS919 was issued to 11 Squadron on 18 May 1967. (BAe)

was 'unacceptably high'.] On the end of the KC-135 boom was a basket, which went into an Omega shape and this put more stress on the connection. Our weak-link safety device just behind the nozzle in the probe (which broke off in emergency) was too weak to mate with the KC-135.'

Initially, 23 Squadron's pilots, 75 per cent of whom had had previous experience of in-flight refuelling, had the lion's share of the KC-135s (by the end of April only nine pilots in 'Tiger' squadron had completed a minimum of three in-flight refuelling sorties). However, the CO, Squadron Leader John Mcleod, admitted that it had also 'broken the largest number of probes – a weakness which would be largely eliminated by a current modification'. Bob Offord confirms. 'We had to have our probes "beefed up" (the weak link was made stronger). From then on, the Americans would ask during tanking if we had a "beefed up" probe.' Pilots in 111 Squadron at Wattisham, however, reported that 'initial contacts in the "boomed" KC-135s proved relatively easy compared with the Valiant tanker'. However, the CO, Squadron Leader George Black, wrote, 'the kinking and shortness of the KC-135's hose and drogue (seven feet) [had] proved more strenuous in probe rivets' and that remaining in contact for prolonged periods of up to five minutes had been 'more exacting and tiring than Valiant refuelling'.'

Then, in May, several sorties were flown with the flight profile being one hour with the KC-135, followed by forty minutes on PIs. During 24-28 May, preparatory to their deployment to Cyprus, 56 Squadron at Wattisham, which had just converted from the F.1A to the F.3 in April, began their *Billy Boy* refuelling practice with five tanker missions involving three pairs of Lightnings being allocated to each tanker. However, one sortie was cancelled owing to Lightning unserviceability, and two were lost when the KC-135 was forced to return to base with a probe end stuck in time drogue. Four probes in total were lost in the twenty-seven sorties achieved.

When a Tanker Training Flight was formed at Marham in July, 55 Squadron could get on with the task of training pilots in 74 Squadron. Nine successful sorties were carried out with nine pairs of F.3s. 74 Squadron's need was urgent, as four pilots would fly the receiver aircraft in the forthcoming in-flight refuelling exercise *Forthright 22/23*, to Cyprus in August. This would be the first occasion that the Victor tanker was used for an operational overseas deployment. The F.3s left Leuchars for Wattisham on 13 August and took off from the Suffolk station the next day, in-flight refuelling to Akrotiri. All four Lightnings arrived on schedule after an average flight time of four hours ten minutes. In the meantime, six pilots from 19 Squadron at

F.3s of 56 Squadron lined up at Luqa, Malta, in 1965. Nearest aircraft is XP746/K, which first flew on 26 March 1964 and joined the squadron on 15 April 1965. It joined Treble One Squadron on 4 August 1970 and was struck off charge in April 1975. (Graham Vernon)

Leconfield converted to high-level in-flight refuelling and then carried out low-level in-flight refuelling trials from five of the K.1A tankers in preparation for 74 Squadron's return to the UK in August. Low-level tanking was possible but extremely difficult and was best carried out over the sea, where conditions are relatively smooth. The Victor's wing was prone to flexing in turbulence and the whip effect at the basket end of the drogue was quite frightening if a Lightning was not on the end to tone it down. Dave Seward agrees:

'You had to refuel cross-controlled because the vortex coming off the Victor's wing always forced the Lightning's wing down. (We always used the Victor's wing positions, the rear, central position only being used by the bigger aeroplanes). So, if you were going in on the starboard side, you had to feed in using the left rudder and right aileron to keep your wings level and keep yourself from being thrown out of the wing vortex. If you went in on the port side you got the same sort of problem, but it was exacerbated in that your probe, being on the left-hand side, meant that you had to be between the Victor's pod and his fuselage. You didn't have much room to play with if you started to buck up and down. People just got used to it. The problem came when we would demonstrate flight refuelling to a student using a T.5. Flying it from the right-hand seat when you were on the left wing of the Victor trying to get between his pod and the fuselage was difficult, especially since you flew the T.5 with your left hand and you had your right hand on the throttle! It worked but you had to work hard at it You became more confident with practice but after becoming proficient at flight refuelling you got into a few bad habits. I, for instance, started off by religiously not looking at the basket and kept a general sight picture, but as you got more used to it once I had trapped the basket I would automatically have a quick look at the probe and nudge it in.

'At OCU the instructors were all flight commander material, but they did not practice flight refueling at night so no one was current. For this reason, 11 Group said that we couldn't be used operationally at night. However, we went up and did prods at night using a Victor until everyone was night qualified. When we told them, 11 Group demanded to know how we had become night qualified. I said we just went up and did it. How else did they think we had become proficient? It was rather like in the 1950s when you couldn't land at Gibraltar unless you had landed at Gibraltar before!'

Just how difficult tanking could be was tragically brought home on 27 April 1964.

F.6 XR725/A, flown by
Squadron Leader Ed
Durham, and XS936/B
flown by Flight Lieutenant
Geoff Brindle, both of 23
Squadron, are refuelled by a
214 Squadron Victor tanker
over Niagara Falls during
their visit to Toronto at the
end of August 1968. Both
F.3s flew non-stop from the
UK to Goose Bay, Canada,
on 27 August 1968. (MoD)

Flight Lieutenant George Davey had been the last of 92 Squadron's Lightnings to take his turn at air-to-air refuelling practice with Victors over the North Sea. Davey repeatedly failed to take on fuel and eventually had to abort. Unwisely as it turned out, he chose not to divert to nearby Coltishall, but decided to try instead to return to base with the rest of his squadron, which had now departed. He reached Binbrook, but on finals his cockpit canopy failed to de-mist and he was prevented from making a visual approach. As Davey entered the circuit for a GCA approach, his Lightning crashed out of fuel, at Beelsby near Binbrook, too low for him to safely eject.

By October 1965 the Lightnings were able to use all six Victor tankers. During the month, four F.3s of 74 Squadron at Akrotiri, in Operation *Donovan*, were refuelled all the way to Tehran and back, where, on 17 October, they took part in an IIAF (Imperial Iranian Air Force) Day. That same month a 23 Squadron detachment was made to Cyprus to take the place of 29 Squadron's Javelins, which, when UDI (Unilateral Declaration of Independence) was declared in Rhodesia, were sent to the troubled region. For Flight Lieutenant Bob Offord it meant a return to the island he had last visited with 56 Squadron. 'This time we stayed three months, with crews rotating back and forth to the UK during this period. One of my interceptions, on 24 November, was against Turkish Air Force RF-84Fs, who as soon as they realized they had been intercepted, turned and headed for home. Little did they know it but my radar was u/s. The Turks were always friendly. In fact they would hold up a map and point to indicate that they were going home.'[4]

At the beginning of December 1965, 55 Squadron had been joined at Marham by 57 Squadron, minus their Victor K.1/1As.[5] In 1966, 56 Squadron was tanked to Malta by 55 and 57 Squadron Victors to take part in *Adex 66*, the Malta air defence exercise. In February 1967 Exercise *Forthright 59 60* saw F.3s flying non-stop to Akrotiri and F.6s returning to the UK, refuelled throughout by Victor tankers from Marham. In April, 56 Squadron moved to Akrotiri to replace 29 Squadron's Javelins, a posting which would last seven years (May 1967-September 1974). The Lightnings' journey from the UK to Cyprus involved six in-flight refuellings for the fighter versions and ten for the T-birds, which were often taken on detachment to Cyprus to familiarize new pilots on target interception.

In-flight refuelling from Victors also became a feature used often on QRA (Quick Reaction Alert), 74 Squadron sharing the northern IAF (Interceptor Alert Force)

F.2A XN733/Y of 19 Squadron refuelling from Victor K.1A XH651 of 57 Squadron in 1971. XN733 first flew on 1 February 1962 and was issued to 92 Squadron on 6 June 1963. It suffered a Cat.4 starter explosion in 1968 and was transported by road to Warton for repairs. After conversion to F.2A, on 31 December 1969, XN733 was issued to 19 Squadron and coded 'R'. On 18 June 1970 BAC used the aircraft and it took part in the September 1970 SBAC show at Farnborough. After a spell at 60 MU, XN733 joined 92 Squadron in October 1970 and was coded 'U'. It became 'Y' with 19 Squadron at Laarbruch from December 1970. (Brian Allchin)

defensive duties at Leuchars with 23 Squadron's F.3s (the Lightning's operational range and endurance being improved from August 1966 by the introduction of the F.6). Of course, intercepts were carried out at night and these posed some added considerations to take into account, as Brian Carroll[6] recalls: 'Night tanking always added that extra bit of interest to the sortie. My personal preference was for the tanker to leave its floodlights off (when used they lit up the under surface of the tanker's wings and ruined night vision). This left just the tanker's navigation lights and the small triangles of blue lights on the basket. In some ways tanking was easier in the dark, as one was not supposed to look at the refuelling probe when trying to engage the basket. In the dark you couldn't see it anyway, so it was one less thing to be concerned about.'

In June 1967, 74 Squadron and its thirteen Lightnings were posted overseas, to Tengah, Singapore, to replace the Javelins of 64 Squadron. Operation *Hydraulic,* as it was known, the longest and largest in-flight refuelling operation hitherto flown, began on 4 June when the CO, Wing Commander Ken Goodwin, led six Lightnings off from Leuchars. Five more departed the next day and the last two flew out on the 6th.[7] All thirteen Lightnings reached Tengah safely, staging through Akrotiri, Masirah and Gan and using seventeen Victor tankers from Marham, for what turned out to be a four-year tour of duty in the tropics. During this time, three 2,000-mile deployments were made to Australia non-stop using Victor tankers, the major one being Exercise *Town House,* 16-26 June 1969. The Lightnings also participated in *Bersatu Padu* ('Complete Unity'), a five-nation exercise held in Western Malaya and Singapore in July 1969. Regular exchanges were also flown with RAAF Mirages at Butterworth, Malaysia and two Lightnings were flown to Thailand for a static display in Bangkok.

Meanwhile, 11 Squadron had practised in-flight refuelling (in 1967) and on 29 November, Flight Lieutenant Eggleton had established a record, of eight-and-a-half-hours' flying, refuelling five times, flying 5,000 miles.[8] In May 1968, four F.6s of 5 Squadron at Leconfield flew non-stop from Binbrook to Bahrain in eight hours,

F.3 XP700/K of 29 Squadron refuels from Victor K.1A XH650. When 29 Squadron from Wattisham to Cyprus on 2 March 1970 the F.3s were refuelled no less than six times, and T.5 XV329/Z ten! T-birds were often taken on detachment to Cyprus to familiarise new pilots with the procedures involved in performing successful target interceptions. XP700 had joined 29 Squadron on 16 February 1968 and it was lost in a take-off accident on 7 August 1972. (Cobham)

A pair of 74 Squadron F.6 Lightnings refuelling from a Victor tanker. (Mike Rigg)

F.6 XR759/P, which joined 56 Squadron on 3 September 1971, landing in Cyprus after flying from the UK. Note the white AVPIN panel on the spine to reflect the Mediterranean heat. (via CONAM)

refuelled along the 4,000-mile route by Victor tankers from Marham. In August 1968 two Lightnings from 23 Squadron, fitted with overwing tanks, were required to fly the Atlantic to Canada non-stop to enable RAF solo display pilot Tony Craig to take part in the International Exhibition at Toronto. He would use one of the Lightnings for his solo display – the other was a spare in case of problems with the first Lightning. On 26 August Squadron Leader Ed Durham and Flight Lieutenant Geoff Brindle of 23 Squadron took off in XR725/A and XS936/B respectively and rendezvoused with their first tanker off Stornaway at 0800. Geoff Brindle, however, could not take on fuel and his overwing tanks were venting. Both pilots aborted and it was decided to re-mount the operation the following day after repairs to Brindle's aircraft. At 11.40 hours on 27 August, Squadron Leader Durham and Flight Lieutenant Brindle set out again with their supporting Victors. The first bracket went well, but at the second bracket, about 300 miles west of Stornaway, Brindle again could not take on fuel into his overburgers. Ed Durham continues:

'We decided to carry on. Geoff would just have to refuel more often. I refuelled seven times across the Atlantic. Geoff Brindle did more like twelve or thirteen! The flight took seven hours twenty minutes. Apart from the refuellings and bad weather at Goose Bay, it was otherwise bloody boring. Craig took XS936 back with me in XR725 on 3 September and he had trouble with the overwing tanks on the first refuelling bracket! I said, "We force on". If a tanker did not get airborne we could always divert to Goose Bay. The Victors did arrive every time and after several tankings we reached Scotland again safely.'

On 6 January 1969 Exercise *Piscator,* the biggest in-flight refuelling exercise so far mounted by the RAF took place. Ten Lightning F.6s of 11 Squadron, refuelled by Victor tankers of 55, 57 and 214 Squadrons at Marham, deployed to RAF Tengah, Singapore, (staging through Muharraq and Gan) and back, a distance of 18,500 miles. During the two-way journey, 228 individual refuelling contacts were made during which 166,000 imperial gallons (754,630 litres) of fuel were transferred.

Twelve months later, in December 1969, Exercise *Ultimacy* was mounted. Ten F.6s of 5 Squadron this time flew to Tengah for joint air-defence exercises with 74 Squadron and RAAF Mirages there before exchanging some of their Lightnings for those of 74 Squadron, which were in need of major overhaul. Flight Lieutenant F.S. 'Stu' Rance recalls:[9]

A Victor K.2 of 232 Operational Conversion Unit at Marham refuels F.6s XR724/K and XR769/J of 11 Squadron during an exercise in September 1974. XR769 was built as an F.6 and first flew on 1 December 1965, being issued to 74 Squadron on 2 November 1966. It finished its career with 11 Squadron as 'BD' in 1988. XR724 was built as an F.3 and first flew on 10 February 1965. It was converted to F.6 before being issued to 11 Squadron on 16 June 1967.

'*Ultimacy* provided an apt name for the deployment over Christmas 1969 of 5 Squadron's Lightnings to the Far East. Building upon previous deployment successes, the "planners" had this time done us proud – for only one stop was involved, at Masirah in the Persian Gulf. Deployment time was to be kept to a minimum, too, with less than five days from first aircraft leaving the United Kingdom to the last aircraft arriving in South-East Asia. The detachment was to last for about a month, air defence exercises taking place in co-operation with 74 Squadron, the resident Lightning "outfit" at our host station RAF Tengah. For the return home, starting the second week in January this year, the more leisurely "scenic route" was to be made available, with stops at Masirah and Akrotiri a major planning concession to the pilot's anatomy. The last aircraft was to arrive in the UK by 16 January. It sounded good and anyone who had flown with the tanker force before knew that No.1 AAR Planning Cell at Bawtry would calculate and cosset us, Victor tankers metering fuel with slide rule precision. "We can hack it" and other such detailed planning epitaphs emitted as we studied our "World Mercator" atlases. Where was the Far East, anyway? The Squadron Navigation Officer, a serious-looking first tour Flying Officer, looked pained. No one else had liked the sound of the job! He was eventually heard – did we realise that Singapore was nearly 8,000 miles away, that each leg required some eight-and-a-half hours in the air and that some of it was at *night*! Even the sturdiest "fighter jock" blanched, as a general realisation that "we'll set off on about one-five-oh degrees", just wouldn't do.

'Still, nothing that about a fortnight in the Planning Section didn't fix and on schedule the first wave of aircraft left the Binbrook runway in the pre-dawn and foggy hours of 8 December 1969. For those of us leaving on the third day, the knowledge that a first pair was already enjoying the sun in Singapore hastened the desire for departure from the ever-deepening fog machine that is North Lincolnshire

Victor K.1A XH650 of 55 Squadron refuels F.3 XP700/K of 29 Squadron.

The Victor's wing was prone to flexing in turbulence, and the whip effect at the basket end of the drogue was quite frightening if a Lightning was not on the end to tone it down. Here F.6 XR723 successfully engages the basket from a Victor tanker. This Lightning began life as an F.3, flying for the first time on 2 February 1965. It was modified to F.6 at Warton before joining 11 Squadron on 9 June 1967 it went on to serve with 5 Squadron and then went to 23 Squadron before being SOC on 18 September 1979.

in winter. An 03.45 hours rendezvous in the dark with the Victor tankers over East Anglia and we were on our way. South across a clear France, slipping by a brightly lit Paris, we coasted out over a dawning Riviera at Nice. Italy went by at equal pace and soon a snow-blown but still smoking Mount Etna heralded the turn east along the Mediterranean and the rendezvous with more Victor tankers North of Cyprus. It is perhaps the almost monotonous precision of these link ups with tankers out of "parts foreign" which visibly impress to the pilot in the air and speak for the standard of support from the planning and operations organisations on the ground. We were to be impressed in the same way many more times. More hours went by as in the sun we meandered on our way east, before a final crossing of the Muscat and Oman, which looked sandy enough to make even the most frugal consume the last of his pre-supplied orange squash – a tricky, technical feat in a small cockpit. Masirah at last and our friendly Ops Officer: "Is it serviceable? Sign in – hurry up or you'll be late for tea!" Tea? – I still hadn't had lunch. As the sun slid immediately below the horizon, I felt vaguely cheated.

'I was woken at ten the following morning. Had I heard the news? A tanker man had backed away from a snake up the road and trod on a scorpion. I checked my boots warily before putting them on and repairing to the mess for breakfast. Much to my surprise it was still available and, heartened by a staging post that obviously catered for staging, I spent the afternoon greeting the newly arrived aircraft from the UK for upon their serviceable arrival depended our own successful early departure. All was well and again a pre-dawn launch. This time into 4,000 miles of ocean, South-East to Gan and then due east to Sumatra. Being brave single-seat men, we braced ourselves to the task, ignored the water and concentrated upon the navigation – even if this did consist mainly of reciting the names of the diversion airfields to ourselves for the first couple of hours or so. We made our through connection with the Victors out of Gan on schedule and so came to the greenery of Singapore – a welcome escort being provided in the latter stages by 74 Squadron aircraft. A warm welcome awaited. With Christmas just around the corner, it was necessary to get cracking. First priority was an umbrella, second a briefing and third a flight around the local area. Of the fifteen pilots participating, twelve had not visited Singapore before and were unfamiliar with the problems of operating in the Far East theatre at the tail-end of the monsoon season. We soon got wet and the message.

'On 18 December Exercise *Antler* took place and together with 74 Squadron and 63 Light Anti-Aircraft Regiment, 5 Squadron aircraft helped provide the Singapore Air Defence Force against an enemy force comprising 45 and 81 Squadron Canberras, 20 Squadron Hunters and 75 Squadron Mirages of RAAF Butterworth. Victor tankers were also available to provide tactical air-to-air refuelling in the battle against targets at both high and low altitudes. A useful and rewarding exercise. Following the exercise, there was Christmas and more Tengah hospitality, both individual and general, for the squadron personnel. With our stay in the Far East now rapidly sliding by, only the New Year was left and it was time to refit our ferry tanks for the long homeward journey.

'With pairs of aircraft leaving Tengah daily from 8 January onwards, Masirah rapidly became the focal point of our operations on the route home. The planning called for a build-up of aircraft at Masirah before moving on to Akrotiri. It was here therefore that our "man on the ground" became vital to the efficiency of the recovery. Acting as co-ordinator with the operations rooms thousands of miles away in the UK, meeting and despatching aircraft, looking after accommodation and messing and the arranging of briefing and transport all make for a busy day. They are essential tasks, however, in taking the "staging load" off the route pilots and in ensuring their adequate rest. During our week's operations in the Gulf, every assistance was provided

Above: XN724 was built as an F.2 and
flew for the first time on 11 September
1961. It went to Boscombe Down on
22 May 1966 and then to 33 MU on 5
September 1963. On 20 October 1966
XN724 went to Warton for conversion
to F.2A and was issued to 19 Squadron
at Gütersloh, where it was coded 'F'. It
is seen here while refuelling at 30,000ft
from Victor XH621 at RAF Marham,
Norfolk, in November 1973. XN724 was
withdrawn from use in December 1976
and became a decoy at Laarbruch.

Right: In 1974 when Flying Officer (now
Squadron Leader MBE) Clive Rowley
was flying F.2As from Gütersloh with
19 Squadron, his probe tip 'rimmed' the
Victor tanker's 'basket', didn't engage and
pushed it sideways. A very large lateral
'whip' developed in the tanker hose and
'clobbered' his Lightning before all 55 feet
of the hose fell off. The hose was found
some weeks later in a German farmer's
field and returned – unfortunately! Clive
commanded the LTF from February 1986
to April 1987 and the BBMF at Coningsby
from 2004 to 2005 (his tenth display
season as a Fighter pilot with the Flight).
At that time he had amassed over 7,000
hours total flying, mostly on fast jets
including the Hunter and all marks of the
Lightning. (Tony Paxton)

for Lightning and Victor operations by the station permanent staff. It was perhaps only fortuitous that Masirah managed its first serious rainfall for nearly six years during our short stay!

'Leaving at first light on 11 January, it was on to Akrotiri for the staging aircraft. After an overnight stop, enjoying friendly hospitality and co-operation of the resident Lightning Squadron, it was homeward bound for a wintry recovery into the United Kingdom. Ah! The welcome sight of the Marham-based tanker who had come out from the UK to take us on the last stage of our journey back to Binbrook. Four days later, with all ten aircraft in the UK, it was all over. The successful conclusion of the most ambitious Lightning deployment yet, which had demonstrated our flexibility to operate in the Far East after short notice. The route experience gained had been immense. Now, with only fast-fading suntans as a reminder, we study the maps again. Perhaps they'll send us to Cyprus this year …'

In February 1971, 23 Squadron tanked from Victors to Cyprus, to take part in practice air defence of the island and ACM (air combat-manoeuvering exercises). On 25 August that year 74 Squadron disbanded at Tengah, Singapore, and 56 Squadron acquired all of the 'Tiger's' remaining F.6s. Starting on 2 September these were flown over the 6,000-mile route, a 13-hour trip, to Akrotiri. They staged through Gan and Muharraq and completed seven air-to-air refuellings with Victor tankers. 56 Squadron was relieved in June the following year by 11 Squadron, which deployed to Akrotiri for a one-month detachment, enabling 56 Squadron to fly to Britain to complete MPC (Missile Practice Camp) at Valley before returning to the island.

'During their early time on a Lightning squadron,' recalls Tony Paxton, 'most pilots took right-seat rides to watch the more experienced hands operating the aeroplane and its weapons system. The Lightning was an easy aircraft to fly. It had to be. The task of operating the radar by day and night in all weathers was quite demanding enough without having a tricky aeroplane to fly as well. So every opportunity was taken to allow the junior guys to watch the combat-ready pilots do their stuff. Inevitably, there would be a chance to fly the aircraft from the right seat. Realising the problems involved, it was obvious that the in-flight refuelling probe could not be seen from the instructor's position. However, there was a well-kept secret about tanking from the right seat. If the angle made by the windscreen centre strut and the coaming was used as a reference point and the aeroplane flown forward so that the tanker's hose passed behind the reference point, the pilot flying from the right seat could not miss making contact with the basket! Many a junior Lightning pilot has been struck with awe and admiration when, after the instructor has uttered those words with a resigned tone, "I have control", he has then made contact smoothly at the first attempt and condescendingly given control back to the hapless learner who knows that the newly revered demigod in the right seat can't even see the probe or basket!

'All military fast jets are controlled by a stick in the right hand and throttle(s) in the left; the trainer versions are generally configured in the same fashion and, indeed, the T.4 was. However, the T.5 was different. For the right seat occupant the throttles were mounted on the right-hand side of the cramped side-by-side cockpit and the flying controls were operated by a stick with the left hand. This arrangement could cause some coordination problems during certain phases of flight, particularly formation flying and landing. During my course to become a weapons instructor, known in the Lightning force as an IWI or Interceptor Weapons Instructor, but later standardized as QWI (Qualified Weapons Instructor), I remember very well my conversion to the right seat of the T.5. I had coped pretty well with flying the aeroplane "back to front", but I had been concentrating very hard. The time came to return to Binbrook during my first right-seat ride in control. I was determined to fly a good approach and touchdown so I was concentrating very hard to send the correct messages to the appropriate hands.

All went well during the initial phases of the instrument approach; air speed 175 knots with the aircraft stabilized on the descent in the landing configuration. Approaching the runway threshold a slight reduction of power to cross the end at 165 knots; then a further reduction of power and a slight increase in back pressure on the stick to flare and touch down at 155 knots. I was delighted; an almost perfect landing. However, then I relaxed big mistake because I reverted to instinct. Because of its high approach speed the Lightning used a braking parachute to shorten the landing roll. The brake 'chute is stowed under the lower jet pipe at the extreme rear of the fuselage. To prevent damage to the canopy the nose wheel must be firmly on the ground before the 'chute is deployed. Therefore the after-landing actions are to lower the nose wheel quickly onto the runway by pushing the stick forward, simultaneously reducing the power by pulling the throttles rearward. Yes, you've guessed it, after my near-perfect touch down I "lowered the nose wheel" with my right hand and "reduced the power" with my left. The result was that we rocketed skyward because in my "relaxed" state I had, much to the amusement of my instructor in the left seat, engaged re-heat and pulled the stick back! Much chastened I flew a reasonable circuit with an acceptable touchdown and managed to carry out the correct actions to bring the aircraft safely to taxi speed. I bought a few beers that evening.'

Cyprus featured high on the agenda again in 1974. In January six F.6s were sent to the island, where on 15 July a Greek-led coup by the Cyprus National Guard overthrew President Makarios of Cyprus. Five days later, Turkey invaded the northern part of the island. After two days of fierce fighting, the United Nations arranged a cease-fire. The coup led to a dramatic increase in Turkish air activity around the island and Lightnings of 56 Squadron flew over 200 sorties, 20-27 July, 110 of them fully armed battle sorties, to protect the Sovereign Base Areas.

During 1974 when Flying Officer (now Squadron Leader) Clive Rowley was flying F.2As from Gütersloh with 19 Squadron, he was photographed with this tanker hose coiled like a snake. Clive explains: 'We didn't get much tanking practice as Germany-based squadrons – spookily enough the tankers were only available on Fridays, meaning that the crews had to stop at the weekend! On about my sixth ever tanking-sortie (with gaps of several weeks between each) I think I was probably getting overconfident about this "tricky" skill. When I attempted to connect with the hose trailed from this particular Victor tanker I used all the wrong techniques, including looking at the "basket" just before connecting. Seeing that I was going to miss to the right I put on a large "bootfull" of left rudder to slide my probe into the "basket". Unfortunately the probe tip "rimmed" the "basket", didn't engage and pushed it sideways. As I backed off I was surprised and horrified to see a very large lateral "whip" develop in the tanker hose, which grew as it snaked towards the HDU (pod) and grew further as it snaked back towards me. Next thing my Lightning was "clobbered" by this hose with a life of its own. There was a loud bang as it hit me somewhere on the intake and my aircraft was tipped 90 degrees of bank towards the Victor's fuselage – rather frightening! I levelled the aircraft to straight and level and having achieved this and averted any collision risk I was appalled to see that the hose – all 55 feet of it – had fallen off over Germany! I transmitted, "Tanker Call-sign, your hose has fallen off!" This didn't go down well! A visual inspection by my leader reported possible damage to the intake.

'After a slow-speed handling check I landed back at Gütersloh safely. Unfortunately the stainless steel double skin of my intake had been dented and the skins squashed together. They were talking about several months to repair it. I was not popular. Meanwhile, I spent the weekend worrying about the tanker hose. Had it, for example, caused a multiple pile-up on an *Autobahn* with significant loss of life? No news was good news, but the aircraft damage was still threatening the previously good

F.3 XR749/Q, which joined 5 Squadron on 30 October 1972, tanking from Victor K.I XA939 of 214 Squadron. XR749 first flew on 30 April 1965, and it joined 56 Squadron on 31 October 1967. Much later this aircraft operated with 11 Squadron and the LTF, before being used for BDR (Battle Damage Repair) duties at Leuchars, after making an emergency landing there on 17 February 1987 while en route to Lossiemouth (Tony Paxton)

An F.6 of 5 Squadron refuelling from a basket deployed from a USAF KC-135 tanker's boom in October 1978. (Tony Paxton)

A pair of F.6s of 5 Squadron approaching a KC-135 tanker. (Tony Paxton)

relationship with the boss. BAe Warton sent an expert panel beater called "Ted" and his expertise saved the day (and my "bacon"). My "punishment" was to buy "Ted" lots of beer, present him with a framed picture of the aircraft and have my photograph taken with a Victor hose wrapped around me. The hose was found some weeks later in a German farmer's field and returned to us – unfortunately! So you see it was a punishment!'[10]

The night of 26 November 1974 was a busy one for Derek 'Furz' Lloyd.[11]

'HMS *Glamorgan* was sailing in the Iceland/Faeroes gap as the capital vessel of a Surface Task Group (TSG) taking part in a joint maritime exercise in the North Atlantic. Leuchars-based Lightnings and Phantoms were providing air defence and Vulcans, Buccaneers and Canberras were attacking the TSG. It was a Tuesday night of the second week of the exercise and I had already taken part during day-flying the previous Friday. The daylight mission had been in support of HMS *Hermes* as she sailed north abeam Aberdeen. This night mission was with Air-to-Air Refuelling (AAR) and involved manning a Combat Air Patrol (CAP) in 'Q' country, way up north of our normal operating area, where we would usually be intercepting Bear Deltas on their way to and from Cuba.

'Unlike the day mission, I was launched as a solo fighter direct to the tanker. All went well with the take-off and climb but the radar dropped off line as I levelled at height. I had just topped out at Flight Level (FL) 340 having climbed all the way up through thick cloud. The left front console dimmer was still distracting and I eventually decided to turn it off altogether. It was a clear moonlit night above the weather system, but I knew I would probably have to descend back into cloud to refuel. Therein lay the first problem: a tanker join in the weather with no radar. I toyed with the idea of asking the Victor to climb to attain Visual Meteorological Conditions (VMC) above the cloud. But relations with the tanker force were not at their best during this period of air defence operations in the UK and I would probably stand more chance of getting blood from a stone. At least I had time to think about it as I trawled north recycling the radar.

'The next problem was an intermittent feed from the ventral. This was relatively unusual in an F.6 and I didn't notice it until both flaps had fed and the mains had dropped a little. It wasn't until a full fuel check somewhere off the coast by Buchan that I realised I had about 800lb trapped underneath, both flaps empty and a slight imbalance in the mains. Selecting Flight Refuel ON and OFF seemed to help, but I had to continually attend to this as I monitored the fuel feed until the ventral emptied. So now I had no radar and a suspect ventral feed. Alarm bells started to ring because I

Easy does it! (Tony Paxton)

was going to be operating in an area where diversion airfields were a long way away and a problem with ventral feeding would be less than desirable. However, previous experience suggested that my action of periodically depressurising the system would see me airtight and I pressed on northbound – still recycling the radar.

'I had to start thinking about the tanker join. The brief was for silent procedures and Buchan had been as discreet as expected on my way north. I was still flirting with cloud tops but the weather seemed to be getting better. As I turned onto a north-westerly heading the Victor turned port about and faced up for a 180-degrees intercept. I picked the Victor up on radar at about twenty-five miles as it came onto the screen from the right. I looked out and saw a set of lights in that direction. I mentally relaxed knowing I would be able to join visually. It seemed as if I was sliding down the top of the clouds as they fell away during my descent. Clear of the weather, there were now only scattered layers of cloud around me and by the time I was behind the flying "Blackpool Illuminations", I was clear of all cloud with only patchy areas well below.

'I may as well not have bothered to set up the cockpit. The lights were so bright on the Victor that all adjustment for night vision was well destroyed before I got close to it. Cleared by the captain to join directly behind, it was with some trepidation that I realised that there were no hoses – at least no wing hoses; only the centre hose trailing out the back.

'In well over 1,000 hours flying in the Lightning I had never tanked from the centre hose at night. I had no problem coming to terms with this; after all it should be easier without the potential distraction of the very slight "leans" which were common to flying on the wing without a visual horizon at night or in the weather. However, I had no idea what visual cues to use when closing in and this could be quite adventurous. I carried out the pre-refuelling checks and motored on in.

'The size of the Victor only really became apparent within a hundred yards or so and then during the latter stages of a join-up there was a definite sense of being overwhelmed by the graceful lines and "crescent" wings. Turbulence from the disturbed air started to interfere with flight within about fifty yards or so and if joining on a wing station increasing amounts of aileron and rudder trim had to be used to maintain straight and level flight. At night, there was the annoying distraction of rotating anti-collision lights but fortunately, by approaching from directly behind and underneath. There was not a problem on this occasion. With great satisfaction I made contact at the first attempt and started to take on fuel.

'With a clunk, I disengaged and the basket rocked away as I backed off. Full to the brim, I quickly turned to take up a vector the Navy had been pestering me to do

Fill her up! (Tony Paxton)

Two of 5 Squadron's Lightnings refuelling from a Victor over Greenland. (Tony Paxton)

whilst I was still in the process of topping up. Passing the "Gate" of the TSG's defences in excess of Mach 1, I was rather pleased this was only a peacetime exercise. They appeared to be making a real hash of the procedures they should have been using, and I was being steered over the fleet at high speed towards the threat. Without cast-iron identification I would not have done this in war!

'Soon I was able to pick up a faint contact which closely resembled the air picture being described by the fighter controller on board *Glamorgan* and I called "Judy". Now in control of the intercept I adjusted the geometry to lag the target in the stern and set myself up for a shot. I never identified the "blip" but at about two miles I got a good acquisition and fired about a quarter of a mile later before breaking away starboard.

'I switched off the Master Arm Selector (MAS) and carried out a set routine of checks. I was not surprised to notice the same problem with the fuel and I depressurised the ventral. Whether it was because I was now far away from home at night, or perhaps a genuine lack of reaction to my switchery, I was under the profound impression that no fuel was transferring. I watched the gauges for a little longer but was immediately distracted by a pairing to another target. I judged that I didn't need to worry too much about it at this stage; after all the tanker was close by and if necessary I could top up early to ensure that I had enough reserves for a safe transit south.

'I don't remember this second intercept but I do remember my concern when the radar dropped off line again. The A/A TACAN was clicking away with random indications, the fuel was well and truly imbalanced with about 800lb trapped in the ventral and the Navy had stopped talking to me. Now I had a problem. I turned roughly in the direction I thought the tanker would be and ferreted around in the left leg pocket of my immersion suit for my IMC "aide-memoire". The very small, reduced photocopy of several hundred frequencies used by the RN is easy to read in a crew room or briefing room but in the extremes of a poorly lit cockpit even my "alleged" 20/20 vision was not coping too well. Inevitably, I read the first collector frequency incorrectly and spent what seemed like hours talking to no one before I realised that something was wrong. Then the clips of my green aircrew folder popped open as I turned the page and the list of frequencies was lost on the cockpit floor forever. I fortunately remembered the initial contact frequency and tuned into that once more. Across the airwaves I could hear the other controller with verbal diarrhoea chatting away to the tanker and with some relief I waited for a break in the conversation.

'Within minutes, the fuel seemed to have sorted itself out; I had topped up to full from the tanker. The radar was working; the cockpit had that warm and cozy feeling again and I was back in business.'

An anonymous Lightning pilot wrote about another Combat Air Patrol in an exercise overseas with the Royal Navy:[12]

'... I was allocated an aircraft and a wingman at ground readiness. After an hour or so, we were brought up to cockpit readiness, for the Combat Air Patrols (CAPs) had detected a low-level raid and there appeared to be a running battle in progress about eighty miles south of us. The two-seater squadron had formed a quorum, back-tracked along the enemy's attack path and were shooting up the ship and anything trying to take off from it. Our own CAPs were mixed up with the enemy strike, which was progressing, via move and counter-move, towards the airfield. We checked in on telebrief and, in response, the SOC crackled into life:

'"Alert 2 Lightnings."

'"49 Alpha and Bravo", from Base Ops. This was it; those were our call signs:

'"49 Alpha and Bravo, vector 270, make angels one zero, call stud 52. Six plus Fakers heading north fast and low. 240-40 miles from you and mixed up with chicks. Your mission to intercept and exercise destroy. Gate, gate, scramble – acknowledge."

'Scramble start, check Bravo's canopy coming down, wave off the marshaller and watch him scuttling for the slit trenches. Pre-take-off checks complete, take the far side of the runway and we're off. A check in the mirror and there is Bravo about 100 yards behind and left. After take-off, check right for ten seconds and reverse – there's Bravo in battle formation on the left.

'"Weapons and cameras! Stud 52 go."

'"Bravo", as he checked in.

'"Loud and clear. Mission 49 – two chicks, gated angels ten. Tiger fast twenty."'

'From the SOC: '"Roger left 250, your target's track 773, 11 o'clock twenty – heading North – reported line abreast one mile with escort 5 miles astern in a mix-up with chicks. I'll bring you in from the south, out of sun."

'Good planning! I hope we have plenty of overtake speed. Perhaps that's why we are at 10,000. Then, from my wingman:

'"Bravo – I hold 2 – ten left 52 miles, low, line abreast."

'"Roger – I hold them – going down – call visual and watch for the escort."

'Then I saw them, two dark-grey banana shapes, intermittently merging with the sea:

'"Tally ho – twelve o'clock 6 – only two, in on the left one."

'"Bravo out – tail clear."

'"Alpha – they've seen us and are going right."

'Their smoke trail was now visible and thickened as they accelerated to avoid us. Then, again, from my number two:

'"Bravo, your tail clear. Can I take the other one?"

'Something stirred in the recesses of my mind:

'"Negative, stay together, look for the escort."

'"Copied – no contact – your tail clear – watt one, two escorts three miles astern no threat yet, but closing in the turn."

'I checked behind number two and called:

'"OK Bravo, engage the escort and keep them off me. Your tail clear. Splash on my first target, going for the other."

'Then silence for about a minute – too long. The second missile saw and fired on the second target.

'"Splash on both. North of you about four miles, 5,000ft. Joining you in a right turn. Bravo – report."

'I yo-yoed out right, craning my neck for sight of the escort and my number two. Then I saw them; two different dark-grey shapes in my 9 o'clock low, turning right underneath me. Bravo's g-strained voice huffed something about having the escorts tied up in a turning fight and my memory stirred again. Where is he? Forget the escorts for a moment. There he is! Filling my right windscreen. Break! Phew, too damned close. I was shaken and felt that enough was enough.

'"Bravo, haul-off east, cover me."

'He feinted at the opposition, who countered and ran off to the north, presumably to join their two charges. Realistic tactics, I suppose – we could argue their demise at the debrief. Breathing heavily, I advised SOC of the two that got away and they reassured me that they were now SAM targets.

'Bravo and I reformed into defensive battle formation and went looking for the rest of the excitement. It was then that my mind started to clear and yielded up its stored memory. "It's the one that you don't see that gets you."'

Following a subsequent Whitehall defence review, all 56 Squadron's Lightnings had gone by the end of January 1975 and only the SAR helicopters of 84 Squadron remained on the troubled island. However, Lightnings did return to Cyprus again, albeit on five-week detachments, when its importance as an Armament Practice Camp was fully realized. Each pilot would fly a series of cine-camera work-up flights against a banner towed by a Canberra. When the pilot was considered safe, he would fly nine live gun firings on the banner. Scoring was completed by tipping the head of each 30mm round in a special semi-drying paint, which, when it hit the banner, left a stain around the hole that left no room for doubt. To avoid confusion on multiple sorties, each pilot's bullets would be tipped with a different colour paint.

An anonymous Lightning pilot described his APC in Cyprus.[13]

'It was a lovely summer's day in Cyprus, tailor-made for flying the Lightning – dark and dirty North Sea nights were a million miles away, and who needs a radar when you can see 100 miles anyway? We were engaged in an Armament Practice Camp, firing air-to-air against a towed banner: this was in the days of the straight banner tow, so the Canberra trundled backwards and forwards just south of Akrotiri, which was always visible. I'd been doing quite well, thank you, and was determined to maintain my position as leading shot, so I set out on this sortie determined to be very pedantic about my firing parameters and really annihilate the flag. I was very disciplined – pass after pass I refused to fire because the pipper wasn't quite on the front of the spreader bar, or the speed was ten knots fast, or whatever. My No.2 fired out and departed for RTB and I'd still only fired about half my rounds. In time, the fuel started to run down a bit, but – no sweat – I looked over my shoulder and there was Akrotiri, so close you could almost touch it, so in we go again … Another twenty or so rounds later, and the fuel was getting decidedly down. But I still had at least another couple of passes to go, and – quick look – yes, Akrotiri was still a short glide away; OK another couple of passes should do it. However, the fuel pucker factor was obviously affecting my ice-cold judgement a bit, 'cos the tracking on the next two passes was a bit dismal, so no fire and try them again. Look over the shoulder again. Still OK. No hassle to get home. Pull up and idle/fast idle cruise descent back onto finals. No problem: I won't make minimum landing fuel on the downwind leg, but pulling up and starting recovery with minimum landing fuel is showing willing, and besides, fighter pilots are always ace at running the fuel just right. Now I'll just get these last two passes sorted …

'The guns were finally "fired out" and I pulled up, turned round and pointed at the island.

'Gata Radar, 44 complete for recover'.

'Roger 44, pigeons 060 55 miles'

'55 miles! Bloody hell. It got suddenly cold in the cockpit, in spite of the sunshine. Next mistake, I failed to climb to a sensible recovery height – a cringing animal at controls convinced that he couldn't afford the fuel to climb. Next mistake, I failed to transfer remaining fuel/shut down No.2 engine – more worried about reputation and landing on one than on saving petrol, even at that stage. In a remarkably calm voice, I told Air Traffic that I would be joining downwind to land, precautionary (first smart thing I had said/done for about three hours).

'Some long time before reaching the circuit, both pumps captions came on steady – inevitable really, you can't expect transfer pumps to keep pumping fuel to the collectors when they're not surrounded by fuel. I slid onto the high downwind, only breathing once every ten minutes, and flew a sort of glide approach – I don't really know why, I suppose it seemed familiar from JPs and Hunters, although it wouldn't be a lot of use with sixteen tons of ominously silent aluminium. Halfway round finals, both FUEL captions came on (for the unlucky who haven't flown the Lightning, it means the collector boxes are empty: every other time I've seen it, the associated engine flames out shortly afterwards). I didn't twitch at all: I'd frozen completely at that stage. To my amazement, the mighty Avon thrustmasters kept pushing me along, and after a couple of lifetimes, I touched down at about the right speed and place. Drag bag, brakes and adrenaline and I managed to exit at the first turn off, 3,000ft in

– who said the Lightning needs long runways? I didn't dare shut one engine down, 'cos I didn't know which one was going to stop first, so I taxied in very fast, jammed the brakes on hard on the chocks (to make the fuel gauges plus-up). The fuel gauges still didn't read anything remotely respectable, but it made me feel marginally better.

'I managed to climb out without falling down the ladder and signed-in in a shaky hand; "It's a fighter pilot's 800lb-a-side, Flight Sergeant" I said, giving him a knowing wink. He gave me a lugubrious look back. Afterwards, whilst I was into my second mug of coffee (I'd spilt most of the first), he 'phoned up to tell me how much fuel he'd put in: I knew then that he was having me on, because everyone knows the Lightning doesn't hold that much.

'Plenty of morals in this little tale: find 'em yourself. For me, I've run short of fuel on occasions again since then, for much better reasons, but I've never run as short as that, and I've always reacted better – climbed, shut down engines, diverted, and so on. I'm grateful that on this occasion I started my recovery from the western end of the area, with the standard Akrotiri 25-knot wind to help me along, as well as help me stop quickly on landing. It was a hard way to learn, but since then I've always been fuel/distance/time conscious, and I doubt that there're many Lightning pilots who haven't learnt in similar ways.

'And after all that, I only got half my previous score on the banner: there's another moral in there somewhere!'

The APCs continued right up until 1987, tanked there and back, as always by the ubiquitous Victors, who were always on time and on target!

---

1 Brian Carroll writing in *Lightning Review*, March 1993.
2 XH667 and XH620.
3 XH602 and XH648.
4 Bob Offord himself went home at the end of 1965 and in 1966 was posted to 226 OCU as an instructor.
5 In fact the first of six, XA937 did not arrive until 14 February 1966. On 1 July the third and final Victor squadron, 214, formed at Marham and by the end of the year was equipped with seven K.1/1A three-point tankers.
6 Writing in *Lightning Review*, June 1993
7 XS416, the T.5 trainer which did not have overwing tanks, remained behind at Leuchars, while another, XV329, went by sea from Sydenham, Belfast. XV329 returned by sea to the UK in August 1971 and had to be written off in December when it was discovered that acid spillage from the batteries had corroded the airframe.
8 By now a further twenty-four Victor K.1A three-point tanker conversions were in RAF service, and in 1968 twenty-seven B.2 and SR.2 versions were converted as K.2 tankers to replace the K.1 tankers at Marham.
9 'Exercise *Ultimacy*: A Lightning Pilot's Eye View' *Air Clues*, April 1970.
10 With over 6,000 hours of flying time, Clive is currently a specialist aircrew instructor with 56 (R) Squadron and one of the five fighter pilots in the BBMF, at Coningsby.
11 Writing in the *Lightning Review* January 1995.
12 'I Learnt About Flying From That', *Air Clues*, September 1976.
13 'I Learnt About Flying From That', *Air Clues*, June 1988.

CHAPTER 5
Quick Reaction Alert

The Lightning's most demanding role was to intercept, supersonically, enemy aircraft penetrating NATO airspace at altitude and, if called upon, shoot them down with air-to-air missiles and cannon. If the deterrent was to work effectively, RAF Fighter (later Strike) Command had to station Lightnings, and later Lightnings and Phantoms, on immediate readiness, twenty-four hours a day, 365 days a year. Quick Reaction Alert (QRA), as it was called, was just that, with intercepts possible at 40,000ft just minutes after a re-heat take-off. It was all very well having the world's most advanced supersonic interceptor with this capability, but if sorties were to be successful, then pilots needed to apply completely new techniques *vis-à-vis* radar and weaponry. Initially, the missile and radar systems were beset with teething problems, and it fell to pilots like Bruce Hopkins at the AFDS at Coltishall to carry out trials work on the Lightning's radar and fire control systems.

'At the start, in 1960, we had problems with the fire control computer', he recalls. 'Once the radar was locked on we had a very simple analogue computerized steering programme to do the intercept. The theory was that we tracked the dot on the scope to obtain the optimum pursuit path for firing. The trouble was, it was bloody useless! You could do a manual intercept far better. So, we threw the steering programme away and developed a system of intercept using the basic B radarscope display. This became the basis of all Lightning AI (Airborne Intercept) work. Unless you had a high closing speed, the intercept bracket was about two miles from the target. The skill came in making the intercept at subsonic speed. If you got it wrong, you had to go to re-heat to make up the distance.

'We did a hell of a lot of work on intercepts, high-level then low-level, where the radar did not perform too well due to ground clutter. (Although the AI pulse radar at this time had a maximum range at height of twenty-five miles, at sea level it sees less than five miles.) Once we had got what we thought were the basic techniques, we started fixing the supersonic intercept mission. Now we really had fuel problems! It meant that there was less time to get the radar intercept right. Our radar scanned horizontally at 45 degrees with a beam width of two to three degrees, so we had to search vertically for the target by use of a scanner elevation control. As we moved the elevation lever the radar dish looked up and down. This is known as the "elevation search". Of course, supersonically, we had less time to search for the "blip". Then we had to lock on to the target using the trigger switch and we went into the intercept with it locked on.

'From February 1961 onwards we started missile firing trials at Boscombe Down. At first, we used telemetry-fitted Firestreaks with the explosive removed, against pilotless, remotely controlled Meteor targets. Then, in March, on the Aberporth ranges in Wales, I fired at Australian-built Jindiviks. Major Bill Cato, our American exchange pilot, Jim Reynolds and I carried out a whole series of Firestreak firings during 1961.

Jim Reynolds and I would fly a Javelin FAW.8 to Boscombe Down on the Monday (which we also used to go back and forth to Coltishall for spares etc.) and fly back to Coltishall on the Friday after a week of missile firing exercises. We must have been the most expensive commuters in the world. We had competitions to see who could transit between Coltishall and Boscombe the fastest. The ground rules were, you were not allowed to break any airframe limits or air traffic rules. After take-off from [runway] 22 SW, you would cruise in re-heat at about Mach 0.94 and make a straight-in approach at Boscombe. Jim Reynolds finally got the time down to eighteen minutes, seven seconds!

'We fired a total of five Firestreaks. This all proved very successful. Then we did quite a bit of gun firing, which wasn't so successful! All we proved was that the pilot attack gunsight was very basic. It was OK if we did approaches from behind, but it was not so good under g conditions using lots of angle. In fact, it was only any good from line astern. Still, guns were a very useful weapon to have, the basic philosophy being missiles for long range (one mile minimum) and guns for within a mile of a target. I was always a member of the "let's keep the gun" lobby. The Lightning, though, was never a good aircraft for gun fighting. All our air-to-air gunnery was done on the "flag", i.e. the quarter attack. With a couple of hundred rounds you were lucky to get twenty per cent of the rounds on target in a Lightning; this compared with 40 to 50 per cent on Hunters.'

Bruce Hopkins left AFDS in September 1962, being posted as a Weapons Instructor on T.4s to the Lightning Conversion Squadron at Middleton St George. Promoted to squadron leader, he left 226 OCU (the LCU had expanded) at the end of January 1964 on a posting to the Air Ministry. A series of staff appointments and a two-year exchange tour with the US Navy on the F-4J Phantom meant that he would not return to the Lightning force until 1972, when he was given command of 23 Squadron at Leuchars. 23 Squadron was a key element in Britain's air defence. The front-line squadrons were backed up by a first-class ground-controlled defence system. No.11 Group's Air Defence Ground Environment (ADGE), with its headquarters and operations centre at Bentley Priory, near London, provided early warning of Soviet aircraft and missile threats. Tu-95 'Bears', Tu-16 'Badgers' and occasionally M-4 'Bisons' and Il-18 'Coots' of the Soviet Long-Range Air Force and Naval Air Force, flying reconnaissance missions around the North Cape of Norway and on towards the central Atlantic and the British Isles, would be investigated in the UK Air Defence Region by 11 Group using QRA interceptors. Usually the Soviet aircraft practiced their war roles of maritime surveillance, anti-shipping and anti-submarine warfare and simulated strikes on mainland Britain.

The UK ADR, contained entirely within NATO Early Warning Area 12, forms part of a unified air defence system under SACEUR (Supreme Allied Commander Europe), which extends to cover three other NATO air defence regions. Three Master Radar Stations (from 1975, key Sector Operations Centres [SOCs]), with control and reporting facilities, were grouped around radar units at Boulmer, Buchan, Scotland and Neatishead, Norfolk. These were fed with data from six NATO Air Defence Ground Environment (NADGE) stations via digital link with the Air Defence Data Centre at West Drayton and the Air Defence Operations Centre at Strike Command HQ, High Wycombe, forty miles west of London. Here sat the Air Officer C-in-C Strike Command, who also wore the NATO 'hat' of COMUKADR (Commander UKADR). Further long-range, low-level radar coverage was provided by twelve Shackleton AEW.2 Airborne Early Warning aircraft. From 1975 onwards, data was also fed into the system from the control and reporting post at Benbecula on North Uist and from the reporting site at Saxa Vord. The Ballistic Missile Early Warning System (BMEWS) station at Fylingdales in Yorkshire provided additional links.

At the 'sharp end' four armed Lightnings (from September 1969, Lightnings and Phantoms) sat in a 'Shed' near the end of the runway. Two fighters were at Leuchars

The Lightning's *raison d'être* was to intercept the high-flying Soviet bombers that approached British and NATO air space. In both the UK and Germany the Lightning was kept at a permanent state of high readiness, called QRA (Quick Reaction Alert) and Battle Flight, respectively. In the UK the readiness state was ten minutes and in Germany it was five minutes. (MoD)

in the Northern QRA all year round, the other two at alternately Wattisham and Binbrook (later, Coningsby's Phantoms were also used) in the Southern QRA. In Germany in September 1965 19 Squadron's Lightning F.2s began performing a QRA role at Gütersloh, and in December that year 92 Squadron's F.2s at Geilenkirchen joined them in the role. In January 1968 92 Squadron moved to Gütersloh and together with 19 Squadron carried out interceptor duties until replaced by Phantoms, in December 1976 and March 1977 respectively.

On QRA seven ground crew, one or two from each trade and a SNCO (Senior NCO), would attend each pair of Lightning interceptors in charge. Two pilots dressed in full flying kit, minus their life preservers and helmets, but including their immersion suits during the winter, were at ten minutes' readiness. This meant that an aircraft had to be airborne within ten minutes of the 'scramble' order. (In keeping with the Second World War fighter spirit, 'scramble' signalled a take-off, while that other popular term, 'buster', which originally meant 'through the gate', was used to describe re-heat. Targets were known as 'trade', another throwback to the war.) At nights, it was relaxed to thirty minutes. Even then they had to don their flying kit.

Brian Carroll[1] recalls. ' "Hunting Bears" for most folk generates visions of big brown beasties or even the polar variety in off-white; but for us, the pilots who manned the Northern Quick Reaction Alert Force, the vision was quite different. We knew precisely what to expect, something in silver with a wingspan of 167.7ft, 162.4ft in length, 39.75ft high and weighing in at around 185 tons, all propelled by four turbo-props, each producing 14,795 EHP, and the whole capable of moving along at 525mph (456 knots). They were bristling with a number of mean-looking cannon which at times were pointed our way, quite un-nerving as they attempted to track us as we flew around the Bear examining it for any new equipment or changes from the current information.

MoD publicity photo of two Lightning pilots on QRA running to their Lightnings. (MoD)

'Northern QRA was a vital part of the defence of the UK. Over the years we spent many hours on standby, either relaxed at a thirty-minute state or in the cockpit, ready to start engines and be airborne within two minutes. At night we slept next to our steeds, having earlier carried out a full pre-flight, including setting the cockpit switches for a fast get away. It was surprising just how quickly one could move from being asleep to being airborne; less than five minutes was the norm. Let me then take you through a sortie from, say, a thirty-minute state of readiness all the way to a successful interception and a recovery back to home ground.

'We usually operated in pairs and would be dressed and ready to move at a moment's notice. Our immersion suits would be on but unzipped, as they were on the warm side while sitting around, though essential should one be unlucky enough to come down in the North Sea. The QRA pilots would, at the thirty-minute state, be in the crew room along with the rest of the squadron, often carrying out one or another of their secondary duties or simply relaxing with a good book. The phone rings; northern radar has requested two aircraft to he brought up to a ten-minute state. We are at most only five minutes' stroll from our aircraft, both of which have been checked over and are ready to go. We take another look around them and chat with the ground crew who are also on standby in the alert dispersal.

'At this stage the alert may come to nothing; the "intruders" are known to play cat and mouse with us, flying close enough to wake us up and then turn away before we scramble. This time we are brought to cockpit readiness and a few moments later instructions are passed to scramble. The usual information is passed, giving a vector to fly, height to climb to, whether they wish us to make a re-heat or standard climb out, and the range of the target.

'Four Avons thunder into life, all systems are go. Almost as one, both aircraft roll from the alert hangar, air traffic automatically clearing us for an immediate take-off

Entering the "active", both aircraft smoothly apply full cold power and surge down the runway. A glance across at my No.2, all is OK, a nod of the head and we both engage full re-heat. Airborne, clean up and turn onto the climb out vector, my No.2 moving automatically into battle formation as soon as we are clear of any cloud. From now on there will be little if any R/T communication between the aircraft or the ground; silent procedure is the name of the game. Standard battle formation is established as we fly north.

'The intruder (at this stage we are not aware of its identity) is over 400 miles away, so for the next forty-five minutes or so there is little to do but fly the required track and monitor our on-board systems. The occasional visual signal is passed between us, confirming that all is OK. We already know that a tanker aircraft has been scrambled ahead of us and that shortly we will achieve a RV (rendezvous) allowing us to top up our tanks. This, too, is a well-rehearsed procedure; no chat between us and the tanker, the aim being not to let the target know until the last possible moment that we are on our way.

'It is now thirty minutes or so since take-off and we have contact with our mobile fuel store. As lead, I take us both into a stern position then, leaving my No.2 there, fly up alongside the tanker's cockpit to let them know we have arrived (they saw us coming anyway). Again, a visual OK from the tanker captain that we are clear to top up. Dropping back, I wave my No.2 onto the port hose whilst I take the starboard one. Full tanks, and we are on our way, now flying a closer tactical formation to allow hand signals to be passed between us. A wave to the tanker crew as we accelerate away, they will follow us for a while and then set up a loiter pattern allowing us to meet up later for more fuel should we need it and, right now, being so far from home, we certainly will.

'Range from base is now approaching 430 miles, and the silence is suddenly broken by a cryptic message from ground radar. Our target is fifty miles dead ahead and coming our way – if he holds that heading we should be right with him in just over three minutes. But no, he has already started turning away; not, we discover later, because of us, simply a routine turn to keep him 430 to 500 miles from our base. This is going to be a long chase if we maintain our present cruise speed, so with tanks still nearly full we crack the burners and accelerate. We both check our weapons, missiles and cannon; one never knows if they will be needed. Cameras, including the hand-carried 35mm, are re-checked and ready for use.

'Still nothing more from the ground, so (briefly) I activate my airborne radar and there is a nice fat blip, not too far away and closing nicely. Radar back to stand-by again, just in case they realise that they are being scanned. Conditions are ideal to surprise our Russian friends. The Bear (as it turns out to be) is flying just above a thin cloud layer only some 1,000ft thick, so we close in from below, preventing his rear lookout from seeing us. Another quick look into the radarscope confirms that we are approaching 2,000 yards. I signal my No.2 to maintain his position at 2,000 while I close to 500 yards before popping up through the dud layer. The effect is dramatic. Ivan in the rear blister obviously reports my presence and the captain immediately throttles back, slowing the Bear very quickly.

'A brief flip of speed brakes and a tight high 'g' roll bleeds off enough speed to remain astern. I'm now very much aware of the twin cannon in the tail that are starting to track me as I close in. The adrenaline tends to flow a little faster at this stage! This particular interception was, in fact, the most northern intercept that had been made at that time; they hadn't realised we were using tankers, so thought that they were out of our operating range. Time now for a little fun and games with their rear gunner/photographer.

'As I close alongside the rear fuselage I can see him clearly in the side blisters, manhandling a somewhat cumbersome camera mounted on a tripod. He's hoping for some pictures of our Lightnings and with luck he won't get any. My 35mm camera is somewhat easier to manage as I switch easily from side to side, rolling

Scramble! Air and ground crew race to their waiting and fully armed F.2A at the start of another intercept sortie. On QRA each pair of Lightning interceptors would be attended by seven groundcrew, one or two from each trade and a senior NCO in charge. Two pilots dressed in full flying kit minus their life preservers and helmets, but including their immersion suits during the winter, were always at ten minutes' readiness. (Richard Reeve)

F.2 XN778/F, which joined 19 Squadron on 9 January 1963 after flying for the first time on 9 November 1962. In 1968 this aircraft was converted to F.2A and it joined 92 Squadron on 30 April 1974. XN778 flew for the last time on 5 April 1977 after which it became a surface decoy at Wildenrath.

F.2As of 19 Squadron in the early 1970s. Top left is XN778/H, which joined the Squadron on 9 January 1963. Next is XN784/R. (MoD)

F.2s of 92 Squadron in very close formation. XN789/G, the nearest aircraft, which first flew on 11 March 1963, arrived on the Squadron on 26 April 1963. In September this Lightning began conversion to F.2A and became the first F.2A received by 19 Squadron on 15 January 1968. It finished its career in 1977 as a surface decoy at Brüggen. In Germany in September 1965, 19 Squadron's F.2s began performing a QRA role at Gütersloh, and in December that year 92 Squadron's F.2s joined them in the role, at Geilenkirchen. (via Tony Aldridge)

over and under the Bear, taking pictures all the time. Meanwhile, I manage to keep my would-be "happy snapper" nicely out of phase; no sooner has he positioned his camera on the port side than I am on the starboard. This continues for a while as I collect a comprehensive number of photographs to add to our ever-increasing library. Meanwhile, Ivan is looking somewhat knackered; still, I saved him a fortune in film!

'Time now to bid farewell to my budding Russian cameraman. I give him a wave and receive one back (a friendly wave, too, not what you might think!) Calling my No.2 to rejoin, we break away, taking up a heading for a rendezvous with our tanker. No need now to keep R/T silence. We are in fact 540 miles from home and the Lightnings are feeling thirsty and in need of another drink. The tanker is 100+ miles south of us, so I give him a call to head our way for a while to save a little time to the refuel point. Allowing for turning manoeuvres, we should be ready to make contact with the hoses in about fifteen minutes.

'After a while I obtain a good radar contact on the tanker and call him to reverse his direction so that we can roll in astern at a mile. Closing, we are cleared to make contact. As we did on the outbound leg, my No.2 takes the port hose while I load up from the starboard. We don't need full tanks this time, so with base and diversion weather good and with no on-board problems we only partially refuel. A few words of thanks to our tanker friends and we wing our way back to base for a routine approach landing. We had been airborne for around three hours, the sortie was textbook and all concerned feel that another job has been well done.

'Of course, not all QRA missions are carried out in such ideal conditions. Poor weather certainly puts added strains on the pilots. At night it can get very interesting trying to identify an unknown target, usually without any lights, and quite liable to pull odd manoeuvres just to add interest to the whole exercise.

'Back at home base, time for a coffee or two and a debrief. The film meanwhile has been rushed away for processing – it turned out to be a regular, standard issue Bear "D". Nothing new had been added, but then no news is, as they say, good news. While we were away, other pilots had been standing QRA duty, another pair of Lightnings ready, as we had been to launch at a moment's notice. And so it went on round the clock; a lot of waiting around, but exciting when things moved, and very satisfying to successfully make a good interception and let the Ruskies now that we were on to them all the time.'

Pete Nash, a ground crewman occasionally on QRA at Wattisham, recalls:

'Sometimes a klaxon, just like those World War Two submarine diving alarms, would rend the air, meaning that a scramble was imminent and cockpit readiness was required. The pilots would let us groundcrew rush out first, punching a button that opened the front and rear doors. First out would hit the button, even if his aircraft was the second and furthest away. Beforehand, all jobs were allocated so each knew what he had to do. One would start the Houchin (ground power set) and press the power buttons. The second would go round the other side and remove the Master Armament Safety Brake, then stand clear, while the third would help the pilot strap in. If a launch was ordered, then the pilot only waited long enough for a thumbs up from the ground crew to indicate that the "fireman" had extinguished any flames from the starter exhausts, before he released his brakes and taxied out. The power lines and telebrief [through which the pilot was given his orders] were anchored to the floor so, as the aircraft moved forward, they were disconnected. As he left the "Q-shed", the pilot lowered his flaps and trusted air traffic to clear the runway for him because he didn't stop. On to the runway he then engaged double re-heat and away he went. A QRA scramble had priority over all other local traffic. Meantime, "Q2" would sit at cockpit readiness until "Q1" was well on his way and declared that his aircraft was serviceable. Only then would he stand down to ten minutes.

'For the ground crews, QRA was a rest. We did a week continuous, sleeping in the accommodation next to the aircraft shed, doing the flight servicings when required, an

F.2 XN726/D, which joined 19 Squadron on 7 June 1968. This aircraft first flew on 29 September 1961 and joined the CFE at Binbrook on 14 February 1963. It was damaged by a lightning strike on 27 March 1972. It flew for the last time in April 1977.

engine run every so often and watching telly, playing board-games, or fixing our cars. It was the easiest job on the squadron! If an aircraft went unserviceable then it either had to be fixed or replaced; half an hour ago, if not now!

'Before the flight servicings could start we had to contact the fighter controllers for permission to take the aircraft "off state", and then we were only allowed one hour to fix it otherwise we had to change aircraft. Another aircraft had to he armed and ready; usually on the flight line with a pilot close by, while the "Q" aircraft was fixed. When it came to meal times we went to the head of the queue and our Land Rover was parked right outside the mess doors, ready for an instant call back for a scramble. Wattisham shared the Southern QRA with Binbrook. Leuchars was always on Northern QRA.'

Flight Lieutenant Bob Offord was posted from 56 Squadron to become the A Flight Commander on 23 Squadron at Leuchars in September 1964, a move that meant transition to the F.3:

'The F.3 was a different aircraft in many ways. It had a totally different instrument layout; the engines were bigger and it had a faster autopilot that worked. It had height and heading hold and could be used for turning. It also had a priority for automatic ILS, although it was set up for 3 degrees (the Lightning liked 2½ degrees), so it was very rarely used. Our preferred approach was GCA, which would be 2½ degrees and, in some cases, manual ILS. The autopilot was like having another pilot, and it let the aircraft look after itself more while you looked after the radar. The AI 23B doubled the range and V-bombers now appeared on screen much sooner. I could also now carry Red Top.

'At Leuchars, 23 Squadron had sixteen pilots. Flight Lieutenant Ian Thompson, the B Flight Commander, and myself did not operate as separate flights. We would chop and change and took it in turns to do the day and night shifts. We operated a pair of Lightnings on QRA, 8am to 8pm. It was intensive, especially for the "plumbers", though in the summer we gave up night flying, because, flying at the heights we flew, it does not get dark enough. Normal take-offs were carried out on cold power, at 150 knots IAS and you became airborne at 165-170 IAS. (The front wheel would not retract above 165-170 IAS.) Then it would be a 10-degree climb out at 450 knots, pitching up to 22 degrees on the Initial Altitude Indicator, invariably to 36,000ft (at the tropopause, the height at which the stratosphere begins), where we did most of

F.6 XS897/S, which joined 56 Squadron in June 1971. It flew for the last time on 14 December 1987.

our work. QRA used re-heat take-offs, so getting the gear up was more critical. So too was fuel, but from October 1965 onwards we used Victor tankers. (The Lightning was short of fuel the moment you started the engines!) Acceleration and the rate of climb were phenomenal – from brake release to 36,000ft took just two and a half minutes. And you did it at a 47-degrees angle. Also, the seat was angled at 23 degrees, so the combination of the two made you feel that you were lying on your back!

'On head-on supersonic interceptions (with another Lightning) we tried a closing speed of Mach 3-4. Head-on attacks were very exciting and set-up had to be very good! For a successful 'shoot-down' to happen, three parameters were needed. First, the trigger had to be pulled (first, because we had to do this up to fifteen miles' range, then hold it until the interception), when the missile saw the target, in range and "fired". There was no audible sound that the missile had "locked-on" but a circle in the sight, which collapsed once you were in range, indicated that you were in range (the Red Top would normally see the target before it was in range). I carried out head-on attacks in daylight, never seeing the target visually. After the attack we rolled down and went home. During my time on the squadron no Russian aircraft were intercepted, but from 1966 onwards they started in a big way, right around the clock.'

One of the 23 Squadron pilots on QRA at Leuchars at this time was Flight Lieutenant Tony Aldridge, a former *Black Arrows* and *Blue Diamonds* Hunter aerobatic pilot, who hailed from Edinburgh. He recalls.

'The normal briefing for a rotation take-off was: after rotating the aircraft off the ground, level off and retract the undercarriage as soon as possible. Fly level until reaching approximately 220 knots and then pull back sharply on the stick, pulling approximately 3g in the process – 3.5g being the maximum. At around 60-degrees, climb, maintain speed in the order of 180 knots until chosen altitude is reached – usually around 2,000ft – then ease forward or wing-over and resume normal climb.'

During the weekend of 26 March 1966 a long-range QRA exercise was held involving two Victors of 55 squadron and two Lightnings. All crews were held at 30 minutes' readiness to attempt the interception of Soviet reconnaissance aircraft passing between the Faeroes-Shetland gap. No operational scrambles were called but the aircraft were scrambled in order to practice the planned procedures. On 30 March Flight Lieutenant Tony Aldridge and his No.2 Paul Reynolds took off, flew the sortie and then made their

High above the North Sea on 15 September 1972, one of the Soviet's long-range reconnaissance aircraft is intercepted and shadowed by F.6 XR753/A flown by Squadron Leader Bruce Hopkins, CO of 23 Squadron, from Leuchars. The photo was taken from a Phantom of 43 Squadron also stationed at Leuchars. XR753 was built as an F.3A and first flew on 23 June 1965. It joined 23 Squadron on 10 August 1967 and in March 1968 it was modified to F.6 standard. XR753 finally became a BDR (Battle Damage Repair) aircraft in May 1988. (MoD)

supersonic tactical recovery. During the supersonic descent both pilots were looking straight down into the centre of St Andrews as Tony Aldridge recalls.

'We (the operational pilots) were trying to work out a descent to the airfield that would allow the maximum time at altitude for the sortie followed by the shortest time back to base and on the ground. My idea was to do the descent at supersonic speed, followed by a break into the circuit for landing. To this end I started a vertical descent a few miles from the airfield, aiming a couple of miles short of the runway. Speed built up rapidly to something in the order of 1.5M and then power was eased off. The descent was continued at about 80 degrees nose down. Mach number decreased as we got lower until it was time to pull out. I ended up over the end of the runway at about 1,000ft and 600 knots, before breaking into the circuit and landing – an extremely quick way to get from altitude and onto the ground, which is what we were trying to achieve. However, the shock waves created when going supersonic don't go exactly where the aircraft is pointed, as I had hoped, but beyond it. Therefore, if you want to drop a bang on a place you aim short of it, exactly as I had done – unintentionally. We dropped a bang on the airfield and also on the Ancient and Modern [*sic*] golf course at St Andrews, which is a very sensitive establishment. The golf club's head person was straight on the phone to our station commander, who called the OC Flying who in turn called our boss. Squadron Leader John McLeod called me and we had a fairly one-sided discussion about the situation.'

Squadron Leader (later Group Captain) Ed Durham flew QRA at Leuchars as a flight commander in 23 Squadron during 1968-70. 'It was one of the loneliest feelings there was' he recalls, 'being 600 miles north of Lossiemouth and looking for a tanker to refuel from.' (As many as six in-flight refuellings could be required on a long-range QRA sortie.) It could sometimes be quite hectic too, although in a given period, not all

An 11 Squadron F.6 on QRA. The Q Shed, a self-contained unit which housed both aircrew and ground crew in an adjacent bungalow, was built away from the airfield hangars, next to the main runway, in order that the aircraft minimised taxiing time prior to take off. (Malcolm English)

flights were QRA sorties. On 25 February 1970, Squadron Leader Durham intercepted two 'Bear-Ds' on a night QRA. He had already flown four sorties the day before and three more followed on the 26th and the same number two days after that.

John Bentley of *Flight International* visited Wattisham and 29 Squadron in April 1970 and wrote about QRA.[2]

'Wherever you are, whatever you are doing as you read this article you can be sure that an element of 29 Squadron, part of the RAF's Strike Command, is alert, waiting for the word at Wattisham, the squadron operates Lightning 3s as part of the "Quick Reaction Alert" (QRA) force. Two aircraft stand on a special "ready" pan, armed and ready to go at 10min notice, 24 hours a day, with air- and groundcrew of 29 Squadron, waiting in their ready rooms at the same notice.

'Once an alert is sounded – a strident hooter has replaced the wartime gong – the two pilots belt for their transport and drive across to the pan, where, strapped in, they are ready to be airborne within two minutes. Groundcrew supply external power to the aircraft during these waiting periods and the pilots get their briefing via a plug-in telebrief direct from the relevant operations room. Their job is to maintain the integrity of UK airspace in the southern half of England (the northern sector is served by aircraft from Leuchars). The Lightnings are a "known armed presence", who can be seen to intercept any aircraft approaching the UK without a flight plan or who crossed into the air defence zone without warning.

'Many of the alerts are practices – intruders simulated by Canberras from RAF Germany – but there are "quite a few" visitors from Russia. Some are long-range maritime flights from the far north which fly past Norway and turn over the Shetlands. Some visitors are clearly testing the readiness of the QRA force. Others listen for the signatures of current NATO ECM devices and there are the electronic-intelligence gatherers, which fly around listening to radio and radar frequencies. There are even some practice bombing runs. Whatever they are doing the Lightnings intercept, identify and accompany them out of the area, armed with cameras and live missiles. Nobody has yet refused to go.

'The squadron is also on call to reinforce certain overseas theatres both inside and outside NATO, including Germany, the Near East Air Force and the Far East

Air Force and annually visits Malta and Cyprus on alternating years as part of this commitment. The object is to train the squadron personnel in both the physical job of rapid deployment and in integrating with a different theatre of operations. The job which would be required in the eastern Mediterranean would be somewhat different from that in the conventional NATO environment.

'NATO bases in other countries are also visited by 29 Squadron regularly in order to exercise the squadron groundcrew in servicing the aircraft of other air forces and vice versa. The visits are also an opportunity for the pilots to gain an insight into the air defence environment of different parts of Europe and to exchange experience. The countries taking part include the Benelux group, plus Germany, Norway, Denmark and, surprisingly, France which, although outside NATO, still participates in the exchanges.

'Tom Hamill and I met 29 Squadron earlier this year in Cyprus where they were on a month-long detachment which seemed to us to be one long exercise from dawn until well into the night. The fact that we were in Cyprus was largely irrelevant; it could have been anywhere and there were few days when we didn't hear the QRA hooter.

'The 12 aircraft had been flown out from Wattisham direct to Cyprus in 5hr, air-to-air refuelled by Victor tankers from Marham. The trip could also be done in stages, but the refuelling exercise is well worth the trouble and has the advantage that if a transport aircraft is sent along at the same time the squadron's groundcrew can arrive at almost the same time as their Lightnings. The whole squadron can be operational within hours of arrival at the new base.

'As part of the mobility concept the squadron always has to keep a proportion of its aircraft serviceable and has a 'fly-away' pack-up of spares and equipment permanently available. The exact number of aircraft which must be serviceable is determined by Strike Command, as is the state of alert at any given time. If the alert state is raised to a level above that of aircraft readiness the engineer officer has to mobilise all his groundcrew to make ready the necessary number of aircraft in the shortest time. All flying has to stop until the required number is on the line.

'The 15 pilots carry out a minimum of 20hr flying each month, training in the various roles in which they have to be proficient during daytime and at night. The squadron has a typical range of ages and experience (unlike the Phantom squadrons, whose pilots seem to have a higher average age) from the CO Wing Commander Brian Carroll and his flight commanders Squadron Leader Dave Kuun and Squadron Leader Dick Bell, down to the junior pilots, somewhat more excitable and not long out of Sleaford Tech.

'A new pilot receives a six-month intensive training course on both the aircraft and its weapons systems. If he is up to scratch at the end of that period he is made 'combat-ready' – capable of leading a flight of two aircraft on any of the squadron's flight profiles, day or night. As he progresses and gains more experience he is given more responsibility and will eventually be allowed to lead a four-aircraft flight.

'Each of the more experienced pilots also has a second specialisation, which he uses to instruct the other pilots in the squadron. One of the most important of these is the interception weapons instructor, whose responsibility is to see that each pilot gets a really thorough training on all the tasks which the squadron does. Others specialise in airframes, engines, electronics, navigation and aircraft recognition. There is no point in sending a Lightning pilot up to intercept something if he is not going to recognise it when he arrives.

'Flying training itself is varied but strictly governed by mandatory requirements for specific tasks to be done on a certain number of occasions each month. In the UK most of the training concentrates on interceptions, but when on deployment the squadron makes use of the different environments and aircraft available to practise combat missions against different aircraft and at varying speeds.

F.3 XP758/D of 23 Squadron. This Lightning first flew on 10 July 1964 and joined 23 Squadron on 14 September that same year. It later flew with 111 and 29 Squadrons and was scrapped in 1975.

Formation of 5 Squadron F.6s at Binbrook over Spurn Head. The nearest aircraft is XR764/L, which first flew on 4 November 1965 and joined 5 Squadron on 1 March 1966. It joined 74 Squadron in 1970 at Tengah and was transferred to 56 Squadron in Cyprus on 10 September 1971 but twenty days later, on 30 September, it crashed into the Mediterranean about twenty-nine miles Southeast of Akrotiri, after re-heat fires and stiffening of the controls. Flight Lieutenant Richard Bealer ejected safely.

'Visual identification of strange targets is practised by making an approach to an intruder from behind and at some 300 yards' range identifying him visually. At night this has to be done in whatever light is available. On all occasions a radar lock-on has to be achieved. The aircraft, which are put up against the QRA force, include Canberras, Phantoms, Buccaneers and Sea Vixens. All fighter pilots have an intensive aircraft recognition course at OTU and when they come to the squadron they are kept in practice by continuous refresher training both simulated and live.

'Normally the squadron operates with the local air-defence radar network, which will vector the interceptors on to a target until the Ferranti Airpass radar has picked it up. Once this has been done the Lightning can be flown into its tail position to identify without itself being seen. The Lightning, although it has been around for some time, is still able to climb to height quicker and accelerate to supersonic speeds faster than its new stablemate the Phantom and is therefore ideal for the QRA role. Its greatest attribute is said to be its handling qualities; particularly in the transonic bands it is highly manoeuvrable.

'It is also praised as a very effective missile vehicle, carrying Red Top or Firestreak. The Ferranti Airpass AI23B radar is a pilot-interpreted system, which means that the pilot must position himself within brackets which are displayed in order to make an effective missile firing. To do this he can fly a computed flight path, also displayed, or position himself manually. The technique in an attack is to approach a target either very high or very low so that the attacker cannot easily be seen. For very high-level attacks the technique is to accelerate to supersonic speed near the tropopause and then climb at attack speed to the height required.

'While mock attacks on other Lightnings, or whatever is put up against them, are carried out on deployment overseas, live missile firings are made at RAF Valley, Anglesey. At these missile practice camps the usual deployment techniques are exercised for the benefit of the groundcrew, while some six pilots at a time are given at least one live missile firing against a magnesium flare target which is towed behind a drone from Llanbedr. Said one pilot: "It's quite exciting. You can hear the rocket motor igniting even over the noise of your own aircraft and you can feel the reaction."

'The engineers of the squadron have changed probably more than any other branch since the war. On 29 Squadron they practise what is known as "opportunity servicing." In effect this means that every component has a latitude band of flying hours instead of a fixed limit. Every job that has to be done has a card on which is listed the number of other jobs on the aircraft which can conveniently be carried out at the same time if the components concerned have reached their servicing latitude band.

'It is done in this way mainly because of access problems on the tightly packed tube known as the Lightning. There are few external access panels; most are in the engine and jet-pipe bays. The servicing schedule for the squadron is so complicated that two men spend their time doing nothing else but planning it. On top of this routine servicing is the periodic check system and the never-ending programme of modifications and mandatory instructions.

'If possible before it goes on a detachment the squadron carries out progressive servicing on all the aircraft so that all will set off from Wattisham with a clear number of flying hours ahead of them in which no routine servicing needs to be done. Once it arrives at its destination the squadron's problems are mainly concerned with the backing available at the station. If there is a Lightning squadron based there, as there is at Akrotiri, an arrangement is made to borrow any special gear required – even down to such mundane items as steps and tail parachutes. If no Lightning squadrons are resident it takes eight C-130s to hump all the gear which is needed, plus many second-line servicing personnel from Wattisham. Much of the heavy gear is peculiar to the Lightning: Lox trolleys, slings, wheels, ventral tank trolleys, etc. With only nine landings per tyre, quite a few of these are needed too.

1. Line-up of 74 'Tiger' Squadron F.1s at RAF Coltishall, summer 1960. The 'Tigers' were the first operational squadron in Fighter Command to be equipped with the Lightning, in February 1960. (BAe)

2. F.1A XM171/A of 56 Squadron in Firebirds livery in 1963. (via Edwin Carter)

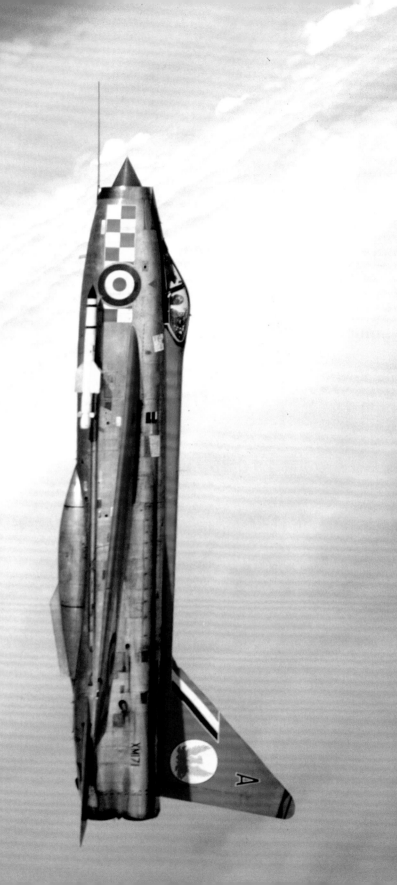

Above: 3. 56 Squadron, the *Firebirds*, here taking off from Wattisham in June 1963, became the second of the official Fighter Command Lightning aerobatic display teams. The team's name was derived from the squadron's 'phoenix rising from the ashes emblem'. (Richard Wilson via Brian Allchin)

Left: 4. F.1A XM171/A spectacularly flown by Flight Lieutenant Brian Allchin, photographed by Richard Wilson from the *Firebirds*' T.4 flown by Flight Lieutenant John Curry on 2 September 1963.

Above and Below: 5. & 6. T.4 XM997 of 226 OCU from RAF Coltishall over the North Sea in September 1965. (Jimmy Jewell)

15. From the cockpit of T.4 XS417 at dusk on 6 July 1965. (via Tony Aldridge)

16. T.5s XS449 and XS422 of 226 OCU taking off from RAF Coltishall in 1965. (Dick Bell)

17. Sunset in the 1960s at RAF Coltishall. (Peter Symes)

18. F.1A XM215 of 226 OCU in 1966. It was withdrawn from active OCU use by June 1974.

19. *'Tiger'* Squadron at rest at Tengah, Singapore, in 1968. (Dave Roome)

20. Night falls at 60 MU, Leconfield, Yorkshire. (Dick Bell)

21. A 23 Squadron F.6 shadowing a Tupolev Tu-20 Bear-D in July 1968. (Bruce Hopkins)

22. F.2A XN773/E of 92 Squadron taxi-ing at RAF Coltishall in 1968. (Adrian Savage)

23. F.2 XN781/J of 19 Squadron in RAF Germany in the mid-1960s. (MoD)

24. Three F.2As of 19 Squadron getting airborne at Gütersloh, September 1971. (Brian Allchin)

25. F.2A XN724/F of 19 Squadron over Germany in 1975. (MoD)

26. F.2A XN727/W of 92 Squadron in RAF Germany in 1977. (MoD)

27. Lightning landing at dusk. (Dick Bell)

28. F.2A XN784/R of 19 Squadron coming into land in 1970. (Dick Bell)

29. F.3 XP756/E of 29 Squadron *en route* from Wattisham to Cyprus in February 1970. XP756 was lost on 25 January 1971 when it crashed into the North Sea off Great Yarmouth after a re-heat fire. Captain 'Bill' Povilus USAF ejected safely and was picked up by a USAF Jolly Green Giant from Woodbridge. (Dick Bell)

30. F.1A XM177 of the Wattisham TFF (Target Facilities Flight) in September 1971. (Dick Bell)

39. F.6 XS901/T of 56 Squadron fitted with overwing tanks, on a test flight from 60 MU Leconfield in 1972. (Dick Bell)

40. F.6 XP750/H of 111 Squadron.

41. Lightnings of RAF Germany airborne from Deccimomanau, Sardinia, during the APC to the island in November 1975, beautifully photographed by Geoff Syrett from a Canberra of 85 Squadron.

42. F.3 XP696/S of 226 OCU take off at RAF Coltishall. (Dick Bell)

43. F.6 XS928/K of 5 Squadron in 1977. (Tony Paxton)

44. F.6 XS928/K of 5 Squadron in 1977. (Tony Paxton))

Left: 45. F.6 of 11 Squadron viewed from a KC-135. (Tony Paxton)

Below: 46. F.6 XS898/J of 5 Squadron, fitted with overwing tanks, refuelling from a basket deployed from a USAF KC-135 tanker's boom in October 1978. (Tony Paxton)

47. A 92 Squadron F.2A on a fast fly-by past the tower. (Dick Bell)

This page: 48. & 49. Superlative
self-portraits.(Tony Paxton)

50. F.2A of 92 Squadron.

51. XR727/F and XS931/G of 11 Squadron in experimental camouflage scheme. On 25 May 1979 XS931 crashed in the North Sea off Hornsea following control problems. The pilot ejected safely.

52. Lightning taking off into the night sky. (Dick Bell)

53. 11 Squadron from Binbrook in formation in 1980. (MoD)

Above and overleaf: 54. & 55. Lightning Sixteen. (Overleaf photograph Dick Bell)

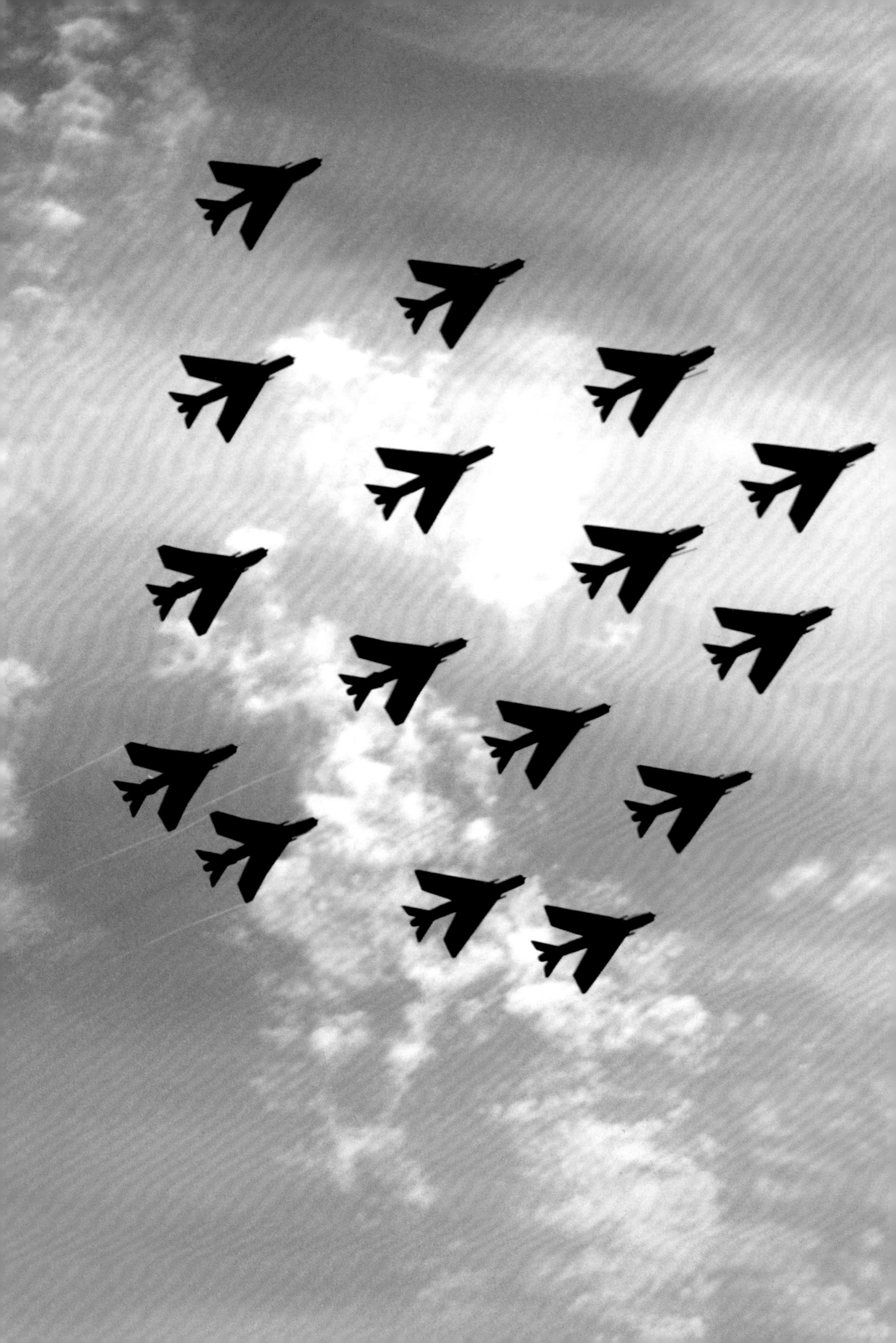

56. F.6 XR755/J of 11 Squadron in 1980. (Tony Paxton)

57. 5 Squadron's F.6 XR769/AM and Tornado F.3 ZE292/CA in December 1987. On 11 April 1988 XR769 crashed off the Humber Estuary following an engine fire. Flight Lieutenant Dick Coleman RAAF ejected safely. (Tony Paxton)

58. Gear Up! (Dick Bell)

Formation of Treble One Squadron F.6s. The nearest aircraft is XM188/F, which first flew on 27 March 1961 and joined 111 Squadron on 31 May that same year. Next in line is XM216/P, which first flew on 28 July 1961 and joined the squadron on 29 August that year.

Formation of 23 Squadron F.6s. The nearest aircraft is XR754/M, which first flew on 8 July 1965 and joined 23 Squadron on 29 February 1968.

'The supply organisation was highly praised by the SEO Squadron Leader Peter Babler. He said that the priority demand system worked very well. Stores are listed in a central computer at Hendonand can be called up by signal. The computer sorts out which is the nearest available replacement component and routes it to the squadron by priority air movement and the 'Earlybird' network of road movement in the UK.

'The squadron has started a scheme known as the 'welfare group' which has aroused interest in other squadrons. It is similar in outline, although not as formal, to the naval system of divisional officers. In 29 Squadron each pilot is responsible for the general off or on-duty welfare of a number of airmen, about 12 per pilot. One of the problems of a mobile squadron is that personal problems tend to be magnified because the men are often away from home base for a long time. So far the scheme which has been in operation for eight months, seems to have gone some way to ameliorate the problems.

'Flying the Lightning is regarded as being not too difficult because the aircraft is said to have no vices, It had always seemed to me to be a hair-raising aircraft, particularly in those stream landings, which used to be made at the SBAC show. "We shan't be pulling much more than 3g at altitude, so you shouldn't have any trouble," was the line. The squadron's champion Kockinelli-taker strapped me in the right-hand seat while the pilots of our four-aircraft flight were completing their self-briefing.

"Have you ever flown before?" asked my pilot Squadron Leader Dick Bell (well it was a change from "are you all right?" and there were a lot of TV camera teams in Akrotiri that week). He seemed reassured: "Oh, well you can do it all then, can't you?" Actually, to save him stretching too far there were a few things I was able to do, such as starting the first Avon, having two wet starts on the second and then finally starting that one.

'I hadn't flown in formation for a number of years and the old regime of formation starts and canopy closures, R/T checks and taxiing began to bring back that once-familiar slight apprehensive stomach-tightening tension which always used to accompany me along the taxi track and into the air until the formation closed up and I was too busy to worry.

'But it was not my responsibility in the T.5 and I was able to relax as we trundled along, the last of four, at some 30 knots to the runway end. We lined up four abreast, nicely positioned in echelon port and for one stimulating moment I thought we were about to do a formation take-off. That would have been quite a run, as my pilot was on the dead side. "We shall be doing a stream take-off at five second intervals; full re-heat followed by a max rate rotation climb as soon as possible after getting airborne," said Squadron Leader Bell. "You've probably seen them at Farnborough. The thing is to unstick the aircraft and let it accelerate to the appropriate speed then just pull hard back on the stick to rotate the aircraft to about a 70-degree climb angle. She'll climb at that angle at a steady speed, no trouble.'

'"Leader rolling," came the call. A loud rumble, quickly followed by the even louder crackle of twin Avons on re-heat, came from our right. "Two, three, four, five ..." Dick, the senior man in the flight, was counting his young pilots out as a check on their own efficiency. Another burst of noise as number two surged forward. The leader was already airborne, wheels tucking in nicely. "Come on number three," growled Dick under his breath, then, as three rolled forward, he began the countdown for us. Full re-heat in a Lightning feels just as it sounds – a smart kick in the back. Once I had accustomed myself to the rate of acceleration I looked for the others. Three was airborne, just rotating into the climb, a split-second transformation from rear profile to planform, but where were the first two ...?

'Hell's bells. I couldn't see the leader but two looked to be going up literally like an arrow at about 10,000ft in the clear sky above Akrotiri. Then we were airborne at about 160 knots, wheels coming up; Dick held it at about 200ft while the horizontal

Flight Lieutenant Tony Aldridge of 23 Squadron gets ready to taxi out at RAF Leuchars in 1965. (Tony Aldridge)

Thumbs-up from Flight Lieutenant Tony Aldridge to XP763/M. (Tony Aldridge)

tape ASI slid along until the cursor showed 240 knots. Then a hard pull-back on the stick and we were pointing what appeared to be vertically upwards. "We lose about 10 knots on the rotation, you'll notice, but she'll hold 230 knots all the way up." Sure enough she did and once the rotation was complete the ride was unexceptional, if you are used to being launched in a rocket. The feeling of lying on my back and being propelled by two crackling afterburners straight up to the troposphere is something I shall remember for quite a while.

Once we were in the climb the three aircraft ahead came into view. We seemed to be number four in an elongated tail chase pushing upwards at the rush, with the noise of the pressurisation competing with that of the afterburners. At about 30,000ft, some 70 seconds after rolling, the leader peeled off left and levelled off, shutting down his burners and setting course for our exercise area. His three followers turned inside him and joined up in battle formation before splitting into two pairs for the mock attacks which we were about to practise.

'When Squadron Leader Bell had positioned us 400 yards behind number three he gave me control of the stick and told me to hold the same relative position. Wisely, I left control of the throttle in his hands. We soon began yo-yo manoeuvres, diving through the transonic speeds just below the tropopause then pulling quickly up in a surging climb still at supersonic speed in a simulated zoom attack.

'After a couple of these we split into two pairs, numbers one and two being vectored away by radar in preparation for an attack on us. It was not long before number three started jinking ahead of me. From my left came relaxed comments to close up, go more to the left and most of all, to pull harder. The Lightning really is a delightful aircraft to fly between M0.9 and M1.3, the range in which we were operating. I had no trouble in keeping lateral position by quick applications of aileron followed by opposite aileron to counter the drift. As soon as I saw number three bank I could follow him quite easily.

'But when we began pulling g in turns or in climbs the leader tended to creep up the windscreen while I craned my neck watching him through the canopy and pulling hard back on the stick. In the thin air some long-forgotten reflex was telling me not to pull too hard in case I developed a g-stall. "Pull harder," came the voice, this time somewhat more concerned in case we lost number three altogether. Dick took over and repositioned us, before handing back to me.

'Chat on the R/T warned number three that our attackers were somewhat close, on my side it seemed, but I saw nothing until Dick pointed out two arrows far below us. "They are just preparing to zoom up on us," he said. "Watch for number three taking avoiding action."

'Then we began another series of twists, turns, climbs and descents. I shall never know whether we did evade our attackers – I was too busy trying to keep number three in the centre of my half of the windscreen. When the turns became really tight Dick pushed in the re-heat, felt, as well as heard, and we wound round even tighter. In the end, just as it was our turn to make an attack, somebody had a radar failure and someone else was low on fuel. So we met our targets head-on and turned in behind them in a tight upward supersonic arc until we were all four strung out in a descending tail-chase. At least, downwards was the general direction. Number one took the four of us through a downward and seemingly never-ending corkscrew. Sea, clouds and sky reared themselves continuously across the screen. I had forgotten what it was like to be at the back of a tail-chase, watching the three in front making their moves to follow the man ahead. And then, as the three began to drift as a group from their position on the screen, remembering that I too would have to do something before they disappeared entirely.

'It was during one of these lazy moments in the descent that I absentmindedly

Flight Lieutenant Tony Aldridge of 23 Squadron, flying T.4 XS417, maintains close formation with F.3 XP763/M, on take-off from Leuchars in July 1965. XS417 was the first production T.5 to fly, on 17 July 1964. XP763 first flew on 11 September 1964 and was issued to 23 Squadron on 27 October 1964. It went to 60 MU in July 1966 and later flew with 56 and 29 Squadrons, before being SOC and scrapped in March 1973. (via Tony Aldridge)

23 Squadron F.3s in formation break, with XP736/F nearest the camera. Next is XP737/L. XP736 crashed into the sea thirty miles off Lowestoft on 22 September 1971. Flying Officer Phil Mottershead of 29 Squadron was killed. XP737/L first flew on 1 January 1964 and joined 23 Squadron on 21 October 1964. It later joined 226 OCU and was displayed at Farnborough in September 1970 by 'Oscar' Wild. In July 1972 it caught fire in the spine during a flight from Coltishall to Binbrook; it was repaired and in May 1976 joined 11 Squadron. On 17 August 1979 it crashed into the Irish Sea after Flying Officer Ray Knowles abandoned the aircraft when the port main undercarriage leg failed to lower when attempting landing at RAF Valley. Knowles ejected safely. (via Tony Aldridge)

allowed us to drift upwards through the wash of number three, 300 yards ahead. The buffet was so startling and strong that I really thought we had hit something. It didn't worry Dick though and we pressed on downwards towards Akrotiri.

'Dick took over again as we closed up for a line-astern formation before our final run-in. There is something about line-astern flying, especially in a group of four or more, which is quite fascinating to watch. The twin jet pipes of number three are five feet forward and above the canopy. Above him are two more pairs of jet pipes. A movement of the leader is repeated and magnified by number two, who is followed by number three, by which time the leader has settled down again. Number four, if he is lucky and experienced, can watch the two ahead of him snaking about, while he retains his position relative to the leader and damps out the oscillations. If he doesn't he can find himself having a somewhat undulating ride.

'We tightened up considerably in the short echelon starboard run-in to Akrotiri for the two-second break. When it came it was less stressmaking than I had anticipated and the approach and landing which followed was very smooth.

'Afterwards at the debriefing it was interesting to listen to the four analysing what had gone on and being mildly critical of themselves and of each other. For the leading three it had been a working flight and for Squadron Leader Bell it had been a check-ride as wing man to a young section leader. Those readers who remember the fighter squadrons of wartime days and the stories afterwards in the crew room, with hands and fingers expressively used to demonstrate who has done what to whom, will be pleased to know that little has changed. The youngest pilots still discuss their tactics in hurried, strident tones while their elders listen and say little. The senior pilots still worry about aircraft availability and whether so-and-so will be able to complete his programme of flying exercises.

'Plus ça change ...'

Wing Commander Bruce Hopkins, CO of 23 Squadron since May 1972, sometimes took part in his squadron's QRA[3] commitment at Leuchars, as he recalls:

'At one time all my pilots had done at least two intercepts against Soviet aircraft. Eric Houston did twenty-four scrambles that resulted in intercepts, 1972-75. The QRA shed was at the end of the runway and we would go there for twenty-four hours at a time and sit and wait. We'd sit in the crew room, kitted up and sleep there in proper beds in our underclothes. Our immersion suit, g-suit and Mae West's were laid out. We would get a build-up – in other words, a recognized air picture. A typical scramble would begin with one of the Norwegian radars plotting a Soviet aircraft transiting the Northern Cape and on into the North Sea. It could be a training flight. Bears were always going to Cuba via the Faeroes-Scotland-Iceland gap – or an intelligence-gathering sortie. Every time we had a naval exercise in the area you could always guarantee Soviet aircraft would monitor it. Sometimes we would go weeks without any Soviet aircraft, then get a dozen in a four-day period. The plot would be picked up by Saxa Vord, who would "tell in" to Strike Command at High Wycombe, who would organize resources. Tankers would usually be called in to support us. You therefore knew well in advance when you would be scrambled and if and when you would get a tanker. First we were brought up to cockpit readiness. The ground controller would relay all relevant information, together with your call sign and that of the tanker. The type of call depended on the circumstances. The aircraft was always fully armed. We would carry a hand-held camera in the cockpit.

'Usually, one aircraft could be scrambled, but both pilots would be in their cockpits in case of a problem. Once airborne, we would first get to a tanker and then stay with him and refuel until the actual intercept. (A typical sortie would be five to six hours and involve several rankings, or brackets.) Once the intercept was set up, we would cast off from the tanker and head for the target. We would intercept, investigate and

Right: Flight Lieutenant Tony Aldridge after a 23 Squadron sortie. (Tony Aldridge)

Below: T.4 XS417/Z, which joined 23 Squadron at RAF Leuchars on 20 December 1965. In June 1966 it suffered an AVPIN explosion in the spine during pre-start cockpit checks. It was repaired and made its last flight on 16 April 1987.

F.6s of 23 Squadron at a very wet RAF Leuchars. The nearest aircraft is XR725/A. Note the Canadian maple leaf painted on the fin to denote the aircraft flown to Canada by Ed Durham in August 1968.

shadow, take photos and feed information on new aerials aboard an aircraft etc., back for intelligence gathering. Flying a Lightning and taking photos of a manoeuvering Bear was not the easiest job in the world and we developed a technique. First we would fly under the Bear, or the Badger, etc. and take photos from all angles. Sometimes, to make life even more difficult, they would trim in to you or away from you. Sometimes the guy at the back would wave. At night they shone lights at you to find out who you were. Although international airspace reached to within 12 miles of the coast of Britain, usually, the Soviet aircraft never came within 100 miles.

Squadron Leader Dave Seward was also asked to take photos of Soviet bombers from the cockpit while on QRA intercepts. 'I think that the Lightning cockpit was built around Roly Beamont, a 4ft 8in monster who had hands like meat plates and not for six-foot tall chaps like me! Trying to turn around in the cockpit when your head is almost touching each side and wearing an immersion suit and oxygen mask etc. to take a photo with your Vivitar was, shall we say "difficult"? Taking photos whilst flying the Lightning 1A, whose early autopilot was an AFCS giving just heading and attitude hold, was even worse. At that time QRA was a lot of sitting around on the ground. At Wattisham, whenever we were used 56 Squadron reinforced the Northern QRA. On Christmas Day 1962 the Russians put lip a stream of "Bears" and the odd "Bison" round the North Cape and we were up and down and landed at Leuchars. The Russians could be sheer bloody-minded. Commanding officers did not do normal QRA but generally speaking, we did Christmas Day and Boxing Day duty.'

In December 1973 the 23 Squadron CO, Wing Commander Bruce Hopkins, leading from the front and volunteering for it, did a Christmas and Boxing Day stint, from 0900 hours on Christmas morning to 0900 hours on Boxing Day. All was quiet until 0400 hours on Boxing Day morning when he was scrambled to investigate a plot over the North Sea. As usual, he expected to first make a rendezvous with a tanker. (Tankers were usually available at a high readiness state, in order to keep the interceptors airborne for as long as required – sometimes up to seven or eight hours.) 'However', he recalls, 'There was no tanker available and so I did not have enough fuel to get to the intercept point. It was a "Bear" making the Cuba run. I flew out for forty minutes in the hope that I would get a look at it but the target profile probably turned away. A year later on 17 September 1974 I intercepted two "Badgers" flying together, going north. The training

F.6s of 23 Squadron in 1968. The nearest aircraft is XR755/O, which joined the squadron on 10 December 1965 as 'A'. It was converted to full F.6 standard in 1967 and when it returned to 23 Squadron, on 23 May 1968, it was re-coded 'O'.

and probing flights continued and each time we would send Lightnings up to investigate. Sometimes they were one of "ours". Sometimes they weren't. It was hard work but I enjoyed it, Comparing the Lightning with the Phantom was like comparing a sports car with a ten-ton truck. The Lightning handled beautifully and had a responsive feel to it, whereas the Phantom did not have that preciseness of control.'

Bruce Hopkins left 23 Squadron in April 1975. Seven months later, in November 1975, Group Captain Ed Durham arrived at Gütersloh having forsaken ('not reluctantly') a desk in MoD London earlier that year, to take command of 92 Squadron at Gütersloh. Group Captain Durham recalls. 'I had spent some month's refresher flying and was looking forward to taking my first command of a fighter squadron. All my time in the RAF had been spent in air defence in the United Kingdom and I had already flown three tours on the Lightning. To return to flying after an absence of six years was a tremendous thrill in itself but to be given a famous fighter squadron to lead and at an overseas location was real icing on the cake.

'In the UK the threat we faced was largely a long-range bomber one, at medium to high level and at some distance from the UK mainland. In Germany it was a totally different matter. The threat was at low altitude, had a substantial self-defence capability and could well be dedicated to defensive counter air – in other words we, the fighters, were their prime target. Generally speaking we were heavily outnumbered as well. Such considerations tended to concentrate the minds of 2 and 4 ATAF fighter crews and the impetus was skill though realistic training. Ground Control was a bonus and we spent much of our time in the low-level combat air patrol patterns although we talked to "Backwash" and "Crabtree" [GCI stations in Germany] occasionally.

'"Lightning Alley" was some obstacle fir the ATAF fighter-bombers to penetrate and affiliation training was achieved regularly under the "Dial a Lightning" concept. All we needed was a 'phone call from some base like Laarbruch or Brüggen to say that so many Jaguars would be south of Soest at 1200 and there would be at least two Lightnings on visual patrol ready to do battle.

'There is no doubt in my mind that my flying at Gütersloh was some of the best I have done in my Air Force career. Low-altitude operations are exciting and stimulating in themselves but to add to these the extra bonus of air combat not only increased the flow of adrenaline but also revealed the sense of responsibility innate in

Left: Queen's Birthday Flypast on 13 June 1970 by eight Lightnings of 111 Squadron, three Vulcans, four Phantoms and a Nimrod. (Brian Allchin)

Below: F.3 XP741/D of Treble One Squadron in 1971. This Lightning first flew on 4 February 1964 and joined 11 Squadron on 22 December that same year. It went on to serve with 5 and 11 Squadrons and the LTF. (BAe)

our young fighter pilots of the day. Mostly they were given free rein to do the job and with very few exceptions they responded in an effective and mature way. I was very proud of all my men on 92, aircrew and groundcrew alike, and I felt very privileged to be their commanding officer. We met every challenge, such as tactical evaluation, which came our way. I would also pay tribute to the other squadrons on the base for their contribution to the outstanding combat capability of the base and also for the friendly rivalry that helped to make life as good as it was.'

In 1972 an article appeared detailing QRA in RAF Germany.[4]

'... On every Station, some personnel will have been on duty throughout the night – in the Ops Room, the guardroom and so on. But at Gütersloh, just 80 miles from the East German border, the centre of quiet activity is a warmly-lit, miniature hangar a few yards from the runway threshold. Inside, behind heavy steel doors that open electrically at the touch of a button, sit two silver Lightnings – fuelled, armed and ready to go. In a small annex two pilots, dressed in bulky rubber immersion suits, pressure vests and all the other paraphernalia of a modern jet fighter pilot, have probably been playing cards all night; a few feet away in another room, the groundcrew doing the same thing. This tiny world is the Battle Flight, RAF Germany's first line of defence, and the scene is much the same 24 hours a day, 365 days a year, be it Christmas, Easter or April Fool's day.

'While the rest of the Station begins its daily tasks, life in the hangar continues along the same lines. Across the airfield, the pilot's colleagues are beginning their day's work by attending the daily weather briefing, and the long-suffering met man is enduring his daily dose of ribbing from the crews. (With the possible exception of the NAAFI, the met men are the pilots' favourite Aunt Sallies.) Within the hour, the first wave of Lightnings is roaring into the sky, and the day's training programme is under way. In pairs or singly, the Lightnings accelerate down the long runway with an ear-splitting roar, twin jets of flame from their re-heated engines scorching the concrete as the wheels leave the ground, some heading for special areas where, at great heights, they are allowed to go supersonic. Then they will chase each other around the sky on practice interceptions, guided by the disembodied voice of a man sitting miles away in a darkened room, watching the green blips that are the Lightnings on his radar set. The days when fighter pilots depended on the evidence of their own eyes are long past; with two Lightnings approaching head-on at supersonic speed, by the time the pilots spot each other it would be too late to avoid a collision. Others will be practising similar interceptions at a much lower level, while still more could be heading for a rendezvous with a converted Victor V-bomber from Britain, its bomb-bays now heavy with fuel. Once in contact, the Victor streams three long hoses, each with an inverted cone at the tip, and the thirsty Lightnings nose in, their pilots carefully juggling the controls in order to spear the cone with their refuelling probes. Once "plugged in", the fighters guzzle fuel at a fantastic rate and within a remarkably short time, gorged, they pull back and swing off to continue their exercise. The Victor, much, much lighter, turns for home, reeling in its hoses as it does so.

'Meanwhile, away to the east, a small civilian aircraft, carrying businessmen from Southern Germany to a conference in Lubeck on the Baltic, is creeping slowly eastwards away from its planned route; the pilot's radio navigation instruments are giving him a false reading. Eventually the aircraft crosses an invisible border in the sky, and inadvertently enters the Air Defence Identification Zone, within which aircraft must not fly without special authority: its purpose is to prevent just such an occurrence from turning into a border incident. In another darkened room, another man at another radio set has been monitoring the aircraft for some minutes. Attempts to contact it by radio have failed and as it enters the ADIZ the controller reacts. An alarm bell rings loudly in the miniature hangar near Gütersloh's runway, and cards

F.3s XP740/B and XP762/C of 111 Squadron flown by Ken Edmond and Rod Dowd respectively during a sortie from RAF Wattisham in 1972. XP740 first flew on 1 February 1964 and joined Treble One Squadron on 30 December 1964. XP762/C first flew on 3 September 1964 and joined 111 Squadron on 26 January 1963. (Ian Robins)

F.6 XS936/B of 23 Squadron at Leuchars, in March 1974. XS936 first flew on 31 May 1967 and was issued to 23 Squadron on 18 August 1967. On 28 August 1968 it was one of two F.6s which made the non-stop, air-refuelled, 7-hour 20-minute flight to Goose Bay, Canada, as a reserve Lightning to F.6 XR725/A, flown by Squadron Leader Ed Durham, which appeared in an air show at Toronto. Flight Lieutenant Geoff Brindle flew XS936/B to Canada and back on 3 September. This aircraft entered the Binbrook store in November 1975 and thereafter continued to serve 11 and 5 Squadrons and the LTF. XS936 last flew in October 1987 and was scrapped in April 1988. (Bruce Hopkins)

pilot, because be has an engineering honours degree from Imperial College.

'But what does make a fighter pilot? Aylward has the answer pinned on his wall at home. "On the hunt he becomes part monster scanning with the eyes of a falcon, has the reaction of a cat, the instincts of a barracuda, the cunning of a fox – and the ability to rotate his head 360-degrees on all axes."

'Paxton obtained a Private Pilot's Licence when he was 17. At 30 he is an old hand on Lightnings with nearly 1,300 flying hours, but admits: "I had dreadful air sickness problems, which had to be ironed out by RAF doctors. To help me they had to use a device known as a 'spin table'."

'Squadron Leader Mike Champion, Stu Gosling's fellow flight commander – as Devon schoolboys they served together in the Air Training Corp's Exmouth Squadron and then he did an exchange tour with the US Marine Corps – is intoxicated with the opportunity as he puts it, "to turn and burn and fight". This enthusiasm has withstood considerable pressure to return to the West Country and take his place in the family chemicals business.

'Steve and Pax and Mike are the sort of pilots to be seen in the glossy advertisements for RAF officer air-crew – products of a campaign to appeal to a young man's yearnings for the elitist role of an interceptor pilot.

'If there is a common denominator among the Lightning pilots it is the determination to succeed in this lonely, quick-thinking, quick-reaction profession; the "press-on" quality, as his predecessors would have described it, discovered while at Biggin Hill Officers and Aircrew Selection Centre where graduates are assessed for the three years of training. The selector will also be looking for mental agility, physical coordination and an ability to take the stresses of flying: in short, as the RAF says, "flying aptitude".

'Generally, graduates will have had pre-entry training – flying solo in university air squadrons, which, in the thirties, spawned many Battle of Britain pilot. Those entering straight from school will probably have belonged to local ATC squadrons. So, by the time he reaches RAF College Cranwell for initial officer training, the future fighter pilot may well have flown solo and will already know a great deal about the service and what it expects of him.

'There follows 100 hours basic flying training in the Jet Provost to wings standard and for all his ambition to become a fighter pilot it is not until the young officer has qualified for his wings that he moves for advanced training into what is known as the "fast jet stream". For Aylward's fledglings this meant training in the Gnat.

'The opening verse of No.11 Squadron's song, written before PAYE and when the RAF still policed an Empire, goes:

> *They call us Legs Eleven*
> *We're a shower of bloody skates.*
> *We never pay our Income Tax,*
> *We never pay our rates.*
> *But from the Nile to Singapore*
> *You'll find our empty crates...*

'Nowadays much of the talk in the crew room is about mortgages, decorating and digging the garden. Although there is a comfortable mess and adequate married quarters, the majority of fighter pilots – there are only three bachelors in the squadron – prefer to buy a house and live off the station. They feel that "with inflation we cannot afford not to buy a house. By the time we leave the service we'll be priced out of the market."

'Nevertheless, Aylward's younger pilots feel a close spiritual affinity with the Few. "We are in the same tradition," says Flying Officer Bob Pickett, 25. He is just a little toffee-nosed about brother officers crewing the Phantom, which accommodates a navigator as well as the pilot. But the aging Lightning – the prototype flew more than 25 years ago – will eventually be superseded by the two-seat multi role Tornado and the single-seat interceptor will have vanished from the RAF. The prospect of company in the cockpit does not appeal to Lightning pilots.

'If the example of the Few is not consciously fostered it remains an abiding inspiration. In the mess ante-room Spitfires joust with the Luftwaffe over the fireplace. No.11 Squadron, which will celebrate its 65th anniversary in September, was not in the Battle of Britain but it flew Hurricanes and Spitfires later in the Second World War and each new pilot browsing in the squadron museum at one end of the crew room finds he is part of a tradition which goes back to 1916 when Albert Ball, the First World War ace, flew Nieuport Scouts with No.11.

'The self-confidence, energy and dedication of Doug Aylward's young pilots would reassure any Battle of Britain veteran. Here and there the confidence borders on cockiness. Aylward accepts that a young fighter pilot, by the very nature of his task and training, will be rather pleased with himself, but discipline is assured by each pilot's desire to uphold the standards of the squadron and earn the approval of the Boss.

'The flying workload means formal parades are few and far between. "We should have more. It does no harm at all to bring the squadron together in this way," says Aylward.

'Absence of drill practice makes preparation for the station's annual exercise – it has the privilege of marching through the streets of Grimsby – something of an ordeal. Defending Britain is more of a round-the-clock responsibility for a fighter squadron today than it was during the Battle of Britain, which was fought mostly in daylight. No.11 Squadron is split into day and night flights: Q pilots and ground crew sleep in the Q shed; pilots sometimes remain there for 24 hours and ground crew can stay for a week at a time.

'Aylward lives in married quarters as on the station because of his responsibilities, so they let their house in High Wycombe. As with so many fighter pilots' wives, Anne Aylward comes from a RAF family. Her father was a serving officer in Malta, where she met Doug, and her two sisters married into the service. She has a nine-year-old daughter, Annette and seven-year-old twins, Douglas and Nicholas.

'In a sense she is also mother of the squadron. Improvements in service pay – average for a flight lieutenant: £11,000 – have enabled her to give up part-time jobs selling shoes and temporary secretarial work to devote more time to the unwritten responsibilities of the Boss's wife, but Aylward says: "Fighter pilots' wives put up with the hell of a lot."

'Pilots are lucky if they can take three or four weeks of their annual six-weeks' leave. *And* everyday social arrangements are often disrupted. "Sometimes the pressures are too much." says Aylward. "They know it themselves and a pilot knows he must talk about it to avoid getting killed. This is gratifying." Certainly none of the stress-has anything to do with hell-raising.

'On most nights the bar, dining and anterooms of the mess are quiet, the acres of deep armchairs sparsely inhabited only by the bachelors and bean stealers (an officer who has bought a house elsewhere and rejoins his family at weekends). So mess life contracts with that of the forties. Denis Rowee of the Lightning simulator team who, at the age of 58 is in the RAF for the second time round, recalls: "Life in a Spitfire squadron was like belonging to a good flying club. Great fun and sometimes a bit amateur. Now it has all become very much more professional."

'Such perilous activities as climbing round the high-walled bar have been abandoned. As Aylward says: "Operational pilots are scarce enough without aggravating the

F.6 XR755/F of 5 Squadron lifting off from RAF Binbrook in March 1971, in preparation for the squadron's defence of its unofficial title of 'Europe's top' in the annual NATO Air Defence competition. To retain the Hudleston Trophy, the symbol of air defence supremacy, 5 Squadron had to fly high and low, day and night, and both sub- and supersonic missions.

F.3 XP743/B of 29 Squadron in 1972. (BAe)

shortage." Several pairs of flying boats are suspended upside down from the bar ceiling; they belong to pilots who have ejected.

'Flight Lieutenant Dave Wheeler displays less of the traditional fighter pilot's bravura than most. At 33 he is their senior, apart from Aylward, who is 38. He is unusual in that he joined a fighter squadron after flying four-engine Shackletons and after a long spell as an instructor. Each pilot has a secondary duty, which adds to his work load. As the squadron's Qualified Flying Instructor, Wheeler checks the flying standards of each pilot twice a year.

'Flying Officer Ray Knowles, 25, is a short breezy Irishman from Belfast. After getting three A levels, he spent eight years in the Air Training Corps, then made a good living as an itinerant bricklayer in Europe before returning to the RAF. He has had his share of scrambles and the big brown boots hanging upside down testify to the day his Lightning failed to return from the Irish Sea.[6]

'Away from the service taboos of the mess, pilots and their wives find the local pub, the Blacksmith's Arms. Neutral ground. Here, the most experienced of pilots will unwind sufficiently to admit to moments of fear. Stu Gosling, nudging 1,300 hours on Lightnings, lights another cigarette and looks over his brimming pint: "Fly low – down to 250ft – over the North Sea at night and dark fears can run through you. But you go on flying."

'In 11 Squadron the burden of its share of Q is the prime cause of its heavy workload and the frequent condition of "Zorbin" – last minute changes. But as training and secondary duties have to be fitted in as well, and with only six other fighter squadrons defending Britain, some of the pressures on a young Lightning pilot can be appreciated.

'At times this summer Strike Command interceptor scrambles totalled as many as seven in one morning. Unlike fighter sorties of 40 years ago – never lasting more than an hour or two – today's scramble, often interrupting a spell of 24 hours sleeping, eating and waiting in the Q shed, lasts almost as long as an office working day. Such long periods airborne may be undesirable but shortage of pilots and aircraft make them necessary and the facility of air-to-air refuelling make them possible.

'The progress achieved in the use of radar since the Second World War reduces the wear and tear on today's pilot. Although in the early stages of the Battle of Britain the regularity and accuracy of their interception surprised enemy raiders, radar and the controllers' communications with fighter squadrons were rudimentary. Forty years on Fighter Control remains the nerve centre of the nation's air defence but the efficiency with which controllers can track Soviet aircraft and scramble and guide supersonic interceptors for hundreds of miles, until they are on the tail of an intruder, would be unrecognizable to the Few.

'Of course the zenith of a mission for each member of 11 Squadron is just that – to be on the tail of a Soviet military aircraft and, for all the assistance he receives from fighter control, achieving it remains a taxing business for a single-seat interceptor pilot. Stu and Audrey Gosling are having coffee with the Aylwards when the phone rings. "Six taken off from Murmansk and coming round the top. Badgers and Bears. Hodge has scrambled." No one, least of all 27-year-old Flight Lieutenant Pete Hodgson, really expects that on this sortie he will be lucky enough to notch up his first meeting with a Soviet aircraft.

'As he heads north of Scotland, his eyes on the radar and instruments, he grabs a crew-room sandwich from the packet under the canopy.

'Danish radar on the Faroes and a Shackleton early warning aircraft help to point him at two blips moving through the Iceland gap. Today there is no need to depend on the cockpit radar for there, 450 miles north of Scotland, 700 miles from base, dead ahead at 30,000ft, contrails advertising their presence, cruise huge Soviet Bear reconnaissance bombers.

F.6 climbing away on full re-heat. Once airborne with the undercarriage selected and locked up and at a safe climbing altitude, a turn onto the climbing heading could begin. When the speed reached 420 knots, the angle of climb was then increased to 18 degrees to maintain 450 knots. (Ken Johnson)

'Closing, munching his last sandwich, Hodgson reaches for the hand-held camera. At this moment pilots say they feel rather like tourists taking snaps. "To take our pictures," Hodgson said afterwards, "we move up on the left-hand side of the Russians. International rules of the air oblige us to approach on the left. It is also a matter of courtesy for the Soviet pilots sit in the left-hand seats of their cockpits. It makes it easier to exchange waves and smiles." And this was a happy, smiling occasion, especially for the Soviet crews who congregate in their observation blisters.

'Hodgson kept company with the Bears for three minutes and then it was time to turn for home. As it was, the sortie had been so extended that his Victor fuel tanker was dry and the Lightning could only reach Lossiemouth in Scotland. After refuelling he flew on down to Binbrook in time to potter in the garden before supper. It had been as near a perfect peacetime working day for a fighter pilot as the RAF could make it.'[7]

1 Writing in *Lightning Review*, June 1993.
2 'Have Lightning, Will Travel. When The Hooter Blares, Everybody Moves – 29 Squadron's Mobile Quick Reaction Capacity.' *Flight International*, 28 April 1970.
3 On 1 April 1971 the term 'QRA' was replaced with Interceptor Alert Force (IAF).
4 *RAF Germany Today* RAF Souvenir Book 1972.
5 'They Inherit The Skies: Are Britain's front-line fighters as ready as they were 40 years ago?' *Telegraph* Sunday Magazine, 27 July 1980.
6 Lightning F.3 XP737 of 5 Squadron, which was ditched in the Irish Sea off Valley, Wales, on 17 August 1979 after the port undercarriage failed to lower. Flying Officer Raymond T. Knowles ejected safely.
7 5 and 11 squadrons at Binbrook remained equipped with the Lightning, serving until 31 October 1987 and 30 April 1988, respectively, when they were replaced with Tornado F.3 aircraft. Binbrook remained equipped with the Lightning and these served until 31 October 1987 and 30 April 1988, respectively, when they were replaced with Tornado F.3 aircraft.

CHAPTER 6

Tiger Tales

Flight Lieutenant Mike J.F. Shaw joined 74 Squadron, the 'Tigers', in 1962.

'The Lightning F.1 had replaced the squadron's Hunter F.6s in June 1960 and had rendered all other European fighters obsolete; it was twice as fast and had more than double the rate of climb of anything else in service. This was brought home to me when I first saw a stream rotation take-off of five F.1s at three-second intervals. The technique was something that could not be applied safely to any other aircraft. Namely, to lift off at 175 knots, retract the undercarriage, push forward firmly to prevent too rapid a gain in height, then, at 220 knots IAS, to pull the stick right back until the attitude reached seventy degrees. Provided both burners were still going, this gave a climbing speed of 190 knots and a feeling to the pilot of ascending vertically, as the ejection seat rails were inclined at 23 degrees. At 3,000ft the Lightning could be rolled onto its back and the nose gently pulled to the horizon before rolling out erect and cancelling re-heat at about 250 knots. At that point the nosewheel, which retracted forwards, would finally lock up! To be anywhere in such a stream take-off was an unforgettable experience.

'At first, all the two-seat flying was done in two Hunter T.7s, which were beautiful aircraft to handle but had no resemblance to the mighty Lightning. Pilots were trained for that in the F.1 simulator, which had no freedom of motion but was more than adequate for the job, including radar interception work. So good was it that, on one occasion, descending through 10,000ft, when I felt a twinge of toothache. I remember thinking, "Oh, it'll feel better when I get down to a lower altitude." Pretty convincing simulation, obviously!

'There were some downsides to flying Lightnings. First, there was "practice death": being thrown into the sea at RAF Mountbatten. Pilots were towed behind a pinnace and had to release their harnesses when a whistle was blown, to haul in their dinghy packs, to inflate and then board their dinghies. After about an hour a Whirlwind would appear, pick up a few "survivors", disappear again, then come back and eventually retrieve all the hobbling sea-sick aviators – often closer to the rocks off Plymouth Hoe than they would have liked. Next, there was decompression training at RAF Upwood. The chamber took us up to 56,000 equivalent pressure altitude, requiring us to "pressure breathe". Bulging necks and arms full of stagnant blood, a squeezing mask, pressure jerkin and G-suit. Awful. Worse with the Taylor helmet – up to 60,000ft.

'Then there was the drag across the airfield at RAF North Luffenham behind a rig on a three-runner. This was to simulate being dragged by a parachute. Great. I was one of the first students to undergo a course on the Lightning Conversion Squadron (LCS) at RAF Middleton St George, where new T.4s had just been delivered. (The OC was Wing Commander K.J. "Ken" Goodwin, with, inter alia, flight lieutenants Pete Steggall, Roly Jackson and a huge navigator, Donaldson-Davidson, on the staff.) As I was to be 74 Squadron's QFI, it was important that I had some feel for the T.4, a model (XM974) which

F.3 XP751/B, which joined 74 Squadron on 29 April 1964. It served the *Tigers* until it joined 23 Squadron in November 1966. It was still flying up until 21 October 1986 when a broken fuel pipe allowed fuel to leak into the jet pipe area, causing a fire and damage to the rear fuselage which was not repaired.

provided two-seat Lightning training for the first time and was not wholly welcomed by the largely self-taught squadron pilots. I found, however, that all the pilots flew Lightnings very much in the same way thanks, presumably, to the flight simulator and its staff.

'The Lightning was incredible. It climbed, initially, in cold (i.e. non re-heat) power at 22 degrees attitude at 450 knots LAS and, if a positive re-trimming was not done at about 20,000ft, would slip through Mach 1 in the climb. It took quite a strong pull at that altitude to counter the nose-down effect of the rearward shift of aerodynamic centre when 450 knots became Mach 0.9. With its beautifully made airframe, ingenious main wheel retraction geometry, first-class engines and superb handling, the Lightning was a truly remarkable aircraft. It may have had a thirst for tyres and had operating costs far higher than those of its predecessors, but in the 1960s it was the queen of the European skies and its pilots knew that nothing could match it. If they kept their eyes open – and watched the fuel gauges – nobody could ever get close to them. It's not surprising that Lightning pilots were the most confident (and nauseatingly cocky) that could be found anywhere – with good reason!

'What the Lightning did lack was fuel. It carried only 7400lb at start-up, including a 250-gallon ventral tank. The contents of this tank usually exhausted a few minutes after levelling off at 36,000ft, where most of the standard Practice Intercepting (PIs) took place – near the normal tropopause.

'Recovery was usually through a "dive circle", a circle centred on a point eighteen nautical miles out on the duty runway, with a radius in nautical miles equal to the height of the Lightning in thousands of feet. This gave a comfortable descent at 350 knots at idle/fast idle (the No.2 – top – engine was kept at a fast idle setting to provide sufficient bleed air to drive the alternator fast enough to keep the aircraft services on line) for a feed into ILS, GCA, or visual rejoin. Further, the fuel used was only about 400lb from each wing, allowing a dive circle descent with 1,200 1,200lb to be completed to landing with the laid down minimum of 800/800lb. That gave a reserve, to tanks-dry, of little more than ten minutes – enough to cause an airline captain to have a heart attack. Indeed, he would have collapsed before take-off!

'In 1964 74 Squadron was posted from Coltishall to Leuchars to help 23 Squadron Javelins to cover the northern part of the UK Air Defence Region and shortly thereafter re-equipped with the F.3. This had Avon 300s in place of the 200s and an increase in the fin area. The radar was improved. Provision was made for Red Top IRAAM and the guns were deleted. The aircraft was cleared to Mach 2 (the F.1 was limited to Mach 1.7 for reasons of stability, not thrust) and all the pilots did at least one run to that speed. The fuel content was not increased, however, and the bigger engines were even less

F.1 XM147/
J of 74
Squadron
at RAF
Leuchars in
July 1964.
(Group
Captain
P.T.G. Webb)

economical, so the practical use of this top speed was doubtful. Provision was made for in-flight refuelling and the flight instruments were to [RAF standard] OR.946, including a strip (harder-to-read) airspeed indicator cum machmeter. Further, the air intake was not really large enough for the Avon 300s, and the cockpit floor would vibrate on take-off as they gasped for air. Overall, the F.3 was not the advance that we had hoped for, although it still flew nearly as well as the F.1 but with a CG (centre of gravity) which was noticeably further aft (heavier engines, no guns?).

'My average length on a sortie on the Lightning F.1 was forty-two minutes. During my tour with 74 Squadron I flew just over 350 sorties, about a quarter of them at night.

'We lost two aircraft during the period. One F.1 (XM142) on 26 April 1963 indicated a double power controls failure after an inverted check during an air test, and its pilot, Flight Lieutenant "Jim" Burns, ejected successfully over the North Sea. The second loss [on 28 August 1964] was an F.3 (XP704) which failed to complete a loop overhead the airfield at Leuchars, killing the pilot, Flight Lieutenant G.M. "Glyn" Owen.

'I had two anxious sorties myself, both due to the fact that our T.4 was really an F.1A rather than an F.1 and was fitted with UHF radio, as opposed to VHF. The squadron had all twelve F.1s and its T.4 at Farnborough in 1962, and on its return it was decided to fly VFR at low-level to Coltishall. We settled at 2,000ft AGL initially, with four vics of three, plus me in the T.4 with Flying Officer Peter Clinton, the Junior Engineering Officer, tagging along behind, unable to hear any of the VHF transmissions. We flew over a town (Northampton) under a lowering cloud base, then over Lakenheath at a rather alarmingly low altitude, but it was a Sunday and nothing else was stirring. Then I saw the vic ahead of me begin to climb, so I joined in as a No.4. We reached 30,000ft before we broke cloud. Nobody was talking to me on UHF and I held on tightly to the No.2. The airbrakes extended, so mine went out too and we went downhill until we broke cloud at 800ft, Coltishall in sight. I landed behind the other three in the sub-formation, still without any R/T contact. The other nine were still airborne but appeared very shortly afterwards. The mission had not gone according to plan, but we were all safely home!

'My next UHF problem was at night, when I was flying with a pilot who was not a Lightning man in the right-hand seat of the T.4. All went well until recovery, when Coltishall did not answer my call on UHF and the station's TACAN was off the air. An adjoining station's TACAN was working, so I positioned overhead Coltishall using that and began a teardrop (out-and-back, turning homebound at half the initial altitude plus 4,000ft) let-down. When we broke cloud at about 3,000ft, we were over land. But the TACAN had broken a lock during the inbound turn (not surprisingly, as the beacon was twenty-five nautical miles away) and I could not see Coltishall,

F.1s of 74 Squadron newly arrived at Leuchars, Scotland, in July 1964. The nearest aircraft is XM163/ K, which joined the *Tigers* on loan from July to September 1961 as 'Q'. After receiving modification at Warton in 1962 the aircraft was issued to 74 Squadron on 3 April 1963 when it was coded 'K'. It joined 226 OCU on 13 July 1964. It flew for the last time in February 1972. (Grp Cptn P. T. G. Webb)

who spoke to us for the first time when I requested clearance to land straight in. We touched down, vibrated badly and stopped in 700 yards. The main wheels had not rotated at all. It later was proved that the Bowden cable from the right-hand control column had not released when the pilot on that side had retracted the wheels after take-off, so the brakes were still firmly on. My fault, of course – I should not have let an unqualified (though very experienced) pilot do the take-off. But there was no clue in the cockpit that the brakes had not released. Sometimes, you can't win.

'My next contact with Lightnings, after a tour in exchange with the US Marine Corps, flying Phantom F-4Bs, was on RAF Handling squadron at A&AEE Boscombe Down in 1966-8. As the pilot responsible for the writing and or amendment of the Lightning Pilot's Notes and Flight Reference cards, I had the opportunity to add the T.5, F.6 and lastly, the F.2A to my tally. The T.5 was an odd aircraft, based on the F.3, but with throttles (unlike the T.4) on the right-hand cockpit console for the right-hand seat. This meant that the stick had to be controlled by the left hand, the only fighter where this had been the case. Odd.

'The F.6 was a Mk.3 with a long belly tank, non-jettisonable. It had extended leading edges, which increased the wing area, improved the camber and compensated for the extra weight. It could also carry overwing fuel tanks, which would catch your eye and, until their presence was accepted, prove rather distracting. For ferry purposes only, these tanks made a great difference to endurance.

'The F.2A was, in my view, the best of the lot. It retained two guns in the nose (the F.6 could carry two in its ventral pack, with the loss of some fuel), had the old Avon 200s, which were much smoother than the 300s, and had the F.6-type long ventral tank and extended leading edges. The long tank deadened some of the sound of the No.1 (forward, bottom) engine and increased the start-up fuel to over 10,000lb. It still had the old AI 23 radar, but that was quite good enough for the job. When the F.2A was released to the RAF, I collected the first one from the English Electric factory at Warton, flew in to Boscombe Down and then, as was my brief, took it to the edges of its cleared flight envelope. It was a beauty, handling exactly as expected. Then, in January 1968 I had to take it to RAF Gütersloh and hand it over to 19 Squadron.

F.1 XM135/B. After service with the *Tigers* and 226 OCU this aircraft was one of several at
33 MU at Lyneham in 1966, which was prepared as a supersonic target for Fighter Command.
While carrying out taxi tests on 22 July, Wing Commander Walter 'Taffy' Holden, a forty-year-old
engineering officer and the CO of 33 MU, went for an unscheduled trip in this aircraft when, on
the fourth taxi run, re-heat was inadvertently selected and the F.1 took off! Holden, who had never
flown a jet aircraft before, was not wearing a helmet and the canopy had been removed prior to
the taxi tests. Despite his lack of experience, Holden remained airborne for twelve minutes and he
managed to land safely at the second attempt. XM135 was repaired and used by the Leuchars TFF
before being retired to the IWM Collection at Duxford on 20 November 1974.

It was not fitted with TACAN or IFF; that was a task for Gütersloh. For the first
twenty minutes I could see the ground, but the Continent had solid cloud cover and,
oh dear, Lippe radar didn't answer my calls. I knew that I had a 90-knot tailwind,
and being anxious not no plunge into the Air Defence Identification Zone just to the
east of Gütersloh, decided to forget Lippe and call Gütersloh direct. They identified
me, to my relief, twelve miles to the south after I had set up a prudent triangle. The
subsequent let-down and recovery was immaculate and the squadron CO, Squadron
Leader Laurie Jones, later Air Marshal, intercepted me on the final approach. And that
was the last time, as I knew it would be, that I ever flew a Lightning.'

Earlier, in June 1967, thirteen Lightnings of 74 Squadron, led by the CO, Wing
Commander Ken Goodwin, had transferred to Tengah, Singapore, for what turned
out to be a four-year tour of duty in the tropics. Flight Lieutenant Dave Roome was
posted to the '*Tigers*' that same year. He relates:

'By the time I came to the Lightning in September 1967, the F6 was already in
production for the squadrons, though only thirty-nine were built in all (a further
fourteen were converted from the 3ER [extended range]). The OCU course was
conducted initially on the F.1a and T.4, flying the conversion phase with 1 Squadron
on 226 OCU and the basic radar phase on 2 Squadron. It was during the latter phase
that we received our postings, for those destined for Germany would remain on 2
Squadron, as 19 and 92 squadrons then flew the F.2, later the F.2a and only those
posted to fly the F.3 or F.6 completed their course on the T.5. The first seven tourists
on our course were told that there were four UK postings, all to Leuchars, while
three of us would go to Germany. This caused a small problem, as five of us wanted
Germany and, whilst we might be officers and gentlemen, none of us was going to
give up a Germany posting voluntarily. In the end we drew straws and whilst the
three lucky ones were celebrating, the two of us who had missed out agreed that the
toss of a coin would leave that one with the chance of any "odd" posting that might
come up. The other could be certain that he would go to Leuchars. Some days later, I

Line-up of 74 Squadron. The nearest aircraft is 'A'.

F.6 XS920/L of 74 'Tiger' Squadron on a *Tambour* X-country from Leuchars with a Victor K.1A tanker in the winter of 1967, as a prelude to the squadron's deployment to Malaya that summer. The loss of the Valiant tanker fleet in 1965 resulted in a rapid conversion of Victor B.1 bombers to K.1A in-flight refuelling tankers, the first flying on 28 April 1965. XS920 was issued to '*Tiger*' Squadron on 5 December 1966. (Jimmy Jewell)

F.6 XR768/A of 74 Squadron taking on fuel from Victor K.1A XH650 of 55 Squadron. In June 1967 thirteen of 74 Squadron's F.6s transferred from the UK to Tengah, Singapore, in Operation *Hydraulic*. This was the longest and largest in-flight refuelling operation hitherto flown, staging through Akrotiri, Masirah and Gan and using seventeen Victor tankers from Marham for a four-year tour of duty in the FEAF (Far East Air Force).

XR768 first flew on 24 November 1965 and joined the *Tigers* on 1 August 1966. On 15 December 1970 the Lightning joined 5 Squadron and on 29 October 1974 it crashed into the sea off Mablethorpe following a re-heat fire caused by a fuel leak during the relight attempt. The pilot, Flight Lieutenant 'Tex' Jones, ejected safely.

'A' Flight Detachment, 74 'Tiger' Squadron, at RAAF Butterworth, Malaya, in February 1968. Nearest aircraft is XR771/D, which is now on display at the Midland Air Museum in Coventry. XS927/N was last flown in October 1986 and was scrapped in 1988. XS895/H was finally scrapped in April 1988. (Jimmy Jewell)

F.6 XS894/H of A Flight Detachment, 74 Squadron at RAAF Butterworth, Malaya, in February 1968. (Jimmy Jewell)

The wreckage of XV329/T of 74 Squadron. This aircraft first flew on 30 December 1966. In March 1967 it was shipped to Singapore aboard the Motor Vessel *Calchas*, but the No.1 hatch and starboard tailplane suffered excessive corrosion during the long sea voyage and on arrival was declared Cat.3. The aircraft was shipped back to the UK aboard the Royal Fleet Auxiliary *Robert Middleton*, arriving at Sydenham on 16 October 1971. XV329 was recovered to 'one flight standard' and flown to 60 MU Leconfield on 14 December 1971, where the aircraft was declared NEA (Non Effective Airframe) and in April 1974 it was placed on the dump at the airfield and SOC as scrap.

F.6 XR771/D getting airborne from RAF Tengah, Singapore, in 1968. (Dave Roome)

On the flight line at Tengah in 1968. (Dave Roome)

Above: During 74 Squadron's posting to Singapore three 2,000-mile deployments were made to Australia non-stop using Victor tankers, the major one being Exercise *Town House* on 16-26 June 1969. Here, F.6 XR761/B takes on fuel from a 55 Squadron Victor tanker. (Mike Rigg)

Right: F.6 XR761/B and F.6 XS921/M taking on fuel from a 55 Squadron Victor tanker during Exercise *Town House* on 16-26 June 1969. (Mike Rigg)

F.6 XR761/B, which became 'B' in 56 Squadron, served the *Firebirds* until the summer of 1976, when, after overhaul at 60 MU, it was transferred to Binbrook where it served both 11 and 5 Squadrons. On 8 November 1984 XR761/AC crashed into the North Sea eight miles east of Spurn Head, following pitch trimmer failure after take-off. Both re-heat fire warning lights then came on, indicating that both No.1 and No.2 engines were on fire. Flight Lieutenant Mike D. Hale, the pilot, burned off fuel, intending to land back at Binbrook but smoke and fire caused him to eject. Hale was picked up after twenty-five minutes in the sea. (Mike Rigg)

Flight Lieutenant Dave Roome with Buddist monks at Don Mauang AFB, Bangkok, on 24 October 1970. Two 74 Squadron Lightnings had been flown to Thailand for a static display in Bangkok. (Dave Roome)

Remarkable view of a 74 Squadron Lightning through the periscope of a Victor tanker during an air-to-air refuelling ferry flight from Tengah to Cyprus in September 1971. (Jimmy Jewell)

74 Squadron disbanded at Tengah on 25 August 1971, and starting on 2 September 1971 all remaining F.6s were flown on the 6,000-mile, 13-hour trip to Akrotiri, Cyprus, staging through Gan and Muharraq and completing seven in-flight refuellings with Victor tankers, for transfer to 56 Squadron. Here, on 6 September 1971 over Iran whilst en route from Gan to Akrotiri, Flight Lieutenant Roger Pope piloting F.6 XS897/K comes up close to Flight Lieutenant Dave Roome in XR773/F. (Dave Roome)

was asked by my squadron commander to confirm that I had indeed won the toss. I duly did so and received my posting, to 74 Squadron at RAF Tengah in Singapore!

'During the three-and-a-half years that I was at Tengah many events, both happy and sad, took place. On 23 October 1968 I had the chance to intercept a USAF RB-57F, a highly modified version of the Canberra with a 122ft span and 42,000lb of thrust. This was in Singapore carrying out high-altitude meteorological trials on turbulence prior to Concorde starting commercial services to Singapore. The abilities of this aircraft in the upper atmosphere were demonstrated graphically when he climbed 15,000ft, from 65,000 to 80,000ft, whilst flying a 180-degree turn! He was surprised that the Lightning, which carried out the next intercept, overtook him in a descent through his altitude and advised us that his last run would take some time to set up. This time his altitude was into six figures and he was safe, but it left me with the thought that out in the tropics where the tropopause is in the order of 55,000ft the Lightning could probably achieve above 85,000ft. I was determined to try it when I got the chance, and some months later, that chance arrived.

'There was a Victor tanker returning from Hong Kong and offering about 17,000lb of fuel to us. I went up the east coast of Malaysia, almost to the Thai border, and filled to full. I was now left with a straight run home and the east coast was the area in which we could fly supersonic. Initially I climbed to 50,000ft, which was the subsonic service ceiling of the aircraft, and there I accelerated to 2.0M and started a zoom climb, selecting about 16 degrees of pitch. I levelled off at 65,000ft and let the aircraft have its head, reaching 2.2M before once again flying the same zoom profile. This time I held the climb attitude, though to do so required an increasing amount of aft stick as the reduction in downwash over the tail increased. Eventually the stick reached the backstops and I gently topped out, 200ft short of 88,000ft. From there, Singapore looked tiny and I convinced myself that I could see from the very southern tip of Vietnam over my left shoulder, past the Borneo coast in my 11 o'clock, to the western coast of Sumatra on my right hand side. The sky was pitch black above me and all of a sudden I realised that I did not belong here. With idle/idle, I started a glide back down which would have carried me over 150 miles. A marvellous example of the Lightning's sheer performance; though the pressure jerkin, G-suit and normal oxygen mask would not have been sufficient had the pressurisation failed.

'We also took the Lightning to Australia for the first time in June 1969 for an exercise called *Townhouse*, which was mounted in the Northern Territory, and we were based at Darwin. This provided some excellent flying as the rules were few — the base commander was quoted by the local Press as saying that, if they were to practice the defence of the area realistically, then the aircrew needed freedom and the town should "expect to get boomed". Darwin was still used by the major airlines as a staging base and one sight that sticks in my mind is of a 707 taking off whilst being overtaken by an "attacking" RNZAF Canberra. Giving chase were one RAAF Mirage and one Lightning, which went either side of the 707 as it pulled into its normal, steep, noise-abatement climb. The complaint of the 707 captain was met by the RAAF air traffic controller's statement to the effect that "didn't he know there was a war on?"

'There were many problems with the aircraft during my time on it. By far the worst problem was that of fuel leakage into the fuselage where it had a rather tiresome habit of catching fire. During my time at Tengah I had four fire warnings in flight.

'Also, there was much fun to be had, not least because there was no QRA, very few exercises and several detachments to places such as Butterworth in Malaysia, to Bangkok and across Australia. We had our own tactical air force in the Far East Air Force: Tengah had 20 Squadron with Hunter FGA.9s and three Single Pioneers for FAC work, 45 Squadron flew the Canberra B.15 and 81 Squadron operated in the recce role with the Canberra PR.7. Elsewhere on Singapore there were Hercules,

F.6 XS895 IH comes
in to land at Akrotiri
after the long flight
from Tengah. This
aircraft finished
its career with 5
Squadron. (*Aeroplane*)

Shackletons, Bristol Freighters, Andovers, Meteors, Belvederes and Whirlwinds. North in Malaysia by some 330 nautical miles was Butterworth, which operated two RAAF fighter Squadrons, eventually both with the Mirage III and we used to have a regular exchange, called Tiger Rag.

'There was a long-standing competition for the fastest time from passing the ATC Tower at one base to arriving at the other, which had started way back in the days of Sabres and Meteors. The Hunter had brought the record back to the RAF but the arrival of the Mirage allowed Butterworth to regain the title. Eventually 74 planned an all-out assault, using four Lightnings on their way to start a Tiger Rag. Each took off at five-minute intervals and had several check points on the route north. 11, the lead, passed a checkpoint with more than the planned minimum fuel, those behind left full burner in and so, of course, the back man slowly caught up the lead! Eventually all four passed the tower at approaching 0.999M and the base commander, a somewhat irascible man, took umbrage at this hooliganism and ordered all four aircraft to return to Tengah the next day! They brought back the record though, of 24 minutes for the 330 nautical miles and it was to stay with 74 for the remainder of our time there.

'On 22 October 1970 I was lucky enough to fly one of the two aircraft up to Bangkok for a display there (the boss, Wing Commander Dennis Caldwell, had announced the detachment some time earlier by saying "I don't know who else is going"). We landed to find that the squadron commander of one of the Thai F.5 squadrons had been on the same staff college course at Andover, and Dennis and he insisted on taking us for "Thai Tea" which came out of a very large whisky bottle and didn't involve any water! Now one of the Thai customs is that good friends hold hands, regardless of sex and the Thai grabbed hold of Dennis' hand and refused to let it go. I watched the boss trying to look as if his right arm no longer belonged to him and I, as the Squadron Diarist, tried to get my camera out to record the evidence, only to be given an abrupt "There'll be no photographs!" So another marvellous scoop went down the tubes!

'However, it wasn't all fun, for there were tragedies too, and in one four-month period in 1970 the squadron lost four aircraft and two pilots, a large percentage of a twelve-aircraft, sixteen-pilot squadron. But we always bounced back, a sure sign of a good squadron. On 26 May Flying Officer John Webster was killed flying XR767 doing low-level practice intercepts over the Malacca Straits. He was, in fact, my No.2 that night and was on my radar scope until probably only seconds before impact with the water, though I was not aware that he had crashed for some time, as it was not unusual to see and then lose a radar return. The weather was stormy and he had just flown through a fairly bad rain shower although, as he should have been at 1,000ft above the sea, he should have had no problem. Only a section of overwing tank has ever been found from the aircraft.

'On 27 July Flight Lieutenant Frank Whitehouse crashed in XS930 attempting a "formation take-off" at Tengah. Following a fire on start to XS928[1] in April, caused by a sticky overwing vent valve, we had adopted the policy – agreed by BAC Warton – of selecting the flight refuel switch to flight refuel until after take-off. This prevented the ventral tank fuel pump from starting up on the ground, which normally occurred after 120-160lb of fuel had been burnt after the start, and which had pumped the fuel out through the vent valve. Unfortunately, no one had realized that burning fuel from the wings and not from the ventral had the effect of moving the aircraft's CG aft, and Frank had had a long wait on the ground and a long taxi to the take-off point. By the time he got airborne his CG was outside the aft handling limits, which had the effect of reducing markedly the stick force per g on the control column. When he "snatched" the stick, as we used to for a good "rote", the aircraft over-rotated and stalled. He should have ejected immediately but, with the aircraft virtually at the vertical (I watched the whole incident), it staggered up to 400-500ft purely under the influence of two Rolls-Royce Avons before autorotating and falling out of control. Frank ejected too late and was killed on impact with the ground.

'On 12 August Flying Officer Mike Rigg ejected from XS893/G off Changi when he could not get his port undercarriage leg to lower. The leg did not even leave the bay, as could clearly be seen by the taxi light illuminating the bay as Mike overflew Tengah several times (I was OC Night Flying that night). The area into which the aircraft fell, the designated ejection area, turned out to have been used as an ammunition dumping area by the RN and the Army for years and no amount of pleading could get any salvage divers to go down! The ejection area, though never used again, was then moved to be Southwest of Tengah by fifteen nautical miles.

'Finally, the time came to fold up RAF fighter operations in Southeast Asia and we disbanded 74 and left Singapore in early September 1971. Our departure was in dribs and drabs too, for we ferried the aircraft in pairs via Gan to Akrotiri and gave them to 56 Squadron who had been operating the F.3. I decided that I wanted to go out with a bang rather than a whimper and talked over an idea for a final flypast on our departure. The Victor tanker captain was quite content, for he had plenty of spare fuel and both OC Flying and the Station Commander agreed in principle. They attended the brief, at which I mentioned that I would take a line, which would put me 'between the Victor on the main pan and the ATC Tower'. That is exactly what I did, but the two senior officers were watching from Local, 60ft above ground level, and I was out of sight to them both as I passed! I flew down the pan as low as I dared at about 330 knots and then plugged in the burners over the squadron for the last time and left for Gan, not realising the apoplexy I had left behind! Luckily, OC Flying talked the Station Commander out of his plan to fall in senior flight lieutenants and recall me for a court martial. Instead, my punishment involved removing my authorising status (just prior to my last ever Lightning sortie). I'm still very grateful to Erik Bennett for that generous action.

'So my last single-seat Lightning F.6 sortie, in "my" aircraft, XR773/F was Gan-Akrotiri with seven "prods" taking on 36,000lb from the Victors. At the end of it I sat for a moment in the cockpit and thought back over all the good times I had experienced in the Lightning. What a marvellous, beautiful, powerful fighter it was and quietly thanked it for giving me such never-to-be-forgotten experiences ... then it was over and I went off to the JP 3 to learn to be a QFI!'

---

1 XS928 had to be airlifted to BAe Warton by a Short Belfast for repair after suffering damage caused by a ground fire at Tengah when fuel vented onto the wing. New wings were subsequently fitted and XS928 operated later with 23 and 56 Squadrons before it joined 5 Squadron as 'K' in September 1976. XS928 served with 5 Squadron until it disbanded in December 1987.

CHAPTER 7

Linies

Lingua Franca (the lore of the service) defines a 'liney' as 'non-flying personnel, one who works on the flight line, preparing the aircraft for flight and recovering them afterwards.' Almost exclusively they were and still are to a great extent, the lowest ranks in the RAF: the LACs and SACs (leading and senior aircraftsmen). As such, they are invariably looked upon as the lowest form of life in a squadron, but they are amongst the hardest working tradesmen on a station.

Peter Hayward was one of the ground technicians in 226 OCU at Coltishall and remembers the Lightning as a 'noisy beast of prey which shattered the peace and tranquillity of certain rural counties in England and Scotland all those years ago. The same Lightning that frightened children, old ladies and all manner of animals also gave pleasure to the pilots who flew it and headaches to the technicians who serviced it. The flight line was the "sharp end", as Wing Commander Engineering called it. "How are things at the sharp end today?" he would say. The flight line and was a busy, noisy hive of industry with pilots and ground crews coming and going, aircraft being marshalled in and out, and turn-round, pre-flight and after-flight inspections always going on. Aircraft were refuelled and new brakes installed. Meanwhile, the fog from the LOX (liquid oxygen) trolley crept along the ground like at a latter-day rock festival as oxygen tanks were replenished, followed by the sharp hiss of an AVPIN engine starter and the subsequent acrid smell and eye-watering after-effects of the fumes. This and the ear-shattering blast of the engine starters forms perhaps the most vivid recollections for many Lightning ground crews. The two Avon engines were each started by a small turbine fed by liquid isopropylnitrate (AVPIN). The burnt gases from these two turbines exhausted overboard at high velocity, the No.1 (lower) engine starter vertically downwards and the No.2 (upper) engine starter parallel to the ground underneath the port wing. The choking fumes were extremely pungent and irritated the eyes as well. On a calm day they hung in the air until the aircraft taxied out and dispersed them with its jet blast.

'We were almost deafened out of our ear defenders by one of those big silver bullets coming out of nowhere with both re-heats at full chat. The trouble was, they crept up on you. They crept up so fast that you didn't hear them coming until they'd gone. Then you heard them all right, but that ear-shattering roar of two Avons with the re-heat nozzles fully open and enough fire coming from their rear ends to make you realize that hell was closer to earth than you thought. The steely-eyed jockeys who flew them took great pleasure in showing off the awesome power of the engines and incredible rate of climb of the aircraft. Especially in the aerobatic displays. A take-off with full re-heat would be followed by few seconds of level flight a few feet above the runway until the landing gear was tucked away and the aircraft was clean and moving fast. Then up into a near vertical climb until the aircraft was a speck in the sky, for the mere mortals on the ground anyway. An unimaginable din accompanied all this; it was simply shattering.

Above and below: Flight Lieutenant Brian Mason of 111 Squadron suffered a brake parachute failure in F.1A XM215 at Wattisham on 25 November 1963, and the aircraft caught fire entering the barrier. This Lightning first flew on 11 July 1961 and joined Treble One Squadron on 2 August that year. XM215 was later transferred to 226 OCU (Operational Conversion Unit) at Coltishall and the Binbrook Target Facilities Flight. XM215 was finally scrapped in 1984. (Brian Allchin)

Final preparations and testing of a Firestreak missile prior to firing at the missile practice camp, RAF Valley, Wales, in March 1964. The aircraft is F.1A XM184/A of 111 Squadron, which first flew on 27 February 1961. This Lightning joined the OCU at Coltishall in March 1965. On 17 April 1967 the aircraft suffered a fire on landing at Coltishall as a result of a major fuel leak. Flight Lieutenant Gerry Crumbie was uninjured but the aircraft was SOC. (George Black)

'For the technicians who serviced them it was a love-hate relationship. The noisy beast of prey was difficult, the systems complex, and it seemed that the designers had packed equipment in with hardly a thought as to how to get it out again. Oh, there were plenty of access panels, but it seemed that for even the simplest of jobs one of the engines had to be removed, or the ejection seat, or the radar bullet. "Top hatch off, ventral tank off, bottom hatch off. Fuel leaks, hot air leaks." Then it all had to be put back together again, tested, engines probably run and if you were lucky, if you were really lucky, the aircraft was cleared and handed over to the flight line. A check was carried out on every pre-flight inspection to make sure that the access panels were all properly attached and that no fasteners were missing. On the two-seat versions there were two large hinged access panels just aft of the cockpit. Because they were hinged at the bottom and so opened upwards, they were known as the "elephant's ears". These panels hid the fuse and circuit breaker boxes, which had on occasions to be accessed with the engines running and the cockpit occupied by two pilots waiting to leave on a sortie. This required some degree of acrobatic talent from the electrical technicians, and they could often be seen hanging on to the cockpit access ladder with one hand and fighting with one of the "elephant's ears" with the other. An alternative method was to stand precariously on the inboard section of the wing leading edge, grasp one of the antennas on the top of the fuselage and reach forwards to open the panel. This was no less acrobatic than the first method, but a darned sight more entertaining for onlookers, particularly if the wing upper surface was wet with fuel.

F.1s of 74 Squadron newly arrived at Leuchars, Scotland, in July 1964. The nearest aircraft is XM163/K, next is XM164/L, followed by XM135/B, XM136/C, then XM137/D, 'G', XM147/J and 'F'. XM163 first flew on 23 April 1960 and was issued to AFDS before use with 74 Squadron. XM164 first flew on 13 June 1960 and joined the *Tigers* on 15 July that year. XM135 first flew on 14 November 1959 and was issued to AFDS on 25 May 1960. It was loaned to 74 Squadron at first (as 'R') and became 'B' on a permanent basis in 1964. XM135 went to 226 OCU on 25 July 1964. XM136 first flew on 1 December 1959 and was issued to AFDS on 21 June 1960. It too was loaned to 74 Squadron (as 'S') on 7 September 1961 and, after modifications at English Electric, returned to the Squadron as 'C'. (Group Capt P.T.G. Webb)

'The really hectic times would come during exercises. Aircraft would be serviced for the next flight in record time and from taxiing out, a turnaround inspection could be done in nine minutes. This included completely refuelling the aircraft and instilling a new brake 'chute and a change of crew. The hive of activity continued even when the weather was too bad for flying. "Clampers" was the term used. It meant bad visibility. The activity, however, was confined to the flight line hut. It consisted of endless games of bridge and other card games, darts, innumerable cups of tea and coffee, erotic books and magazines, sleeping and asking if the squadrons could stand down, as the weather obviously wasn't going to improve, was it?

'Most impressive were re-heat runs at night, for which, at Coltishall anyway, the aircraft would be towed into the old Second World War concrete revetments. The reason for this, I imagine, was to reduce the noise for the civilian population that lived within earshot of the airfield – and that, on a still winter's night, was a good number of miles. Even wearing ear defenders, the noise as re-heat was engaged was awesome. First the engine was taken up to full dry power, then the throttle lever was rocked outboard into the re-heat range. This caused a slight reduction in noise as the re-heat nozzle opened, then the bang as the fuel in the jet pipe lit. As the throttle lever was pushed forwards towards the full re-heat position, the ground shook, the walls of the revetment vibrated and the aircraft compressed its nose landing gear leg and pushed its nose wheel hard into the concrete, fighting on its special chocks and with its brakes fully applied against the power of the engine. The visual effects were no less impressive. The jet blast now consisted of a long pattern of large blue and red diamonds roaring its way for about sixty feet out of the re-heat nozzle.'

Pete Nash joined the RAF in September 1967 and passed out as an LAC Aircraft Mechanic (Weapons) late in March 1968, being posted to RAF Wattisham and then

F.2A XN781/B of 19 Squadron underwent a Major Service by 60 MU at RAF Leconfield from 14 January to 12 June 1972, when it was flown back to Gütersloh resplendent in dark green overall on the upper surfaces. (Dick Bell)

Ground technicians winch a Red Top drill round onto the port missile pylon of a 23 Squadron F.6 at RAF Leuchars. (BAe)

Squadron Leader Sam Lucas, 29 Squadron's 'aeros' pilot, climbs into the cockpit of F.3 XP763/P in 1969. Lucas had flown with the *Firebirds* in 1963 while seconded to 111 Squadron. He was also an 'ad-libber' who would often get 'bored' with his show and throw in some unannounced routines! XP763, which first flew on 11 September 1964, ended its days on the Wattisham fire dump following its retirement at the end of 1974. (Dick Bell)

to 29 Squadron on 1 April. He well remembers his introduction to the squadron. As he was led up to the squadron armoury by a sergeant from the station armoury, he looked across the front of Hangar One (29 Squadron's Lightnings were in Hangar Three) to see 29's T-Bird stuck in the grass alongside the runway after bursting a tyre on landing. On a typical squadron the technical personnel would be split into two shifts: one on days, the other on nights. 'A typical working day for the "linies" (about ten or twelve of us)', Pete Nash recalls, 'started at 0700, when we arrived at the hangar. The Line Chief, a chief technician of the airframe ("riggers") or engine ("sooties") trade would have drawn the keys from the guardroom and unlocked the centre fire doors. He would then go to Engineering Control, an office where all hangar servicing and rectification was controlled from and where the Form 700s were kept to find out which aircraft were available for that day's flying. Assisted by his two line corporals, usually from the rigger and scenic trades, he would detail off the towing teams and who was to take out all the ground equipment, etc. The hangar doors would be opened and the aircraft and ground power sets.[1] The towing team would consist of three: a driver, brakeman and chockman.

'The tractor driver had an endorsement on his RAF driving licence stating than he had been examined and found sensible enough to tow aircraft and that his colour perception was safe (CP1), i.e. that he could tell red from green as required by Air Traffic when they changed the traffic lights, or shone a red or green light at him, or, if he was in danger of annoying the Senior Air Traffic Controller (SATCO), a Very light across his bows. The brakeman was certified as having been trained to sit in the cockpit and if the aircraft broke free of the towing arm, to apply the aircraft brakes.

'Linies' of 29 Squadron are seen in special white overalls (which are always worn by groundcrew handling aircraft flown by air vice marshals and above) at Wattisham in February 1970. It is probably apocryphal, but folklore has it that 29 Squadron's 'three-X' marking was the result of the originator being told to paint two Xs followed by 'one X'. For '29', it should of course have read 'XXIX'! (Dick Bell)

On the Lightning this was a squeeze lever on the control column. Upon entering the cockpit he had to ensure that there was enough hydraulic pressure to operate the brakes. 1,500psi had to register on the gauge to operate the brakes at least once. If it was insufficient, then the manual pump handle was removed from the port wheel well and inserted in the pump just in front of and slightly below the port tail plane. Fortunately, it did not take long to pump the reservoir up to the required amount. Sometimes, when a canopy lock had not been used, the canopy would droop down and prevent entrance to the cockpit. When this happened, a small triangular panel behind the cockpit on the port side was opened. Inside was a two-position rocket switch and handle. The switch was pushed away and the canopy was pumped up using the external hydraulic pump, accompanied by an audible warning. If the canopy was to be closed, then the switch was toggled towards the operator and the canopy would drop under its own weight. The handle was to lock the canopy, by pushing it inboard, inflating the canopy seal at the same time if there was enough air in the system.

'The chockman would connect the towing arm to the towing pintle of the tractor. Then he would pick up the wheel chocks, throw them onto the back of the tractor and walk at the wing tips until the Lightning was clear of the hanger, checking that the aircraft would not hit any obstruction on the way. Outside the hangar he would jump on the tractor and ride out to the line. With the nose wheel on the painted mark on the line, the two chockmen placed the chocks in front of or behind the wheels, depending on the slope of the pans. Then they disconnected the towing arm, lowered the wheels, fitted the earthing lead, jumped back on the tractor with the brakeman and went back for the next aircraft. Meanwhile, more linies would be taking out the

T.4 XM973 at 60 MU Leconfield in July 1972. This aircraft first flew on 17 May 1961 and was used for twenty-seven development flights at Warton before being issued to AFDS on 3 August 1962. In the spring of 1963 this T-bird was loaned to 74 '*Tiger*' Squadron at Coltishall and to Treble One Squadron at Wattisham. It left 60 MU on 29 September 1972 as XM973/V of 19 Squadron, finishing its days as a decoy aircraft at Bruggen. Behind XM973 is F.2 XN794/W of 19 Squadron. This Lightning first flew on 16 May 1963 and was damaged by fire on its second engine run. After repairs at 33 MU in September 1963, XN794 was issued to 92 Squadron and coded 'P'. XN794 was withdrawn in 1973 and used as a decoy at Gütersloh. Behind is T.5 XS457 and T.5 XV328/Z. (Dick Bell)

Houchins[1] and the brake 'chutes and wheel trolleys and collecting the LOX (Liquid Oxygen) trolley from the LOX bay. Others would be taking out the fire extinguishers and earthing leads stored in and around the "line hut". Within half to three-quarters of an hour the once-empty line would get cluttered by all the paraphernalia used to operate Lightnings.

'The line was clearly marked out with lines and rectangles. The lines, in yellow, reached back to the taxiway and indicated the ideal path an aircraft should take to arrive at a square where the nose wheel should stop. At various places, red lines were painted, pointing at an angle to the yellow lines. These were for use when live missiles were fitted and indicated the "safe heading" where a missile, if accidentally fired, could head off without damaging anything nearby. The rectangles delineated the ground equipment areas, where the Houchin had to be and where we could safely put LOX trolleys and access ladders etc. With two Avon engines sucking through a narrow annular inlet, there was a very real danger of FOD (Foreign Object Debris) ingestion. Also, with the No.1 engine exhaust at about chest level, any loose, light articles were easily blown about.

'While all this was going on, those not otherwise detailed to get the equipment out would start the "B/F". This was the Before Flight Inspection, where the Lightning was inspected and any replenishment done to prepare it for flight. The B/F lasted for eight hours and if no other inspection was done in the meantime, another B/F was done.

The riggers would check LOX levels, tyre pressures and the condition of the tyres and check for hydraulic leaks and oil levels etc. The sooties checked fuel states, AVPIN starter fuel and engine oil levels etc. AVPIN was a mono fuel. It created its own oxygen as it burned, so it could be used in a totally enclosed ignition chamber. In its liquid state, it had a distinctive sweet smell. Burnt, it had a distinct, sharp odour, shared only with other select AVPIN-started aircraft. [The fuel was not shock-sensitive and tests showed that armour-piercing ammunition might be fired into tanks containing this fuel without any danger.]

'As one of the armament mechanics, or "plumbers" as we were known, I ensured that the Master Armament Safety Break (MASB) in the starboard wheel-well was fitted. Initially this was a quick-release electrical multi-pin plug, later modified to be a push-in-and-turn key. It physically open-circuited some of the armament firing circuits, preventing, along with the undercarriage micro switch, firing of guns or missiles when on the ground. During armament system tests a special tool operated the weight-on-wheels switch and the MASB fitted, or inserted, as required. Next, using a cocking indicator box, I made sure that the manual 4,000lb bomb hook holding the belly tank on was correctly cocked. The missiles were inspected for loose wings and fins. This became a problem with Red Tops later in their life. The wings often became loose on their mountings. This was why in some photos, especially late in the Lightning's career, that the wings were missing.

'The infrared seeker head on the Firestreak was cooled using a combination of Stannag air and anhydrous ammonia. If the Lightning was fitted with Firestreak the missile-pack air bottle pressure was checked and topped up if required and the ammonia bottle fitted. Air pressure was read off a small gauge just in front of the cooling intakes on the right-hand side of the missile pack. Upper and lower limits were 2,500 and 1,700psi respectively. The ammonia bottle formed the rear position of the launch shoe. It was screwed in by a worm drive engaging a thread on the bottle valve. Red Tops were cooled by a replaceable pure air bottle, fitted and removed using an in-built winch through a panel at the front of the pack. The pressure in the bottle was read off a cockpit gauge. Both Red Top and Firestreak missile packs had a misfire indicator viewed through a small round window below the stub pylon. It consisted of a solenoid and plunger that operated when the pilot squeezed the trigger, but the missile failed to launch. The plunger was re-set by turning a cam. Checking it was required on the B/F because the hangar people would often forget to do it if they had been testing the pack. Also on the missiles, the shear bolts were checked for proper engagement.

'The Lightning always flew with two missile bodies fitted: a weighted drill round on the port side and an acquisition on the starboard. It was always that way round to protect the glass seeker head from being damaged by the access ladder being fitted and removed. Sometimes, a metal cover was fitted over the glass to protect it when the aircraft was going to be used for in-flight refuelling. It was rather expensive to replace the seeker when a flailing refuelling hose smashed it if it got on the wrong side. The pilots also preferred to have the missiles fitted. The aircraft was better balanced. Both the Red Top and Firestreak were launched forwards from launch shoes, the electrical services being provided by spring-loaded pins onto corresponding flush connectors. To stop the missiles sliding off they were held in position by a bolt between the missile body and the launch shoe. On rocket motor ignition the bolt was sheared when enough thrust had built up and the missile was launched. On one occasion a catalogue of errors and omissions occurred which allowed a shear bolt to be incorrectly fitted to a Firestreak drill missile fitted to XP755 "E" on 29 Squadron. A pilot reported feeling a jolt and a bang. He looked out of his cockpit and found the port missile missing. The inevitable board of inquiry was convened. It "cogitated" and "deliberated" and came

T.5 XS422 newly arrived on 29 Squadron in 1972. The small square panel open behind the cockpit gives access to the canopy raise/lower switch and handle. In the foreground are two 45-gallon drums. The red and white striped one is for FOD (Foreign Object Debris). The white one is filled with water to be used for dunking anyone caught by the ammonia. In the centre are two old-style towing arms, heavy and awkward to use (later replaced by a lightweight towing arm). The tilt on the Land Rover is painted yellow so that it can be seen by Air Traffic Control. The flat-top trolley contains a main-wheel jacking adaptor, a bottle jack, two brake units and four main wheels. The small box contains a supply of split pins. Behind the wheel trolley is the canvas-sided brake 'chute trolley. The steps at the back of the aircraft are being used by a rigger to fit the cable for the brake 'chute in clips around the jet pipes. If he is following the normal practice he has climbed the steps until halfway and then stepped onto the starboard tailplane. XS422 was Squadron in 1973 and later served with the ETPS at Boscombe Down. (Pete Nash)

A continuing problem with the Lightning was fuel and hydraulic fires. The two engines, No.2 mounted above and behind, No.1 lower, behind the missile pack, had long jet pipes close to the external skin. In an attempt to solve some of the in-flight fire problems 29 Squadron's XS459/T was loaned to BAC in the spring of 1972 for trials, though it remained on the squadron. The safety equipment was removed from the right hand seat, and small reservoirs of blue dye were placed in strategic places around the airframe. A control box operated by the BAC test pilot took the place of the safety equipment and the fuselage was painted with white distemper so that the dye trials could clearly be seen. (Pete Nash)

On its first flight at Wattisham after coming out of ASF, on 12 July 1972, F.3 XP694/D of 29 Squadron suffered a double brake failure on landing and engaged the barrier. The top wire has taken off a small 'shark fin' aerial from the canopy and has ripped into the spine. (BAC)

out with its findings. One of its results was that torque wrenches in the RAF were inspected and calibrated on a more frequent basis. I didn't hear any more about the incident so I assumed that, as the last plumber to sign the flight certificate, I "escaped by the skin of my teeth". The damage done to the aircraft was minor: a few cut wires in the external cable duct and a few dents in the belly tank. The aircraft was soon repaired and back flying again.

'After doing my external checks it was into the cockpit for the seat checks. Fitting the cockpit access ladder was not entirely without risk. On the F.3, 5 and 6 the cockpit access ladders were held in position by four balls on stalks engaging four elongated slots in the fuselage. Often, because of damage, the balls needed a little encouragement to engage the slots. In difficult cases it was accepted practice to jump up, grab the stalk or cross bar and our weight would pull the ladder into the slot. This had tragic consequences for one liney. We were all told of the dangers of wearing wedding rings. One liney had a rather ornate one with crinkled edges. He leapt up to grab the cross hat and his ring caught. He was left hanging, screaming in agony. We got him off and into a Land Rover to take him to sick quarters, where they had to cut the ring off before treating him. When we saw him a few days later he wasn't happy with his wife: she was more annoyed with the damage done to his wedding ring than the injury to his hand!

'Once in the cockpit it was a quick look under the seat for loose articles (any found were by consensus claimed by the finder unless it had been reported beforehand). This is how I came to be the owner of an aircrew torch. Captain Ed Jordan, a USAF officer on an exchange tour, left it on top of the seat. The seat inspection started with a look underneath to ensure that the leg restraint lines were anchored to the floor. This was followed by a look up the left side to make sure that all the pipes and connections were made, then across and down the tight side, before removing the seat safety pins from the guillotine and the canopy jettison and seat firing sears. These were then placed in the stowage on the cockpit coaming port side.

'Then it was turn around, sit down and flick the battery "on", if there was no external power running (third switch down on the outboard bank of switches by your

XP757/M of 29 Squadron landing at Wattisham in 1971. Good tyres were important: at 15 tons the Lightning landed at about 140 knots on tyres about 6 inches wide and inflated to 345 psi. They only lasted for seven landings and many times less that that. For this reason, the Lightning never did 'roller' touch-and-go landings. The *only* time a Lightning took off again after touching down was on the rare occasions that the brake 'chute 'candled'. (Dick Bell)

right leg). Next, check the air pressure for the Red Top pure air bottle and give a quick burst of up and down on the seat raises and lowering actuator. Pure air pressure was read off a gauge on the right console by the knee. It had a red sector reading from 0-2,500psi and green up to 3,300psi. Below 2,500psi the bottle was to be replaced. However, if the system was operating before it went into the red, it was sufficient for the air to liquefy and continue to keep the head cooled. If the electrician wasn't about, or external power was on, I would take the seat pan down to its lowest limit and back up again to make sure that there were no obstructions. If a rigger were about, we'd call out the LOX contents. Below five-eighths would mean replenishment. Finally, I would stand up, turn around and re-tie the shoulder straps over the seat head box. Climbing out of the cockpit I would descend the ladder face first until I could grab hold of the refuelling probe and swing myself down to the ground, before going off to the line hut, sign up and back out to do the next Lightning.

'As the aircraft became available, flying started. A two-man starter crew comprising a marshaller and a fireman, both detailed by the line corporals, was required. While the marshaller followed the pilot on his walk round, stowing the MASB, the fireman removed the intake blank, started and ran up the Houchin and fetched a CO_2 fire extinguisher and asbestos glove. Walk-round completed, the marshaller would follow the pilot up the ladder and assist him strapping in, handing him his shoulder straps and pulling up the kidney pad to sit in his lumbar region. His final act before climbing down was to remove the face screen safety pin and pace it in its stowage. The ladder was removed and placed within the ground equipment area. Removing it entailed lifting it about half an inch and swinging it out and down clear of the refuelling probe. Being top-heavy it was hard to control, so it usually hit the concrete bending the arms at the balls. All was then ready for engine start. The pilot raising and waggling an index finger signalled No.1 engine start. The AVPIN pumps whined and a pitched scream assaulted the eardrums as the AVPIN ignited and spun the engine tip to speed

29 Squadron F.3s on the line at Akrotiri in Cyprus, at the end of their training period in June 1974, prepare to return to RAF Wattisham with refuellings from Victor tankers. At the end of the year 29 Squadron began re-equipping with the Phantom. (RAFPR)

kit ignition. After about five seconds the starter kicked out and the engine ignited and became self-sustaining. The starter exhausted through the bottom hatch, any residual flames being extinguished by the fireman placing an asbestos glove over the exhaust port. The same procedure was followed for No.2 engine, its exhaust coming out just above the cable duct on the port side. The starter frequently failed to ignite. Three failed attempts and the mission was scrubbed, as a half-hour wait was required for the starter system to cool down. Sometimes it would start on the second try and igniting any fuel from the previous attempt.

'With both engines running, two hydraulic system checks were then carried out. Facing the aircraft the marshaller raised both hands, palms together, above his head, opening his arms as the airbrakes were opened and closed. Next, he turned sideways on with arms horizontal, one over the other, lowering his bottom arm to indicate that the flaps were operating. (Only once did I come across an occasion when the flaps operated differentially and the sortie was abandoned.) Checks over, there was a wave from the pilot, repeated by the marshaller, which indicated the time for the fireman to remove the power leads and chocks. Most would then have a final check on the line of seat safety pins in the stowage, making sure that all five pins were in the stowage. The one usually missing was the seat-pan pin. A reminder to the pilot was usually in order before allowing him to go any further. The marshaller then walked out to the other side of the pan centre line and would wait for a flash on the taxi lights to marshal the aircraft out.

'On average, an F.3 sortie lasted forty-five minutes, unless air-to-air refuelling was involved, with a take-off about every fifteen minutes, so the line was a busy place. When an aircraft returned, it was subject to a run-around inspection (T/R). Like the B/F, it also lasted eight hours. If it didn't fly again, we had to do a B/F before it did. When it returned, the Lightning was taxied back onto the line, marshalled for the final turn and up to the nose-wheel mark. At first it was a frightening experience marshalling fifteen tons of metal travelling at about 20mph, especially if your only experience was

19 Squadron groundcrew in NBC (Nuclear, Biological and Chemical warfare) clothing refuel and rearm a Lightning during an 'attack evaluation' exercise at Gütersloh in 1976. These were a regular feature of RAF life at the time when the base 'went to war' to test whether it was ready for any eventuality. The speed with which the groundcrew refuelled and rearmed an aircraft would put the average Grand Prix pit crew to shame! (Richard Reeve)

a Chipmunk or Jet Provost at training school. About 1pm from the final stop point the aircraft was stopped and the tread on the main wheels inspected for bald spots, cuts and depth. Once completed, the aircraft was marshalled forward for the final stop. Two stops were required because the part in contact with the concrete could not be checked.

'Good tyres were important; at fifteen tons the Lightning landed at about 140 knots on tyres about six inches wide and inflated to 345psi. They only lasted for seven landings, on average many times less than that. For this reason, the Lightning never did a "roller" touch-and-go landing. The *only* time a Lightning took off again after touching down was on the rare occasions that the 'chute "candled". (The procedure for a 'chute that partially opened was to jettison it and take off again. Then wait for the recovery vehicle to retrieve it and then land again as close to the start of the runway and be followed by the fire section in case either the brakes caught fire or a barrier engagement was inevitable.) One day we were talking to one of the more experienced pilots about the way they slammed the aircraft onto the runway, so he taught us a lesson. On a later trip he eased it onto the runway. When he got to the end he called air traffic for a party to he sent out to inspect the wheels. The word came back to send the men and equipment to the end of the runway to do a double wheel change. When he took off the tyres were in good condition; they were bald when he stopped at the runway end. The lesson he taught us was that by slamming the aircraft onto the runway, the wheels got up to speed practically instantly. By creasing it onto the runway, the wheels took longer to get up to speed and wore the tread off the tyres!

'While the wheel checks were being done, the MASB was fitted, or removed if it was a pre-key MASB. Soon after engine shutdown the bowser pulled up behind the aircraft. Mostly, these were driven by civilian drivers and such was the relaxed, ready-to-help atmosphere at the time, anyone would help the driver reel out and connect the hose to the refuelling point on the fuselage under the port wing. The sooty would replenish the AVPIN tank in the spine and the brake under the tail would be replaced. The plumber would straighten out the seat straps and carry out an inspection similar to the B/F. If it needed LOX-ing, the rigger donned a facemask and leather gloves and connected the LOX trolley to the charging point in the nose-wheel bay. Clouds of condensation would form on a warm day as the LOX in the aircraft tank was first vented out. The pipes and ranks were flushed and finally, when it was down to the proper temperature, liquid oxygen started to flow into the tank and it filled with LOX.

'Sometimes we would get sprayed with fuel from the wing upper surface when the overwing vents failed to shut off. A shout of "Oi!" to the bowser driver would get the fuel shut off. Above the refuelling point was a rectangular panel with a Perspex insert covering seven lamps. These were the tank indicators; one for each main, flap and belly rank. When the tanks were full, the lamps extinguished. If the wing tanks vented and the light was out, then judicious and skilful application with a General Service (GS) screwdriver handle to the vent shroud followed, to ensure that the valve would slant off. The belly tank shut-off valve also suffered from the same fault. Again, hitting or kicking it ensured that it operated properly. The remaining two lamps were the indicators for the overwing ferry tanks. These were rarely fitted to the F.6 and never on the F.3.

'Another, potentially more serious, problem with a returning aircraft was a leaking ammonia bottle on Firestreak-equipped Lightnings. It wasn't hard to detect a leaking bottle. It stank, like 2,000 wet nappies put into a bin and opened two weeks later! The type used was anhydrous ammonia, a particularly nasty form, with a high affinity for water. It sucked up any moisture, including that of human flesh, if you stood near enough to it. To remove a leaking bottle we were provided with a fireman's breathing apparatus, complete with full facemask and cape over the head and shoulders and a pair of full-length rubber gloves. Another accoutrement of the armourers was a two-wheeled barrow to keep Red Top wing and fin covers. This came in handy for changing ammonia bottles. It was the right height for standing in. So, wearing breathing apparatus and gloves, pushing the trolley, I would approach the leaking bottle, remove it and carry it, hissing and spluttering like an angry cobra, to the grass area behind the line. Along the back of the line and at each squadron line hut was a 45-gallon oil drum with the top cut off and filled with water. If anyone got a burst of ammonia in the face they were meant to be dunked headfirst into the barrel. Fortunately, in five-and-a-half years, I never saw them having to be used.

'Once all the consumables had been replenished and all trades signed their boxes on the flight-servicing certificate, the Lightning was ready for another flight. However, if it was unserviceable and had to go into the hangar for rectification, then an After Flight (A/F) inspection was carried our. This inspection was valid for seventy-two hours, and once it was completed, the aircraft required a B/F before it could fly. If it didn't, then another A/F had to be done. It wasn't unusual for an aircraft that had been in the hangar for a long time, say four days, to require an A/F and B/F before it could fly. This was because the last A/F was over seventy-two hours old and therefore invalid. It had to be done again. In practice the differences between the two servicings was small. For instance, on the A/F the armourers did not have to straighten the seat straps, or ensure that the missile was above limits. So what tended to happen was that one inspection was carried out by each tradesman covering both A/F and B/F inspections. After which he would sign the certificate and start on the next aircraft. Personally, I used the one inspection to cover all three servicings, except on an A/F the ejection seat safety pins were fitted to all five places required to make the seat "safe for servicing" i.e. seat pan and face blind firing handles, main gun, canopy jettison and guillotine sears. For the other servicings on the face screen and seat-pan safety pins were fitted. In the line hut were the servicing schedules. We were each meant to have a copy and follow them every time, but there were insufficient copies to go round, so each inspection was memorized.

'One day [29 October 1971] I finished a turn-round, and standing at the top of the cockpit access ladder I watched a "Tremblers" (111 Squadron) Lightning take off, retract his undercarriage and sink back down, dragging his backside along Runway 23. Tongues of flame and billowing smoke followed as the contents of his 360-gallon belly tank burned off. I later learned that it was XR711 and the pilot was Flight Lieutenant Eric Steenson.[2] [Dennis Brooks, who was directly behind Steenson for this nine-ship, two-second stream departure, flew right through the fire and undamaged,

While 5 Squadron was deployed on its APC (Armament Practice Camp) at Akrotiri, Cyprus, for live gunnery practice in the summer of 1984, three of its 'Barley Grey'-painted F.6s (first adopted in the summer of 1981) had sharkstooth markings added (to XR770/AA [left] the Boss's aircraft, XR754/AE [right] and XS903/AM) to their forward fuselages. XR770 was no stranger to different colour schemes; in 1966 at the SBAC display, it was flown on ten occasions wearing Saudi Arabian markings. On 26 September this F.6 was issued to 74 Squadron, where it acquired the famous *Tiger* black and yellow scheme. 5 Squadron's sharkstooth markings were retained for several weeks after the squadron returned to the UK. (RAF Akrotiri)

and diverted to Coltishall.] On 7 August the following year, XP700/K of 29 Squadron did exactly the same thing, but this time the pilot successfully clawed his way into the air. Unfortunately, the resulting fire destroyed all tailplane control and the pilot abandoned the aircraft. I didn't witness this event; I was on leave.[3]

'So flying continued throughout the day. Wheels were changed and brakes were replaced. On one particular day we were flying hard and by mid-afternoon, things were getting a bit frayed between the flight sergeant in Engineering Control and us on the flight line. D-Delta required a double wheel change and was delayed for its next sortie. The squawk box buzzed. The flight sergeant, irascible and irate, called, "What's going on with Delta?" "Wheels" was the cryptic reply from a harassed line corporal before he switched the box off.

'After the landing run, these were jettisoned at the end of the runway, picked up and bundled into the back of a Land Rover operated by the brake section. They were taken back and hung for a period to straighten out and dry, then re-packed into their curved, metal-backed containers and re-issued. Sometimes, they would fail to release and be dragged back to the line by the Lightning. The container was fitted under No.1 exhaust and two wires led, one either side of the jet nozzles, to a socket at the base of the rudder.[4]

'Wattisham was meant to be the inspiration for one of the exercises held one time at the RAF School of Personnel Management at RAF Newton (called "Little Snoring", after a Second World War airfield in North Norfolk). The exercise was about packing brakes with random chance selected by cards. Apparently, the Wattisham brake section was having a hard time meeting its commitment so a time and motion team was sent in. They arrived at about 12 o'clock as everybody was leaving. When asked where they were all going, they received the reply that it was lunchtime! This did not please the time and motion team, who quickly came up with the answer that, "if they had time to shut down for lunch, then there was no point in them being there to help them with their problem". Whether this was true or not, I do not know, but it was a strong rumour from "rumour control" when I did my management course.

'On days our shift ended officially at 1700 hours (five o'clock), but the night shift started at 1630 hours, so we were away soon after they arrived. Night shift was just a continuation of days with one exception – *Magic Roundabout*! Somehow, it became a tradition that all line work, including see-offs and seeing aircraft in, ceased, so that we could see the Magic Roundabout. Eventually, even the pilots joined in and watched with us. On the few occasions they got their timings wrong they would wait for us, engines running round the back of the line hut for it to end before we would go out and marshal them in. Oh! Halcyon days of ground crew power!

'Finally, flying for the day ended. Noise restrictions meant that flying finished at about 2330 hours. One night [10 December 1972] we on 29 Squadron had finished flying. The last A/Fs were being done and some of us were sitting in the line hut waiting to row the aircraft into the hangar when we saw a blue flash light up the north sky, rapidly followed by the crash alarm sounding over the Tannoy system. We rushed to the windows and saw a Lightning⁵ sliding on its belly along the runway and a shower of yellow sparks. Some of us on 29 shared a block with people from Air Traffic and "rumour junction" was soon alive with the "gen". Apparently, the pilot had done one practice approach, overshot, retracted his undercarriage, gone around again and on his final approach, had called "Finals, three greens" and plunked his belly on the runway. Normally, at night, the pilots could switch on their taxi lights, which were on the main undercarriage legs, but not all did this. So when the pilot called "three greens" telling everybody that all three undercarriage legs were extended and locked, the runway controller in his caravan thought that the pilot had left his taxi lights off, so did nothing. After every incident there is, usually, a procedure change and so it was in this case. Pilots were now to switch their taxi lights on when landing and the runway controller was instructed to fire off a red Very light if he didn't see them. At least this is what "rumour control" said was what was to happen.

'As the aircraft landed from their last sorties they were given the final flight servicing. Any landing sooner and turned round were also A/Pd. Unserviceable aircraft were put into the hangar as soon as possible while the serviceable ones were left for last so that they were down the centre of the hangar and were first to be pulled out in the morning. At about 0100 or 0130 hours, with all the aircraft put away for the night, we linies would go home. We left the hangar night shift to work on for another couple of hours before they too packed up, locked up and went home also. Towards the mid-seventies NATO started to increase its alert and exercise status, calling "no-notice" exercises. I remember that on one of the first we were involved in, the "Directing Staff" (Di-staff) put a cardboard sign on a Houchin that was being used in the hangar to supply power to an aircraft. It read "Fire!" The Di-staff approached a tired, harassed, tradesman with the query, "What are you going to do about that?" The tradesman took one look at the sign, picked up a piece of paper and wrote "Foam", placing it over the "Fire" sign and walked away!

'In March 1974 I left the Lightnings to go on Jaguars with 54 Squadron to form at Lossiemouth and come south to Coltishall, just as 226 OCU was winding up in July-August 1974. By this time practically all of the Lightnings had gone, the few that were left going to fire dumps. Years later, when on 56 Squadron, we were detached from Wattisham to RAF Leuchars for *Red Flag* build up. I drove a Sherpa north. One of my refuelling stops was at RAF Boulmer, near Alnwick in Northumberland. Arriving at the main gate I was surprised and delighted to see XP745 still in 29 Squadron markings; an "H" standing guard over one of the fighter control stations that had, no doubt, controlled it in earlier years. I remarked to my passenger that I wished I'd had a pound for every time I'd serviced it. He brought me back down to earth by sarcastically remarking that I must be old if I'd worked on a gate guard!'

1 'Houchins' – so called from the name of the makers in Ashford, Kent.

2 Who later managed the *Red Arrows*.

3 Flight Lieutenant George Fenton of 29 Squadron was taking part in a formation rotation take-off when he scraped the belly of XP700 on the runway and set the ventral tank on fire. He climbed to 3,000ft at 250 knots when the controls began to stiffen, but which were still operative when he ejected using the SPH. There was some tearing of the pilot 'chute and main canopy and Fenton, who had done a parachuting course in 1967, landed heavily in a cornfield and suffered crush fractures. He had not tightened his harness straps as he felt they were already tight enough for take-off. The F.3 crashed at Great Waldingfield, Suffolk.

4 Tony Paxton recalls: 'The Lightning had a fast landing speed (155 knots) and not very effective wheel brakes. Because of these characteristics the aeroplane was fitted with a brake parachute which was stowed in a housing below the jet pipes at the very rear of the fuselage. It was mandatory to use the 'chute for all landings and a landing without it was a minor emergency. If the tail 'chute failed to deploy the standard procedure was to apply power and go around for a 'chuteless' landing. If returning to base with the minimum fuel reserves then a special landing technique was employed so that the aeroplane would stop on the available runway if there was no 'chute deployment.

   'One very fresh winter's morning I was airborne in the T Mk.5 with a new pilot to the squadron. We had finished the exercise that we had taken off for and were in the circuit at Binbrook. It was time to land; the ground was covered in snow with small snow banks either side of the runway which was clear with a dry surface. After touchdown the brake 'chute failed to deploy so power was applied and we turned down wind for a "chuteless" landing. It was a beautiful day and from the downwind position I could see our brake 'chute lying in the middle of the runway. It had come out of the housing, but for some reason hadn't remained attached to the aircraft. The position it was lying in would cause a hazard to us on our second touchdown so I asked ATC to request the fire section to remove it from the runway before we landed.

   'Our fuel was now down to minimums so it was time to make plans. The diversion airfield was Waddington, about twelve miles to the South West. No problem, because they were used to Lightnings arriving suddenly and short of fuel so I was not unduly concerned. As we made our second orbit of the airfield the fuel situation was becoming critical and because of the snow banks along the runway edges it didn't look as if our "dead" 'chute would be removed soon. Best to make an early decision so I declared to ATC that we would be diverting to Waddington. I shut down one engine (standard procedure) and started transferring fuel so that it would all be available to the functioning engine. We headed towards the diversion airfield on one engine, with a minimal amount of fuel and our braking parachute lying on the runway at Binbrook. No problem, all in a day's work for a Lightning pilot and after all it was such a beautiful, sunny day. We call Waddington ATC and they are expecting us; we are cleared straight in to Runway 21, no other traffic (it was about 0830). Then the bad news! Braking action moderate to poor. This is indeed bad news because we are committed to landing at Waddington. We have no fuel to go anywhere else.

   'Our brake 'chute is back at Binbrook and the normal landing ground roll is extended by 60 per cent on a wet runway. Suddenly we have all sorts of problems but no choices, we are on final approach the speed is good but I reduce it to give us a slower touchdown speed and, hopefully, a shorter ground roll. As we cross the aerodrome boundary I can see that the runway is completely covered in a white shining frost but there is nothing for it, we are going to land. I cross the threshold 15 knots slower than normal and "plant" the aircraft down in the first 100 feet of runway, the nose wheel goes down immediately and I apply full braking (the aeroplane's maxaret units will ensure that the brakes do not lock and cause a skid). We are down safely, all we have to do now is stop! Waddington's 9,000 feet of runway is being rapidly used up and I become dubious about our ability to come to a halt before the end. As the end of the tarmac approaches it is obvious that we are going to go off the end, very slowly, but off the end. The only option is to try and steer onto the taxi way, the aircraft responds with agonising lethargy but we eventually come to a halt with all three wheels still on paved surface and clear of the runway. The engine is shut down and we open the canopy. The silence is deafening. Then I hear the "Da-da … Da-da … Da-da" of an approaching fire engine and we sit spellbound as "Crash One" from the Waddington fire section slides gracefully under our left wing in a four-wheel skid. The tension is released and we both start giggling. Eventually a very embarrassed crew leans a ladder up against the side of the aeroplane and we climb down to *terra firma*. However, it is very difficult to stand up on the frosty surface and we realize how lucky we are not to have gone cross-country in a totally unsuitable vehicle.

5 XP738 of 111 Squadron.

CHAPTER 8

Last of the Lightnings

One of the very best kept secrets during the Lightning's service career was the very high loss rate, which some place on a par with that of the notorious Lockheed F-104 Starfighter.[1] Dave Seward comments, 'If you look at the numbers we lost, the numbers were not great, but you have to look at the total we had, and the total number was also not great. Of the 339 Lightnings built, 109 were lost or written off by a combination of many things, including pilot error, undercarriage failure and fuel or hydraulic leak-related fires. In the late '60s and very early '70s, this became a disease known as "LFS" (Lightning Fire Syndrome), which in 1972 reached epidemic proportions. One of the first instances of LFS occurred on 16 December 1960, when Flight Lieutenant Bruce Hopkins of the AFDS had a lucky escape in F.1 XM138.

'I was on a trial sortie from Coltishall with a Javelin as my target when, suddenly, there was a big thump. I felt it on the rudder bars. Then, nothing. I called the Javelin pilot to check me over. He looked and said he could see nothing wrong I decided to abandon the sortie and recover to Coltishall. During the approach I had restricted elevator control so I knew something was wrong. I did a straight-in approach using elevator trim. The landing was normal. I was rolling out with the brake deployed when the "Attention Getters" started clanging. One of the fire-warning lights was on. At the same time ATC told me I was on fire! I completed the landing run – what else could you do? I stopped, switched off everything, unstrapped, stood up in the cockpit, looked back and saw a conflagration; a great twenty-foot sheet of flame was spewing out! I hurriedly exited. Usually, you needed a ladder to climb down. I just leapt out onto the dummy Firestreak and onto the ground in one bound. I ran! By which time, the fire engines had arrived. What had happened was that there had been a hot gas leak from the No.1 engine near the jet pipe and it had impinged on the fire extinguisher bottle. Of course the inevitable happened. It cooked it and exploded it. The blast had bent the elevator control rods and fractured a fuel pipe. The fuel had spilled all down the underside of the fuselage but the airflow had kept it from igniting, until, that is, I landed and slowed. This incident was very unusual and, as a result, fire extinguishers were modified to include a pressure valve.'

On 28 June 1961 Flying Officer Pete Ginger of 56 Squadron safely abandoned F.1A XM185 near Wattisham after the undercarriage failed to lower. It was the only Lightning casualty that year. In 1962 six Lightnings were lost and in 1963 four more were written off. In 1964, another six Lightnings were lost after in-flight fires, undercarriage failures and pilot- or fuel-related problems. In 1965 another four Lightnings were lost. On 11 January XG335 was abandoned by A&AEE test pilot Squadron Leader J. Whittaker over the Larkhill Ranges in Wiltshire after the undercarriage had failed to lower. Whittaker ejected safely and the F.1 crashed at Woodborough. On 26 June Flight Lieutenant Tony Doyle of 111 Squadron ejected

F.1A XM189/E of Treble One Squadron left the runway during its take-off roll at night on 18 January 1962. XM189 first flew on 30 March 1961 and was issued to 111 Squadron on 1 May that year. In February 1965 XM189 transferred to 226 OCU at Coltishall. It was finally withdrawn from active OCU service in June 1974 and beginning on 10 July 1974 was used as a decoy at Gütersloh. (BAC)

During low-level trials on 25 March 1964, F.2 XN723 was abandoned near the Rolls-Royce Hucknall facility after an in-flight fire. It crashed at Keynham near Leicester; Dennis Witham, the Rolls-Royce test pilot, ejected safely. (BAC)

safely after XR712 shed pieces of tailpipe during the Exeter Air Show. The F.6 crashed near Padstow, Cornwall. On 29 September another 111 Squadron pilot, Flight Lieutenant Hedley Molland, safely abandoned F.3 XP739 on approach to Wattisham after a double engine flameout.

Earlier, on 22 July, XM966, a T.4 used to test the Microcell air-to-air rocket pack, was lost over the Irish Sea when its fin disintegrated during rolling manoeuvres at Mach 1.8 at 35,000ft with the rocket pack extended. English Electric test pilot Jimmy Dell was able to slow the T.4, hoping to recover it to Warton. Graham Elkington, the Flight Test Observer (FTO), ejected without any order to do so from Dell, who had his seat adjusted to the highest position and was thus exposed to high air blast as his head was above the top of the windscreen frame. His eyes were severely air-blasted but his subsequent ejection was normal.

1966 was another bad year, with seven Lightning losses. The one on 5 January was fatal. Flying Officer Derek Law of 56 Squadron was piloting XR721 when it suffered an engine flameout. Law, a Rhodesian pilot whose tour in the UK was almost up, tried to eject, but the system malfunctioned and his canopy would not separate after he pulled the ejection seat-pan handle. With no option but to try to belly land, a procedure which was normally out of the question in a Lightning, he skillfully put his crippled F.3 down in a ploughed field at Helmingham, near RAF Bentwaters in Suffolk, after avoiding high-tension cables. XR721 shed its tail and careered out of control across the fields before clipping a tree on the B1079 Helmingham-Otley road. However, the young pilot was then ejected through the branches of the tree and was killed, his Lightning coming to a halt barely a yard from the front door of Elm Tree Farm Cottages on the other side of the road.

Group Captain Antony J. Barwood of the Institute of Aviation Medicine at Farnborough explains what probably happened. 'The cockpit canopy jettison system had fired when Law initiated ejection but one lock or shoot bolt had failed so that the cockpit canopy could not lift from the front and it had remained held by that shootbolt. Law would then have had no option but to attempt a crash landing. The ground impact was sufficient to shake the cockpit canopy off and thus to remove the interdictor. It would have required a further seat-pan or face blind pull to extract the ejection gun sear after the interdictor had been removed by the separating cockpit canopy. Law may have realised that the canopy had separated and that he could now eject or he might have retained a pull on a handle throughout the incident but this is unlikely as he was flying the aircraft so successfully to effect his crash landing. An unlikely alternative was that it was an impact ejection – the seat being forced up at ground impact, breaking the top lock to allow the sear to move up, displacing the sear to fire the gun, but we had no reported evidence of this.'

Dave Seward, Law's commanding officer, recalls his loss: 'It was part of the bloody game I'm afraid. He did everything right. Somehow, against all the things in the book, he made a copybook wheels-up landing despite having two dead engines and seized up controls. It was a great shame. He was a great pilot and a lovely lad who had great potential.'

During March-June three Lightnings of 226 OCU at Coltishall were lost but all three pilots were uninjured. Then on 27 July F.3 XR714 of 111 Squadron sank back on to the runway at RAF Akrotiri after being caught in jet blast during formation take-off. On 24 August Flight Lieutenant Al Turley of 23 Squadron was forced to eject after F.3 XP760 developed ECU failure, to crash into the North Sea 35 nautical miles off Seahouses in Northumberland. In 1967 another six Lightnings were abandoned including, on 3 March, XP699. Flying Officer Stuart Pearse of 56 Squadron ejected from the F.3 near Wethersfield, Suffolk, after a fuel line failure had started a fire. The aircraft crashed at Finchingfield in Essex. Four days later, on 7 March, T.55 55-710 of BAC crashed on landing at Warton in a strong crosswind. On 7 September Squadron

Leader Ron Blackburn of 23 Squadron abandoned XR766 near Leuchars, after an uncontrollable spin. Blackburn ejected safely, the F.6 crashing in the North Sea, twenty miles east of Montrose. F.6 XS900, which was abandoned on 24 January, was the first of five Lightning losses in 1968. The pilot, Flight Lieutenant Miller of 5 Squadron, experienced trouble after take-off from Lossiemouth when his controls were jammed by FOD, which caused a total loss of power. He ejected safely.

F.53 53-690, which was destined for the RSAF, caught fire at 400ft on its first test-flight on 4 September. The BAC test pilot, John Cockburn, climbed to 4,000ft, intending to ditch the aircraft in Morecambe Bay, when he lost elevator control and had to eject. Cockburn was uninjured but Bill Lawrenson of Stakepool, Pilling, twelve miles north of Warton, who was inspecting the newly laid concrete drive to his cottage, had a lucky escape when 53-690 plunged vertically through his nearby greenhouse! The explosion created a crater thirty-five feet deep and hurled Mr Lawrenson into the air. His wife, who had been working in the kitchen, was thrown into a corner when the wall blew in. The Lawrensons were taken to hospital and treated for shock and lacerations. Obviously believing that lightning does not strike twice in the same place, the Lawrensons still reside in the same cottage thirty years later!

A Lightning fatality occurred on 12 September in Singapore. 24-year-old Flying Officer Pete Thompson, of 74 Squadron, was approaching Tengah in XS896 on the downwind leg and was heard to call, 'Three greens', then, 're-heat light on shutting down No.1'. The F.6 was seen to pitch tip, then roll twice and enter a spin. The No. 1 in the formation told Thompson to eject. The aircraft was now at low level and in the airfield circuit. Thompson's canopy was seen to leave the doomed aircraft but the unfortunate pilot was later found dead twenty feet from the seat, which landed in a mangrove swamp north of Tengah. To discover the cause of the crash, Group Captain Antony Barwood of the Institute of Aviation Medicine at Farnborough and Brian Limbrey of Martin-Baker Ltd were despatched by RAF VC10 to Singapore. Barwood, who joined the RAF in 1941, had seen his first crash, a Vickers Vimy that fell near his prep school at Aldburgh in 1926. He recalls. 'There were several witnesses to the Lightning accident. Some of them aircrew on the ground and in the air, but the key witness was a corporal's wife who was hanging out her washing. She told us what she saw, *not what she thought she thought we wanted her to tell us.* (The best witnesses to aircraft accidents are schoolboys!) She saw the aircraft invert and the pilot eject downwards. All the seat systems had functioned correctly until the seat hit a mangrove tree and slithered to the ground with the pilot just detaching from it. He had a technical problem and presumably hoped to land the aircraft, but had left it too late.'

Two months later, on 29 November, F.1A XM174, flown by 43-year old Flight Lieutenant Edward Rawcliffe of the Leuchars TFF and a simulator instructor, was abandoned after the pilot received a series of fire warnings. These were as a result of a hydraulic fire caused by leaking fluid, which then burned through the controls. As the Lightning pitched downwards, Rawcliffe, who had ejected from a Javelin FAW.4 two years earlier, tried, but failed, to pull the face blind. However, he managed to use his seat-pan handle, which he activated at 1,000ft while the F.1A was doing 190 knots in a 40- to 60-degree nose-down attitude and in a 30-degree bank to port. Both wheels and the flaps were down and the dive brakes out. The ejection seat rotated once, then separated and the deployed. Rawcliffe landed in a hilly scrub fifty yards from the Lightning, which crashed into a quarry at Bulmullo, near Leuchars. A rescue helicopter arrived within five minutes and airlifted the downed pilot to Leuchars, where his only injury was a bitten tongue.

The fire integrity programme begun in 1968, to fit 'Fire Integrity Package' modifications to Lightnings and which went hand in glove with improvements in servicing procedures and engineer and ground crew training, seemed to have an immediate effect, for in 1969

F.1A XM174 of 226 OCU from Coltishall at Wethersfield, 11 June 1966. XM174 was abandoned on 29 November 1968 after a fire in air, the aircraft crashing into a quarry at Bulmullo near Leuchars. Flight Lieutenant Edward Rawcliffe, Leuchars TFF, ejected safely. (Tom Trower)

only one Lightning was lost. XS926 was abandoned fifty-one miles east of Flamborough Head on 22 September by Major Charles B. Neel USAF, an exchange pilot attached to 5 Squadron, after he failed to recover from spinning during ACT. Neel, who had previously ejected into the sea in a F-100 in November 1967, ejected from the F.6 safely and clambered into his dinghy after just four seconds in the water! He was picked up and whisked back to base in a helicopter with nothing worse than two grazed fingers.

In the next twelve months eight Lightnings were lost. 31-year-old Flying Officer Tony Doidge of 11 Squadron abandoned XS918 over the North Sea on 4 March 1970 after a jet-pipe fire overhead Leuchars. Doidge climbed the F.6 to 12,000ft and his No.2 confirmed an aircraft fire. Doidge called, 'Ejecting'. His No.2 saw the canopy go and pilot and seat leave the aircraft, which crashed in the Firth of Forth. The pilot's PSP (Personal Survival Pack) was recovered five hours later floating in the sea, but the lanyard had not extended and Doidge's body was recovered soon after. The weather at this time was very cold indeed and Doidge was wearing no underclothing or other insulation beneath his Mk.10 immersion suit.

Two months later, on 2 May, a RSAF Lightning piloted by 'Slim' Wightman, who was uninjured, was lost. Five days later, on 7 May, F.3 XP742 was abandoned over the North Sea off Great Yarmouth, Norfolk, after an uncontrolled ECU fire during a pair's supersonic attack at 28,000ft. Flying Officer Stu. Tulloch of 111 Squadron had just made a climbing turn to starboard at Mach 1.3 in full re-heat when both re-heat fire warnings illuminated. Tulloch pulled back the throttles, called, 'Mayday! Mayday! Mayday! Double re-heat fire – ejecting!' and pulled the seat-pan handle. The oxygen hose to his mask was broken and his helmet blew away in the ejection but Tulloch, who next remembered being in his dinghy, had nothing worse than a bruised forehead and bruising on the back of his shins and tight ankle.

In a four-month period, May-August 1970, 74 Squadron, based at Tengah, lost three Lightnings, two of the crashes proving fatal.[2] On the night of 26 May Flying

F.3 XP705 first flew on 12 October 1963 and joined 23 Squadron on 28 February 1967 where it was coded 'K'. Prior to this the Lightning had served on 74 Squadron and 56 Squadron. XP705 joined 29 Squadron on 14 January 1971 and it crashed into the sea thirty-five miles south of Akrotiri on 8 July that same year following re-heat fires and loss of control. Flight Lieutenant Graham Clarke ejected safely.

Officer John C. Webster (flying XR767) was killed when he crashed into the sea after becoming disorientated during low-level practice intercepts over the Malacca Straits.

On 27 July two 74 Squadron pilots, Flying Officer Roger Pope and 25-year-old Flight Lieutenant Frank Whitehouse, were briefed for a sortie. Pope had not done a rotation take-off for about a year so the brief for this seemingly almost vertical climb to height was left to Whitehouse. The minimum speed for rotation was 260 knots with a maximum pull of 3g. However, both pilots agreed that the more normal speed of 290 knots was preferable, although they would observe the 3g limitation. Having entered a climb of around 60 degrees the recovery would be effected by a wingover to port. As they walked to their aircraft Whitehouse jokingly said to Pope, 'Don't overstress it.'

Whitehouse wanted to make his rotation take-off as spectacular as possible because he had arranged for a photographer to be stationed at the end of the runway to capture his rapid climb to 20,000ft on film. The two Lightnings lined up in echelon port and Pope released his brakes and accelerated down the runway. At 290 knots IAS, he rotated as briefed. Unfortunately, perhaps because he was rusty, he overdid it a little and registered 4g. However, he was safely airborne and as he gained height he waited for a call from Whitehouse in XS930, which took off just five seconds behind. Unfortunately, the call never came. Whitehouse rotated while still 300ft short of the runway barrier and snapped into an almost vertical climb before starting to roll left. In doing so he probably pulled 5g or more. (Onlookers reported that it was the fastest rotation they had ever seen.) Having reached a height of about 600ft, the F.6 started down again and after what looked like an attempt at recovery, disappeared behind some trees, where it crashed into a Malay village and exploded. Whitehouse; a Chinese farmer, Cheong Say Wai; and two villagers were injured; and 100 buildings were destroyed.

On 12 August Flying Officer Mike Rigg of 74 Squadron was returning from a low-level pairs night interception sortie when the port undercarriage of F.6 XS893 failed to lower. Happily, Rigg ejected safely off Changi and suffered only bruising in the process. Even so, lessons were learned, as Group Captain Barwood explains:

'With plenty of time, the pilot tried everything, high g, hunting and so on, to no effect. He was then vectored out to the ejection area off Changi and ordered to eject. This he did at 12,000ft and at 300 knots. He was surprised to find himself hanging in his parachute harness, his life preserver hard up under his armpits and nothing, apparently, between his legs. It was dark and he was aware of "something" flapping around in front of him. He could see the lights of Singapore and of fishing boats and he could feel the quick-release box of his harness high up on his chest compressing his life preserver onto his face. He inflated his life preserver before entering the water and then undid his QRB to get rid of his harness. He inflated his dinghy and got into it and was quite quickly recovered to Changi, as all the rescue services had been alerted. He was uninjured, apart from scuffing on the side of his body where the straps appeared to have pulled up and across his skin. His harness was not recovered.

I spent about three hours with this pilot, getting a detailed narrative, which he gave very well. Then I questioned him and we had a discussion. He wanted to know what went wrong as much as I did. Next morning I visited the Safety Equipment Section and had a look at an identical harness. From the design of that harness and the way in which the back riser webbing was sewn to the seat loop, it seemed obvious that a load applied at anything but a right angle could overload the corners of the sewn webbing and that it could then peel off. We had no sophisticated method of measuring the load to peel a strap like that. We suspended the pilot with the crutch loops torn and this was exactly the situation he had during his parachute descent. I sent signals to the UK, which were copied to Martin-Baker's factory at Denham, where I went as soon as I got back. A large gathering at all those concerned were waiting. Sir James Martin was livid that I had dared to suggest that one of *his* harnesses had failed, as he said that it had never happened before, in use or on test. I reminded him that two naval Scimitar pilots had ejected over the sea and were never recovered. "This could be the same thing", I said. Steam was coming out at his ears. "Anyway, we have got a dummy fixed up to drop and to simulate the seam parachute opening load."

'I had a look at the harness where I thought that it had failed. It was just as I thought. It was not at right angles. The dummy was dropped and fell straight through the harness into exactly the position described to me by the Lightning pilot. It was like an H.M. Bateman cartoon – so many mouths dropping open! Sir James had gone back to his office and did not witness the drop. I persuaded them to take photographs of the dummy in the failed harness and of the load areas of webbing stitching failure so that I could send them back to the Board of Inquiry in Singapore. The modification to prevent this recurring was extremely simple, well within the capability of every unit with a fabric workshop sewing machine. I sent copies of the photographs to Tengah, together with some of the drop tests we did at Farnborough. The pilot's mistake was that he opted to eject too high – 12,000ft – and too fast – 300 knots. The suggested speeds for a controlled ejection at this time were 9,000ft and 250 knots. The higher altitude and speed produced a *much* higher parachute opening load, resulting in the damage to his harness. This may have occurred before, but had never been seen, as the Navy pilots were not recovered and possibly they fell through their harnesses.'

Another Lightning fatality occurred on 8 September with the loss of XS894. Major Bill Schaffner USAF had completed two tours on the F-102, and as an exchange pilot attached to 5 Squadron at RAF Binbrook had accumulated 121 hours on the Lightning, of which 18 were at night. He had been declared limited Combat Ready after only eight weeks on the squadron, this unusually short period of time being based on his previous operational status as well as his performance this far on the Lightning. Schaffner was qualified in two of the three phases of 'visident', which meant that he would be capable of carrying out shadowing and shepherding tasks only if he was in visual contact with the target. 5 Squadron was participating in a TACEVAL at Binbrook and Major

Left: While attached to 29 Squadron on 25 January 1971 Captain Bill Povilus, USAF, abandoned F.3 XP756 after a re-heat fire. The Lightning crashed off Great Yarmouth. Captain Povilus ejected safely. (Povilus)

Below: On 5 and 6 July 1971 ten F.3s of 29 Squadron flew out to complete a detachment to Akrotiri in Cyprus. In the foreground is XP698/B. Behind is XP705, which was lost on 8 July when Flight Lieutenant Graham Clarke abandoned the aircraft thirty-five miles south of Akrotiri. He was recovered safely by the SAR Whirlwind helicopter. XP698/B and Flt Lt Paul Cooper were involved in a collision with XP747 on 16 February 1972 off Harwich. Cooper was killed. (Dick Bell)

Toting a pair of Firestreak missiles, F.3 XP698/B of 29 Squadron is seen plugged into a Houchin ground power set at Akrotiri, Cyprus, during the squadron's annual missile practice camp. On 16 February 1972, XP698 and F.3 XP747 collided off Harwich during a 29 Squadron sortie. Flight Lieutenant Paul Cooper, the pilot of XP698, was killed. Flt Lt Paul Reynolds ejected safely from XP747. (Dick Bell)

Schaffner was one of the pilots who took part. The evaluation involved 5 Squadron's pilots identifying and shadowing a simulated 'intelligence gatherer' (in this case an Avro Shackleton AEW2 of 8 Squadron flying at 160 knots at the minimum authorized height of 1,500ft) during a period of rising tension. The 'intruder' entered the UK airspace during daylight and remained on station through dusk and into darkness. One by one, the 5 Squadron pilots were scrambled to identify the 'intruder'. Each subsequently completed the task before returning to Binbrook. The TACEVAL continued as darkness fell, by which time it became the turn of Major Schaffner. He had had to endure one hour at cockpit readiness before being scrambled but this was cancelled before take-off could commence. Later, he was scrambled again and got airborne at 2030. The American climbed to 10,000ft and was handed over to GCI. He was then given a shadowing task against a Shackleton at 1,500ft. At a range of 28 nautical miles he was told to accelerate to Mach 0.95 in order to expedite the takeover from another Lightning. Schaffner called that he was in contact with the lights, but would have to manoeuvre to slow down. His voice sounded strained, as though he was being affected by 'g'. XS894 was seen by the other Lightning pilot and appeared to be about 2,000 yards astern and 500-1,000ft above the Shackleton, in a port turn. The Shackleton crew then saw Schaffner's Lightning, apparently very low. Shortly afterwards, Schaffner failed to acknowledge instructions and emergency procedures were initiated. He crashed into the sea five miles off Flamborough Head. A search by the Shackleton and a further ASR search the following day failed to find any trace of the F.6 or its pilot.

At RAF Boulmer SACA. Yates, the controller's assistant for the sortie, recalls. 'What kept it in mind for me was that I had met and spoken to Major Schaffner at length the day previous, when pilots of 5 Squadron had paid us a liaison visit. Major Schaffner approached me while I was on duty in the Master Control Room, asking questions about my duties, the equipment etc. He was far more casual and friendly than the average RAF senior officer, a major being equal to squadron leader in rank. That night there was a queue of aircraft waiting to intercept the Shackleton. We, Boulmer, were

F.3 XP700 (photographed at the May 1967 Mildenhall Air Show) joined 29 Squadron on 16 February 1968 after serving on 74, 56 and 111 Squadrons. On 7 August 1972 it was lost after a take-off accident at RAF Wattisham when Flight Lieutenant George Fenton retracted the undercarriage and sank back down onto the runway, rupturing the ventral tank. The resulting fire destroyed all tailplane control and Fenton was forced to abandon the aircraft. It crashed at Great Waldringfield, Suffolk. Fenton ejected safely. (Ken Hazell)

talking to it on one frequency, while my controller and I had another frequency for the fighters, as their turn came they were handed over to our position for the intercept. The Shackleton was at 1,500ft AGL and in our "clutter" (ground returns) but we could still see it. Major Schaffner checked in on our frequency, giving his call sign, fuel state and exercise weapons fit, and asked for target information. After we gave him this he called "Judy", meaning he could handle the intercept himself and closed for a "VisIdent" as briefed, but didn't respond to any further calls. We later guessed that he had got too close to the considerable turbulence created by the Shackleton's contra-rotating propellers, at that altitude he would not have had time to pull out. After the sortie my logbook was impounded, which was standard practise. It was one of the sadder moments of my Service career. "*Per Ardua Ad Astra*".'

Bill Schaffner's Lightning was located within a few days and was recovered on the seabed at a depth of 190ft, almost completely intact with the canopy closed. The cockpit though, was empty, but the seat was still in the aircraft, the harness release box undone and the harness still in position. The ASI read 176 knots. Group Captain Barwood, who was involved in the investigation into the accident, tells what happened next:

'When the aircraft was raised it was established that the seat-firing mechanism had been initiated but that the cockpit jettison mechanism had failed to fire The cockpit area was completely undamaged, but the visor attachment track on the pilot's flying helmet had contacted the instrument panel. This probably had no effect on the pilot. He had accidentally flown into, or onto, the sea and the very large belly fuel tank with which the aircraft was fitted acted as a boat hull to take most of the impact load. [During salvage the ventral tank and the belly of the aircraft were found to be ripped open and there was under-tail damage.]

'The pilot had attempted to eject, but the canopy mechanism would not fire as the firing mechanism had been incorrectly assembled. (The breech-firing mechanism of the cockpit canopy jettison system had been clamped in a vice, partially flattening the threads, so that when assembled, it was not screwed completely home, so that

F.6 XR726/N of 5 Squadron. Note the day-glo Maltese cross zap on the fin. This Lightning was built as an F.3 and first flew on 26 February 1965, before being converted to F.6 and being issued to 60 MU where it was used by the station flight. It joined 5 Squadron on 29 February 1968 after first being loaned to 23 Squadron, and was damaged by a No.2 engine starter fire at Binbrook on 19 October 1973. XR726 later joined 23 Squadron and on 15 August 1979 lost a rudder in flight but managed to land safely. After further service – and no further mishaps – with 5 and 11 Squadrons and the LTF, XR726 was withdrawn from use in July 1987 and stripped for spares. (Tony Paxton)

The low-level interception role carried out by 19 and 92 Squadrons had a detrimental effect on the Lightning's airframe fatigue life and it was decided to replace them with Phantoms in 1977. 19 Squadron disbanded on 31 December 1976 and reformed at Wildenrath on 1 January 1977 with the Phantom FGR.2. In this photo, taken in January 1977, F.2A XN782/H of 92 Squadron formates over Germany with a Harrier of 4 Squadron also from Gütersloh. (RAFPR)

the firing plunger did not contact the percussion cap with sufficient energy to fire it.) He then opened his cockpit canopy manually using the ordinary post-flight opening mechanism, which is hydraulically operated. He still could not eject, as the interdictor wire had not armed his seat firing mechanism. He undid his combined harness quick release box and climbed out of the cockpit. His dinghy lanyard was still connected and as he separated from the cockpit this extended – fully. At full extension it would check his upward movement, so he released it.

'The pilot's body was never recovered. The cockpit canopy hydraulic pressure system slowly decayed so that the canopy closed, trapping the extended dinghy lanyard line. We did find some broken visor transparency on the cockpit floor. This would have broken when the pilot's Mk.3 helmet had hit the coaming beneath the in-flight refuelling panel and it is possible that a sharp edge cut his life preserver. We shall never know.

'Altogether, night visidents were responsible for the loss of three Lightnings and Keith Murty had a narrow escape when he hit a twin-engined Cessna which had entered UK airspace and was unknown to the air defence network. Neither pilot realized that there had been a collision until the Cessna pilot saw the damage to his wing on landing and associated this with the hump he had felt in flight.'

The year 1971 proved the worst on record with no fewer than ten Lightnings lost. The first, involving Captain William 'Bill' R. Povilus, a USAF exchange officer, occurred on 25 January during a head-on night intercept in XP756. Povilus, who had flown 373 combat missions as a forward air controller in Vietnam, had been attached to 29 Squadron at Wattisham since 1969. He recalls: 'It was a normal pairs take-off, climb-out and positioning, about sixty miles off the coast of East Anglia. Bawdsey CCI control was the radar agency overseeing the mission. (As an interesting note, another American exchange officer, Major Bud Manazir USMC, was on duty with Bawdsey that evening.) After a thirty-mile split to obtain separation, Bawdsey turned both aircraft toward each other and ordered acceleration. I pushed both engines into re-heat and accelerated through the Mach. After what was probably only a minute or two, a No.1 engine fire warning illuminated and I instantly pulled both engines out of re-heat. (I had been checked out as a test pilot in the Lightning and had two previous instances of fire warnings – both had been false). In any event, all other indications appeared normal, but the fire light stayed on and I proceeded through the appropriate drills, shutting down No.1 engine, then jettisoning the belly tank. The light stayed on, so in short order I informed Bawdsey of the problem, turned westerly and asked my wingman to try and catch up. The first indication that I might have real problems was an erratic hydraulic gauge that finally went to zero. Then the machometer motored ever so slowly also to zero – I had no airspeed!

'I kept a hot microphone open to Bawdsey and kept them informed about what was happening. My wingman finally called to say he saw flames at the rear of my craft and recommended ejection. I guess the water temperature that January night motivated me to stay with XP756 as long as possible. As other gauges and indicators also began to fail I knew ejection was inevitable; then I became aware that the rudder pedals had gone totally slack, as if disconnected! Shortly thereafter the aircraft nosed over slowly and I was unable to change its course. A British exchange officer in the States had once told me that, "Fail all else, you can always place your faith in God, Mother and Martin-Baker." I left XP756 to determine its own fate. [The F.3 crashed off Great Yarmouth.]

'I found that my preparations came automatically and without hesitation. I called "Bailing out", locked my knees as I forced against the rudder pedals and I pulled the seat-pan firing handle with both hands as I stiffened to receive the howitzer shell that was about to fire into my butt. The decisions I had made long before that night surely helped save my life. I have long legs and knew I must press as hard as possible against the seat in order to escape with my knee caps still attached – hence the locked knees. I

F.2As of 19 Squadron in formation. XN776/C, the nearest aircraft to the cockpit, joined 19 Squadron on 13 August 1969. It last flew on 92 Squadron on 3 March 1977 and finished its RAF career as a decoy at RAF Leuchars. It is now preserved at the Museum of Flight at East Fortune, Scotland. To its left is XN777K, which joined 19 Squadron on 26 March 1968. It transferred to 92 Squadron in January 1977 and on 6 April was declared non-operational and issued to RAF Wildenrath as a decoy. (Brian Allchin)

F.6 XR765/S of the Leuchars pool which it served from 25 March 1968 to 11 June 1969, with overwing tanks and Red Top missiles. Built as an interim F.6 this Lightning first flew on 10 November 1965 and was converted to full F.6 standard in 1967. XR765 was lost on 2 July 1981 during Exercise *Priory*, when it crashed into the sea thirty miles east of Spurn Head after a double re-heat fire. Flight Lieutenant J. G. Wild of 5 Squadron ejected safely. (CONAM)

had also long ago decided that the bottom handle was the only one for me regardless of situation I always used it in simulator practices and virtually forgot that the top handle even existed.

'As I pulled the seat-pan handle I heard a swoosh of air as the canopy left the aircraft. [The American ejected at 25,000ft at 30 knots]. Everything from then on appeared to happen in slow motion. I felt my hands able to pull just a bit more on the handle (double pull seat) and then I started rising slowly amidst a shower of sparks that were coming from alongside and below me. I can remember glancing at various instruments as I started up and the last I saw of my ship was the windscreen brace as it passed in front of my face. There was no sensation of wind blast as I left, only a feeling of flipping over backwards, then everything happened in "real time" again and I found myself spinning violently in a very unstable fashion. I tried desperately to focus my eyes on the lights that I knew to be the East Anglian coast but was unable to do so due to the spinning and tumbling. It is hard to describe the experience – it was almost intolerably unpleasant, my whole existence consisting of blackness interrupted by brief flashes of light that continually changed position as they streaked by. A dull greyness I interpreted as being a cloud layer. I knew such cloud existed at about 5,000ft and I decided that as I approached it I would pull the manual separation lever; I even felt for the lever to make sure it was still there. Then I felt myself losing control of the situation – losing consciousness – and I made a last-ditch effort to stop the spinning and tumbling by forcing my arms straight out. The motion slowed and then suddenly lurched the other way. A bang occurred behind me and then the opening shock of the parachute suddenly brought me into a completely different environment.

'I was stable and could clearly see the village lights on the coast and the greyish cloud below. In contrast to the trauma of only seconds ago I was quite comfortable now, mentally and physically. The opening shock of the 'chute had pulled my feet out of the boots and up to the leg restrainers in the immersion suit. I corrected this and proceeded pre-landing drills. The mask disconnected quite easily and I threw it away. I then checked the PSP connection (several times) and tried to locate the release connections. I had waterproof gloves on and just couldn't get hold of those releases. After trying many times I almost got panicky for fear of going into the water with the pack still strapped to my butt. I decided to take off each glove in turn and find the release mechanism. I had no trouble at all with my bare hands, but was very careful not to drop my gloves and quickly the PSP was deployed.

Next was the Mae West inflation and then followed what seemed to me the next logical step. I pulled up the life raft lanyard, found the T handle and inflated the dinghy. Again a decision I had made a long time ago; a decision that was reinforced by troubles other chaps had had with the dinghy T-handle once in the water. (American exchange officers flying the Lightning had speculated about inflating the life raft in the air on the way down and having it ready for use once splashdown occurred. I followed this alternative procedure and it was a likely factor in my survival. Interestingly about a year after my incident, the RAF adopted automatically inflating life rafts.)

'I tucked that dinghy under my left arm with the large end facing rearward. I entered cloud, rotated the quick-release box, grabbed it with my right hand and prepared to enter water. I remember coming out of the warm moistness of the cloud but could see nothing – total darkness all around. Hitting the water was a complete surprise and certainly the worst shock of the evening. My left arm rested over the side of the dinghy so I merely swung around and pulled myself inside. Total time in the water couldn't have been more than thirty seconds.

'After about fifteen minutes a red flashing light appeared on the horizon and progressed toward me. I became somewhat elated and knew I must fire some flares for him [an RAF Whirlwind from Coltishall] to find me. That was when I started

T.5 XS417 transferred to 11 Squadron in October 1980 and was used until May 1982 when it was stored. In February 1983 the T.5, now coded 'DZ', was returned to the LTF, but on 13 March 1984 a tyre burst on landing and the ventral tank struck the runway and was ripped off. The aircraft became airborne again and was then landed safely. In June the Lightning was repaired and resprayed and used by the LTF until being withdrawn from service in April 1987. It was stored until December 1987 and finally scrapped in March 1988. (Martin Chorlton)

F.6 XS920 first flew on 25 October 1966, being transferred to 11 Squadron in August 1970 and then being issued to 5 Squadron in November 1983, where it is seen here in Malta. XS920 was lost on 13 July 1984 during ACM when it hit power cables and crashed at Heuslingen, twenty-five miles east of Bremen, West Germany, while following a USAF A-10 at 200ft. Flight Lieutenant Dave 'Jack' Frost was killed.

having trouble getting the pen gun to engage the flares in the kit. I just couldn't seem to screw the gun into the flares. A certain sense of urgency developed as the chopper came closer and closer. I managed to fire off about four flares as the chopper swung around within about a half-mile of me and then headed toward the horizon again. As he left he fired a green flare, but by now he had caused me to foolishly waste half my mini-flares and I was mad at him. As I tried to screw another flare into the gun (just to have one ready) the pen gun came apart in my hand and the parts fell. I "battened down the hatches" for a long night, pulling my head down into the dinghy and doing up the Velcro all the way to the top.

'I spent a good hour inside my little self-created womb and did little things like trying and arranging items in the raft – by feel of course. I knew it fatal to start thinking about my predicament so I kept busy by doing little mundane tasks over and over again. The SARBE antenna was blowing over in the strong wind. I could hear it whipping against the dinghy canopy. I detached the beacon from my Mae West, listened to the reassuring beep-beep and then fixed it down between my legs. I ran the antenna tip through a small hole in the Velcro and thus had about 2ft of straight vertical length for transmitting. A squall came up and the rain pelted my back and the waves broke over me more often. Suddenly I found myself going over into the water. I lunged in the opposite direction and managed to right the dinghy again. I became very afraid of tipping over and crouched down in my dinghy even more.

'I first heard a noise that wasn't the wind and stuck out my head for a look around. Immediately I saw a great number of red flashing lights far off and then saw a large aircraft through breaks in the cloud. Several white flares were dropped about five meters away and my sense of elation was almost overwhelming. I knew it had to be the rescue chaps from RAF Woodbridge with the Hercules and Jolly Green Giants. One flare fired by me quickly brought the search pattern closer. Another flare and another until one chopper headed right at me. I fired off my day/night flare but the helicopter drifted away again. Finally the Hercules dropped a batch of white illumination flares right overhead and a Jolly Green Giant came right alongside. I fired my next to last mini-flare vowing to shoot the last one right into his cockpit if he moved away. A basket was lowered and the chopper pilot kept trying to get it near me. For the first time I realised how rough the seas were – 10-12ft waves and a whole lot of spray and white water.

'I thought about getting out of my raft (standard USAF procedure) but was so entangled in the cords and lanyards that I couldn't get free. When the basket came within about 3ft I lunged for it, literally falling inside with the life raft still strapped to my back. Talk about happy – you have no idea. Up I went and let them pull me inside just like the book says. An NCO took out his knife and cut me free from the dinghy and I was able to stand up though on somewhat wobbly legs. I almost kissed the NCO. We got my immersion suit off (there was about half an inch of water in the boots and my seat was damp) and I wrapped up in a batch of blankets. While laying there for the half-hour trip home I got the shakes – partly from the transition of warming up – but mostly I think from the fears that were finally catching up with me. As I lay there I kept on thanking God and Martin-Baker over and over and over.

'What caused the fire? From the sequencing and timing of events as recorded by Bawdsey that night, the engineering staffs were able to locate quite precisely the source of the fire and the resultant loss of control. The fire originated in the proximity of an elbow in the main fuel line in the firewall between Nos 1 and 2 engines. All F.3s were X-rayed for cracks in the fuel line elbow and I was told several were found to be close to imminent failure. Hydraulic, pitot, static and control cables also ran through the same fire-walled area and as they melted or were burned the respective instrument or control surface failed. I was told that ultimately the tail section probably burned off.'

On 15 September 1985 Flight Lieutenant Bob Bees of 11 Squadron safely abandoned XR760 (seen here serving on 23 Squadron, which it joined on 28 November 1967 after modification to F.6 standard) after a rear fuselage fire. The F.6 crashed into the North Sea seven miles north of Whitby. (BAC)

In Germany three days later, on 28 January, Flying Officer Pete Hitchcock, of 92 Squadron at Gütersloh, entered a spin in XN772 at 32,000ft during combat training. The F.2A had still not recovered by 14,500ft and he decided to eject using the face blind ejection initiation. Hitchcock had some difficulty as his head was high in the canopy, but eventually he got his right hand to the blind handle and then his left. He descended normally with automatic separation and landed in scrub, suffering a crush fracture. The aircraft crashed near Diepholz.

On 28 April Flying Officer Alastair Cameron 'Harry' MacLean of 23 Squadron in XS938 suffered a re-heat fire in the No.1 engine shortly after take-off from Leuchars. He turned back and then received a second fire warning. MacLean put out a mayday and said he was ejecting, making a face blind initiation at 4,000ft and 250 knots, slightly nose-up. There were no problems but after separation front his seat one side of the PSP support was undone. He lowered it gently but it increased in oscillation, so he pulled it up again and inflated his life preserver. Then he lowered the PSP again; this time there was no oscilation and he was able to clamber into the dinghy. He was picked up shortly afterwards, twenty-eight minutes after his Mayday signal. The F.6, meanwhile, had crashed into the River Tay.

In Cyprus on 10 May Flight Lieutenant Robert D. Cole of 56 Squadron abandoned F.3 XP744 shortly after take-off from Akrotiri after he received a zonal fire warning. Cole ejected safely and he was picked up uninjured by a helicopter after thirty minutes. His aircraft crashed eight miles southeast of Akrotiri. Flight Lieutenant Tony Alcock had a narrow escape on 20 May, during a 111 Squadron detachment to Colmar in France when XP752 was involved in a collision near the base with a French Air Force Mirage IIIE. The French jet hit the starboard side of the cockpit canopy and nose of the F.3 as they broke formation in cloud. The Lightning's pitot head was bent in the collision, which

F.6 XS921/L of 11 Squadron in June 1967 with a KC-135 tanker. XS921 joined 11 Squadron on 2 August 1974. On 19 September 1985 XS921, now coded 'BA', crashed thirty miles off Flamborough Head after an uncontrolled spin. Flight Lieutenant Craig Penrice suffered leg injuries during the ejection. (Mick Jennings MBE)

also jettisoned the canopy. Alcock, who received a blow on the right side of his helmet, decided it was time to eject, but he did not pull his seat-panhandle hard enough and the seat refused to budge. Obligingly, the Mirage pilot formated on Alcock's damaged Lightning and led him in to land without further incident. XP752 was later written off. On 26 May Flight Lieutenant Alastair J. MacKay RCAF, who was attached to 5 Squadron at Binbrook, ejected safely from XS902 near Grimsby following Fire Warning 1 after take-off followed by Reheat Warnings 1 and 2. The F.6 crashed nine miles east of Spurn Head. MacKay's was a routine ejection and the Canadian was recovered by helicopter within the hour and treated for neck abrasions and bruising of the shoulder and crutch.

Then, during a 29 Squadron detachment to Cyprus on 8 July, Flight Lieutenant Graham Clarke safely abandoned XP705 near Akrotiri after a Reheat Fire Warning 1 followed by Reheat Fire Warning 2. His ejection was copybook straight and level at 230 knots at 13,000ft – and Clarke was picked up with only a bruised front shoulder. He was flying again ten days later. The F.3 crashed in the Mediterranean.

On 22 September Flying Officer Phil Mottershead, a 29 Squadron pilot, crashed into the sea thirty miles off Lowestoft. During a climb at Mach 1.3 to 35,000ft to intercept 'Playmate' at three miles Mottershead's "Mayday! Mayday! Mayday!" had been rapid and panicky before his F.3 (XP736) fell away to port and spiralled into the sea.

Group Captain Antony Barwood recalls: 'Nothing more was heard. About half an hour later a searching Phantom crew saw an empty, deflated dinghy floating on the sea. This was recovered by the ASR launch and sent to the IAM [Institute of Aviation Medicine] Accident Laboratory at Farnborough. The dinghy pack had obviously been hit very hard with displacement of the CO_2 cylinder under and obvious scuffing and some paint transfers. It looked as though it might have hit the outside of the aircraft. The Radar Unit at Warren reported that they had a plot of the aircraft and that one only left the aircraft when the pilot ejected. They had a plot from an earlier ejection in almost the same spot and that normal ejection showed quite clearly two items leaving the aircraft: the cockpit canopy first, followed briefly by the seat, It seemed likely that this young pilot's ejection seat had failed to fire. The Lightning cockpit canopy was a purely metallic structure, which must be jettisoned before ejection

F.3 XP738 of 111 Squadron was declared 'Cat.5' after belly landing at Wattisham on 10 December 1973.

can proceed. The jettison system is operated by ejection initiation which unlocks the canopy locking mechanism by withdrawing two lock or shoot bolts, operated by explosive cartridges. Explosively operated jacks then lift the canopy from the fuselage sill and the aerodynamic load takes it well clear of the aircraft. As the cockpit canopy separates, it removes the interdictor, which prevents the ejection seat from firing into the partly solid canopy. We had to assume that the interdiction had failed to operate, so that the ejection seat could not fire.

'The pilot may have attempted manual abandonment. To do this he would operate his manual override handle, unlocking his seat restraint harness from the seat structure. His dinghy pack would remain attached to him. This would considerably hamper his efforts to get clear of the cockpit in a high air-blast situation. We assumed that he had disconnected it from both sides and from the dropping lanyard and that he pushed it out of the cockpit and that it picked up its paint markings as it contacted with the outside of the fuselage. I went to Warton with the board of inquiry to see the plots for myself and then went on to Coltishall with the pilot's damaged dinghy and with an identical dinghy. They found me an identical aircraft with exactly the same paint finishes as the lost aircraft. By bashing the dinghy with a wooden mallet onto various parts of the side of the aircraft rear side of the cockpit and the on the inner edge of the wing leading edge, I was able to show that the paint transfers were identical.

'About a month later, the pilot's bone-dome was recovered by a Danish fishing-vessel and returned to Farnborough. The break rivet on the chinstrap had broken, so we assumed that it had been torn off by exposure to air blast. The remains of the aircraft were located on the sea bed and showed that the ejection seat was still in the aircraft at impact, but the seat systems had totally disintegrated and no evidence of a misfire or other malfunction could be found. Six months later, his cockpit canopy was dredged up. It was sent straight to the lab at Farnborough. It was immediately obvious that the interdictor cable had broken. This cable is made of twenty-eight strands of stainless steel wire twisted into four smaller cables which are twisted together to form the interdictor wire. The ends of the cable are swaged onto a steel sleeve (the wire being inserted into a sleeve and then subjected to high, all round pressure, a well-established method of securing a steel cable into a connector). The broken end of each individual outer cable, six forming the outside with one in the middle, had cracked, producing a

F.2A XN733 in formation with a BAC Strikemaster. XN733 first flew on 1 February 1962 and was issued to 92 Squadron in June 1963. It suffered Cat.4 damage at RAF Gütersloh after a starter explosion and was then reissued to 19 Squadron as 'R', later 'Y'. XN733 was withdrawn from use in December 1976 and SOC on 1 January 1977, being put into use as a surface decoy at Laarbruch. (BAC)

six-sided facet. This cracking had occurred at the cable end of a swage and as this end was covered with a rubber sleeve; it was therefore not visible for routine inspection. Every time the cockpit canopy is opened, this cable is flexed slightly. Many repetitive flexings had produced the cracking of the outer six wires forming the strand, leaving one intact central wire in one of the four sub-cables – only one intact wire out of twenty-eight. This single strand of wire failed in extension when the interdictor wire tried to pull the interdictor catch off the seat firing mechanism.

'We were able to reproduce this wire failure by clamping the swaged end so that it was firmly fixed and flexing the cable through 30 degrees, each side. It only required thirty-five flexions to reproduce the identical failure. This was one of the occasions when I went straight to the Director of Flight Safety to get him to ground all Lightnings until their interdictor wires had been tested under load. The interdictor wires were replaced and subsequently redesigned.'

In Cyprus on 30 September Flight Lieutenant Richard 'Dick' Bealer of 56 Squadron was forced to abandon XR764 near Akrotiri after take-off on full re-heat. At 22,000ft Bealer received a Reheat Fire 1 Warning and he throttled back and turned toward base. His controls stiffened and the Reheat Warning Light illuminated. Bealer called 'Mayday! Mayday! Mayday!' as the warning lights refused to go out despite his completing the fire drills. He ejected at 22,000ft and 220 knots and tumbled in his seat to such an extent that he believed his drogues had failed. Thankfully, however, the seat separated perfectly normally at 10,000ft and he entered the water with his PSP under his arm. A helicopter picked him up from a choppy, but warm (65-70°F) sea twenty minutes later. The F.6, meanwhile, had crashed into Limassol Bay southeast of Akrotiri.

Despite the Fire Integrity Programme, most of the losses in 1971 had been due to fuel leak-related fires and so the RAF redoubled its efforts to stamp out the problem. None of the Lightnings lost during 1972 were due to fuel-related fires, and the first

End of an era as the one-dozen F.2As of 92 Squadron fly formation over snow-covered Germany near RAF Gütersloh, for the last time. 92 Squadron inherited some of 19 Squadron's newer F.2As when that squadron disbanded at the end of December 1976. Three months later, on 31 March 1977, 92 Squadron also disbanded, its Lightnings being replaced by FGR.2 Phantoms on 1 April when the squadron reformed at Wildenrath.

F.3 XP707 of 226 OCU where it served from December 1971 until late 1974. This aircraft joined the LTF in 1986 and crashed on 19 March 1987 near Binbrook, during practice aerobatics. Flight Lieutenant Barry Lennon ejected safely.

F.6 XS417/DZ of the LTF at RAF Binbrook which flew for the last time on 16 April 1987.

F.6 XR763 (pictured at RAF Coltishall on Battle of Britain Day on 14 September 1968 when it was serving as 'G' on 23 Squadron at RAF Leuchars) was abandoned on 1 July 1987 near Akrotiri, Cyprus, during APC after a double engine flame-out following ingestion of part of the target banner. Flight Lieutenant D.K.M. 'Charlie' Chan of 5 Squadron ejected safely. (Tom Trower)

F.6 XR755/F of 5 Squadron, which flew for the last time on 18 December 1987.

casualty on 16 February was the result of a collision during a 29 Squadron night supersonic interception exercise from Wattisham. XP747, flown by Flight Lieutenant Paul Reynolds, had slowed to Mach 0.9 at 35,000ft, turning onto 350 homing to Wattisham. As he descended and forty miles southeast of Harwich, Reynolds experienced a bump and pitched nose down but felt that he was being pushed upwards (XP747 and XP698, flown by Flight Lieutenant Paul Cooper, who was killed, had collided). Reynolds' tail controls were lost and he was diving at 45 degrees so he put out a Mayday signal. At 31,000ft he put one hand to his face blind and pulled. Just fifteen seconds later, XP747 crashed. Dry and warm in his immersion suit, Reynolds was picked up by a fishing boat and a USAF Jolly Green Giant helicopter arrived to hoist him aboard, but the RAF pilot declined as he was sick and did not know how to use the Kaman winch used by the USAF.

Two T.5s of 226 OCU were lost, on 6 September and 14 December and brought the year's Lightning losses to five. The first Lightning loss in 1973 occurred on 3 April when XS934 was abandoned near Akrotiri, Cyprus, after an ECU fire during a general handling sortie. Flight Lieutenant Fred Greer of 56 Squadron throttled back at 11,000ft and increased power on one engine. The fire went out but then recurred again and Greer experienced some stiffening of the controls. After pointing the F.6 towards the sea, he called 'Ejecting!' and left the aircraft safely. Another Lightning was abandoned before the year was out and two more, F.6 XR719 and F.3 XP738 of 111 Squadron, were declared 'Cat.5' after belly landing on 5 June at Coltishall and 10 December at Wattisham respectively.

The fire prevention measures taken in the early '70s now began to pay dividends, for after 1973 fire-related accidents were halved, although XR715, the first of three Lightnings which crashed in 1974, on 13 February was lost to 'Lightning Fire Syndrome'. Flight Lieutenant Terence 'Taff' A. Butcher, one of a pair from 29 Squadron at Wattisham exercising at 7,000ft, experienced some difficulty in locating his face blind with his left hand. Butcher finally ejected at 8,000ft and 270 knots. The Southwold lifeboat was alerted in case the Lightning came down in the sea. But it clipped two willow trees in a paddock at Mells near Halesworth in Suffolk and ploughed a 200-yard furrow before ending up in three main sections across a barbed

T.5 XS452/BT of 11 Squadron and F.3 XR728/JS in formation on 13 April 1988, among the last Lightnings to operate in the first-line squadrons during a NATO exercise the following week. After 30 April they and the other surviving Lightnings at Binbrook were used for training purposes only. XS452 first flew on 30 June 1965 and joined 226 OCU at Coltishall on 20 September 1965.

F.6 XP693 in 56 Squadron livery at RAF Wattisham on 3 July 1992, when this aircraft was used as a chase plane for Tornado F.2 and F.3 development. XF693 was built originally as an F.3 and first flew on 16 June 1962. It never saw squadron service, being used exclusively by English Electric, BAC and A&AAE for many kinds of development work.

Saudi T-54 T-Birds, 55-712/B and 55-714/D, which arrived on 22 March 1968 at Coltishall for Saudi pilot training with 226 OCU. 55-712 first flew on 12 October 1967 and was received by the RSAF at Jeddah on 11 July 1969. It served with the LCU and 6 Squadron, crashing into Half Moon Bay on 21 May 1974. 55-714 first flew on 1 February 1968 and was also received by the RSAF on 11 July 1969. After service with the RSAF, it returned to Warton (as ZF595) on 22 January 1986. (Graham Mitchell)

wire fence, just 100 yards from Watermill Farm. Butcher, who landed in a field near the Norwich road, was flown to the RAF Hospital, Ely, where X-rays revealed that there were effectively no injuries, and he was flying again the next day.

On 24 June Flying Officer Kevin Mason of 111 Squadron took off from Wattisham in XR748 and did a slow roll over the station at 8,000ft, when both hydraulic warning lights illuminated and remained on. Mason commenced a slow climb towards the coast, tightening his lap, shoulder outer and negative g straps, but after twelve minutes control was lost and Mason ejected near Coltishall at 18,000ft and 380 knots. The F.3 crashed in the North Sea off Great Yarmouth and Mason also dropped into the sea, having separated from his ejection seat automatically at 10,000ft. Mason could not release his QRB or inflate his life preserver, and he was dragged along for about fifteen seconds. He finally clambered into his dinghy but his harness pulled him out again. A Whirlwind arrived and the winchman managed to release Mason from his harness and pull him aboard the helicopter. On 29 October XR768 had to be abandoned by Flight Lieutenant T.W. 'Tex' Jones of 5 Squadron near Saltfleet, Lincolnshire, after his top engine flamed out off the Lincolnshire coast during banner firing. It refused to relight, but after a fire warning on No.2 was followed by a fire warning on No.1, it re-lit spontaneously. Jones, who had previously ejected from a Gnat on 23 May 1966 after flying into high-tension cables, ejected at 3,500ft and 260 knots. During his descent he dropped his PSP and he was a non-swimmer. Once in the sea, Jones was in his dinghy in ten seconds flat! The F.6 crashed three miles off Mablethorpe.

Lightning losses, thankfully, now began to tail off. In 1975 two were lost, and in 1976 and 1977 only one a year was lost, although the first of these, in Cyprus on 7 April 1975, proved fatal. Squadron Leader Dave 'Quingle' Hampton, a very experienced pilot in 11 Squadron, took off from Akrotiri in XR762 on an AI exercise with another Lightning. Hampton climbed up to 40,000ft and carried out a tail chase down but then lost contact in a barrel roll. Hampton recovered but later lost it again. His No.1 saw him spinning through 12-10,000ft and called, 'Eject, eject, you are

T.55 55-714, one of the
production batch of
six two-seaters for the
Royal Saudi Air Force
at Coltishall on Battle of
Britain Day, 14 September
1968. (Tom Trower)

Royal Saudi Air Force
T.54 54-651 pulls in to
air refuel in 1966. This
Lightning was written off
in 1970 after a starter fire
at Khamis. (BAe)

F.53's 1301 and 1302 of
the RSAF.

F.53 53-696 '226' of 2 Squadron RSAF with a RSAF McDonnell F-15C Eagle.

below 12!' No.1 thought he saw Hampton recover and pull out but the F.6 hit the sea with one large and two smaller splashes. It hit at a shallow angle and the seawater rushed up through the air intake and burst through the cockpit floor, forcing the seat upwards and firing the canopy jettison system. No.1 called 'Mayday' and alerted the Akrotiri helicopter, which arrived at the scene in fifteen minutes. There was no sign of the aircraft but Hampton's body was seen floating face down, his PSP up but without any sign of a parachute canopy. The crewman turned the body over, inflated his life preserver and undid the QRB and tried to resuscitate the unfortunate squadron leader, but to no avail.

In June 1975 T.4 XM99 1 was written off after a ground fire at Gütersloh. In 1976 on 29 July F.6 XS937 piloted by Flying Officer Simon Manning of 11 Squadron at Binbrook suffered an undercarriage failure overhead Leconfield. Eighteen minutes later, off Flamborough Head, he ejected at 7,000ft and 300 knots. A SAR helicopter in the descent area picked up Manning ten minutes after he entered the sea. Manning got his feet tangled in his rigging lines and took a minute to free himself. Apart from some low lumbar pain, Manning suffered no lasting injuries. In 1977, on 24 February, Squadron Leader Michael Lawrance of 92 Squadron at Gütersloh was giving Lightning experience to Squadron Leader Christopher 'Hoppy' Glanville-White, the 4 Squadron Harrier operations officer, in T.4 XM968 when, on the descent to circuit altitude, the undercarriage would not lock down. Lawrance closed down No.2 engine to conserve fuel and applied positive g to try to shake the wheels down, but to no avail. Glanville-White and then Lawrance ejected after the canopy jettisoned, the Harrier pilot sustaining crush fractures and Lawrance spinal injuries.

No Lightnings were lost in 1978, the first clean sheet since 1958. In 1979, though, three were lost. The first occurred on 25 May when Flight Lieutenant Pete Coker of 5 Squadron abandoned XS931 near Flamborough Head after a control restriction caused by FOD, and the F.6 crashed off Hornsea. Pete Coker recalls:[3]

'I was leading a pair on my squadron combat-ready work-up training with Neil Matheson on my wing. I recall the take-off time was about 0830 and the ejection

Formidable weapons load options available to the F.53. Two Firestreak or two Red Top plus two 30mm Aden cannon with 130 rounds each (housed in the forward section of the ventral tank), forty-eight 2-inch spin-stabilised rockets in the fuselage forward weapon bay in place of missile pack and two 1,000lb HE bombs. The rockets are housed within the fuselage in twin retractable launchers that automatically extended outwards and downwards in one second for firing and closed again after attack. The rockets were designed to fire with optimum dispersion for hitting the target. They fired in 'ripple' salvoes whereby two were fired automatically every 25 milliseconds. Single 'ripple' salvos could be fired from first one and then the other launcher, or twin 'ripple' salvoes could be fired from both launchers simultaneously. Each Matra Type 155 launcher (two proposed twins shown here) could carry 18 84mm SNEB 13®^lb rockets. (BAC)

55-411/G-27-79/B, the second of the two T.55s for the Kuwaiti Air Force, in Kuwait in March 1972. This aircraft first flew on 3 April 1969. 55-411 was flown to Kuwait via Akrotiri, Cyprus, and Jeddah in Saudi Arabia (with 53-423) on 3 December 1969 by Flight Lieutenant Adcock and Squadron Leader Hopkins. (Peter Hayward)

55-410/A the first of two T.55s for the Kuwaiti Air Force. (BAe)

took place some fifteen minutes later. Due to a control restriction I was unable to gain much height and spent the time trying to establish the cause of the restriction whilst flying at low level. I do believe I passed quite close to the cranes at Hull before easing the aircraft right towards the sea, but making the turn caused even greater height loss. I do recall passing very low over a town, which I subsequently discovered was Hornsea. After passing over the town, the sea appeared and, with no further hope of recovering the aircraft, I ejected. Unfortunately, my first pull of the handle was too light; it requires up to 75lb force to pull! I left the aircraft at an estimated 200ft and 350 knots with a fair amount of nose down. I was not in the parachute long and did not have time to release the PSP. For some reason, I also broke my leg in two places, which made it even more difficult when I was in the water to undo my PSP. Although I inflated the dinghy, I never managed to get into it! The weather was a beautiful spring day and the sea was calm, although there was apparently about a 500ft deep bank of fog in the area of my ejection. The helicopter arrived some ten minutes later and took me to Hull Royal Infirmary. I am sure that if I had had the time I would have been able to see the coastline and Hornsea in the background, as it was only a mile or so off the coast.'

On 17 August Flying Officer Raymond Knowles of 5 Squadron was on a normal transit flight in XP737 from Binbrook to Valley, where the F.3 was to be part of a ground display for an open day. In the circuit west of the airfield the port undercarriage warning light came on when the gear was operated and the tower confirmed that the port undercarriage was only 20 degrees down. Knowles completed all his emergency drills and attempted to fling the gear down with g, to no avail. Positioned four miles off Anglesey with a 22 Squadron Wessex alerted, Knowles, who had made four previous parachute drops, pulled the SPH and ejected at 9,000ft and 250 knots over the Irish Sea. His PSP finally dropped at 500ft and the life preserver inflated at 300ft.

The winchman aboard the Wessex saw Knowles dragged along for fifteen seconds before safely picking him up. Knowles suffered a very minor neck injury and was in a collar for seven days.

On 18 September XR723, a 5 Squadron F.6 which was on detachment to Akrotiri and was piloted by the Station Commander, Group Captain Pete Carter, received fire warnings on both engines followed by aircraft failure. Carter, who had made a previous parachute drop, corrected his posture, tightened his straps, adjusted the seat height and checked arm and leg clearance as he climbed from 4,000ft to 7,500ft before pulling the SPH and ejecting at 250 knots over the sea. He suffered back pain as the seat fired but managed to scramble into his dinghy after just twenty seconds and was flown by helicopter to land in minutes. XR723 crashed fifteen miles south of Akrotiri. There were no Lightning crashes in 1980 and just one in 1981. On 23 July XR765 was lost when Flight Lieutenant Jim Wild of 5 Squadron abandoned it over the North Sea after a double re-heat fire. The F.6 crashed fifty miles northeast of Binbrook. Wild ejected safely. The next Lightning to crash occurred on 26 August 1983 when XP753 plunged into the sea off Scarborough during unauthorized aerobatics. Flight Lieutenant Mike Thompson of the LTF was killed. In 1984 two more Lightnings crashed. Flight Lieutenant Dave Frost of 5 Squadron was killed on 13 July when XS920 was lost near Heuslingen, West Germany after the F.6 hit power cables during air combat manoeuvres.

On the afternoon of 8 November Flight Lieutenant Mike Hale of 5 Squadron took off in XR761 from Binbrook for a routine training sortie. Almost immediately the pitch trimmer, which keeps the control column forces in balance, ceased to operate. As a result Mike Hale had to maintain a constant forward pressure on the control column. He elected to cancel his planned mission and, instead, circled to the east of Binbrook, over the sea, to reduce the fuel load before landing. After circling for approximately seven minutes he started positioning his aircraft for a landing at Binbrook. However, at about fifteen miles from the airfield, the No.2 engine fire warning indication illuminated. Mike Hale shut down the No.2 engine and again flew the Lightning out to sea. Shortly afterwards, a second fire warning, this time for the re-heat zone of No.1 engine, illuminated. This was followed by a third fire warning indicating that there was also a fire in the No.2 engine re-heat zone. In addition there were indications that the aircraft generator and other electrical services were not operating correctly. A second Lightning inspected XR761 for damage. Its pilot reported that smoke was issuing from the No.2 engine jet-pipe and that an orange-coloured fire was burning between the two jet-pipe nozzles. Meanwhile, the pilot of XR761 noticed that the flying controls were becoming stiff to operate and that the warning indicators in the cockpit showed that the two powered flying control systems were no longer functioning correctly. He was unable to control the aircraft and, just before the aircraft entered a spiral dive into the sea, he ejected. The ejection and parachute decent were normal. However, once in the sea the pilot was dragged for some distance. The lanyard connecting the pilot to his dinghy became entangled in the parachute risers, exacerbating the problem and making it difficult for the pilot to breathe as he was continually being dragged under water. Mike Hale finally disconnected himself from the parachute but in doing so lost his dinghy. He was in the sea for about twenty-five minutes before being rescued by a RAF helicopter.[4]

Two more crashes in 1985 followed these losses. On 6 March XR772 of 5 Squadron was abandoned by Flying Officer Martin 'Tetley' Ramsey off Spurn Head after a possible structural failure and crashed into the sea, twenty miles northeast of Skegness. Ramsey ejected but he was dead when he was recovered from the sea. On 19 September XS921 of 11 Squadron crashed approximately thirty miles off Flamborough Head after an uncontrolled spin. Flight Lieutenant Craig Penrice suffered leg injuries during the ejection. Almost exactly a year later, on 15 September 1985, Flight Lieutenant Bob Bees of 11 Squadron safely abandoned XR760 after a rear fuselage fire. The F.6 crashed into the North Sea seven miles north of Whitby.

Squadron Leader Clive Rowley, OC LTF from February 1986 until April 1987, recalls: 'Flight Lieutenant Barry Lennon of 5 Squadron had been selected as the Lightning display pilot for the 1987 season. [On 19 March 1987] he was conducting a 5,000ft minimum altitude practice over Binbrook airfield in a borrowed LTF F.3 [XP707] when he trialled the effects of a slow feeding ventral and negative g. The resulting manoeuvre, a negative g tuck into an inverted spin, had never before been demonstrated. We were all much relieved that he survived the subsequent ejection and parachute landing on the airfield with nothing worse than a pair of bruised heels to show for it. Within twenty minutes of the accident he telephoned from No.5 Squadron and said, "That aircraft is u/s sir; can I have another one?!"'

On 1 July 1987 during the last Lightning APC Flight Lieutenant D.K.M. 'Charlie' Chan of 5 Squadron abandoned XR763 near Akrotiri. He was flying an air-firing sortie on a target banner towed by a Canberra when the upper wheel from the banner spreader bar came off and was ingested by the Lightning's No.1 engine, which promptly seized. Chan shut it down and headed back to Akrotiri with the No.2 engine now running at abnormally high temperature due to debris damage. At about 2½ miles from the airfield the engine began to lose thrust. When Chan applied full power, the JPT rose to 900°C (the normal maximum allowable JPT being 795°C). XR763 continued to lose speed and at about 250ft and 150 knots, Chan ejected safely. The F.6 crashed in a vineyard close to some houses and exploded in a fireball. (The fin, later recovered almost intact from the wreckage, was erected in the grounds of a bar used by service personnel.)

It was an ignominious end for XR763, which had first flown over twenty-two years earlier. So too had XR769, which was safely abandoned over the North Sea by Flight Lieutenant Dick Coleman RAAF of 11 Squadron on 11 April 1988, after an engine fire during practice air combat with a 74 Squadron Phantom. (The Phantom crew landed and marked up their aircraft with one 'kill'!) XR769 was the eightieth and last RAF Lightning lost to all causes.

Bruntingthorpe airfield, Leicestershire, is now the only place in Britain where one can see a Lightning fire up its Avons. The Lightning Preservation Group has been fortunate in acquiring the former Wattisham QRA shed to house its pair of Lightnings. The Q Shed is one of only three in the UK, the other two being at Leuchars and Binbrook. The Q Shed was donated by Trafalgar House Construction, who also paid for its dismantling at Wattisham. The last Lightnings flying anywhere in the world are Mike 'Beachy' Head's four Lightnings in his family of jets in the Thunder City operation at Cape Town International Airport in South Africa.

---

1 The Belgian Air Force lost 39 Starfighters, the Dutch Air Force 44 and by late 1982 the Luftwaffe had lost 252.
2 In '*Tiger Tales*' Group Captain Dave Roome details all three crashes.
3 In a letter to Charles Ross, Editor, *Lightning Review*, December 1993.
4 The aircraft crashed three miles off Donna Nook. Only a small portion of the wreckage was recovered from the seabed. The wreckage, together with the other evidence available, proved insufficient to determine positively the sequence of events leading up to the fire and abandonment. It was concluded that the Lightning had suffered a persistent fire in the rear fuselage, the cause of which was unknown.

Lightning Units

5 Squadron

Motto: *Frangas non flectas* ('Thou mayst break, but shall not bend me')
Command Assignments: Fighter Command Interceptor Alert Force; UK Air Defence
   Region (Southern)
Aircraft: F.6 (12.65-12.87); F.1A (06.70-09.72); F.3 (10.72-09.87)
Station: Binbrook (12.65-01.05.88)
History: Disbanded at Geilenkirchen, RAF Germany (Javelin FAW9), on 07.10.65,
reforming the next day at RAF Binbrook to begin re-equipment with the Lightning.
T.5 XS451/T arrived first, on 19.11.65, followed on 10.12.65 by XR755/A and
XR756/B, the first (interim) F.6s, so becoming the first RAF squadron to operate the
type. Last of twelve interim F.6s arrived on 08.03.66, the squadron becoming fully
operational late that year. XS894/F, first full F.6 standard aircraft, arrived on 03.01.67,
the full complement being completed by spring 1967. Took part in ADEX 67, being
based at Luqa, Malta, from 6 to 26 October. In May 1968 four F.6s flew non-stop
from Binbrook-Bahrain in eight hours, refuelled along the 4,000-mile route by Victor
tankers from RAF Marham. Won the Dacre Trophy (awarded to the top UK fighter
squadron in weapons proficiency) in 1968 and 1969. Ten F.6s flew to RAF Tengah,
Singapore, in December 1969, for joint air-defence exercises with other Lightnings
and RAAF Mirages there. Participated in local defence exercises in Singapore in
1970, exchanging and returning with some Lightnings from 74 Squadron which were
in need of major overhaul. Won the Huddleston Trophy (best interceptor squadron
in NATO) in the AFCENT Air Defence Competition, 1970 and 1971. 5 Squadron
proved the longest operator of the Lightning, finally disbanding at Binbrook on
31.12.87, reforming as a Tornado F.3 unit at Coningsby, 01.05.88.

11 Squadron

Motto: *Ociores acrioresque aquilis* ('Swifter and keener than eagles')
Command Assignments: Fighter Command Interceptor Alert Force; UK Air Defence
   Region (Northern)
Aircraft: F.6 (04.67-5.88); F.3 (10.72-05.86)
Stations: Leuchars (04.67-1972); Binbrook (1972-05.88)
History: Disbanded at Geilenkirchen, end of 1965, reforming at Leuchars, 01.04.67,
when re-equipped with the Lightning F.6, the third RAF squadron to operate the type.
With the move by 74 Squadron to Singapore, became the main air defence squadron
at Leuchars on 15.05.67. With 23 Squadron formed the Leuchars Lightning Wing,

part of the Interceptor Alert Force (IAF) or Quick Reaction Alert (QRA); the long-range interception of Soviet aircraft in the Northern UK Air Defence Region. One day, April 1970, no less than forty interceptions were carried out on Badgers and Bears. Meanwhile, in-flight refuelling was practised. Flight Lieutenant Eggleton established a record on 29.11.67 of eight hours' flying, refuelling five times and flying 5,000 miles. Took part in the biggest air-refuelling exercise so far mounted by the RAF on 06.01.69, when ten F.6s, refuelled by Victor tankers, deployed to Tengah, Singapore, (staging through Muharraq and Gan) and back, a distance of 18,500 miles. F.6s retrofitted 1970 with twin 30mm Aden cannon in the front section of the ventral fuel tank. Replaced at Leuchars on 22.03.72 by Phantom FG.1s of 43 Squadron, moving to Binbrook, 22.06.72, following the departure of 85 Squadron to West Raynham, to continue in the IAF role. Deployed to Akrotiri, Cyprus, in June 1972 for one-month detachment, relieving 56 Squadron, which completed APC at Valley. Six F.6s sent to Cyprus, in January 1974 following the Turkish invasion. Began receiving additional Lightnings from 226 OCU in mid-1974, following its closure, and from other F.3 squadrons, which began re-equipping with the Phantom FGR.2. 'C' Flight assumed the training task of Lightning Conversion in 1974, the Lightning Training Flight taking over at Binbrook, October 1975.

11 Squadron finally disbanded on 30.04.88 (reforming as a Tornado F.3 Squadron at Leeming, 1.11.88). Squadron Leader Aldington had the distinction of making the final RAF Lightning flight when he delivered one of three aircraft to Cranfield, 30.06.88.

19 Squadron

Motto: *Possunt quia posse videntur* ('They can because they think they can')
Command Assignments: Fighter Command Interceptor Alert Force; UK Air Defence Region (Southern) (1962-09.65); RAF Germany (23.09.65-31.12.76)
Aircraft: F.2 (12.62-10.69); F.2A (01.68-12.76)
Stations: Leconfield (12.62-01.68); Gütersloh (01.68-12.76)
History: Began conversion from the Hunter F.6 to the Lightning F.2 at Leconfield, October 1962, the first RAF unit so to do. T.4 XM988 first aircraft to arrive, 29.10.62. First F.2 (XN755/D) received 17.12.62. Became operational as an all-weather unit, March 1963 with twelve F.2s and one T.4. Took part, July 1965 in in-flight refuelling trials with the new Victor K.1 tankers, winning, that same year, for the second time, the Dacre Trophy (awarded to the top UK fighter squadron in weapons proficiency). Transferred from Fighter Command, 23.9.65, to Second Tactical Air Force, RAF Germany, at Gütersloh (less than 100 miles from East Germany), becoming fully operational in 1966. F.2A Lightnings, able to carry four 30mm Aden cannon or twin Firestreak AAMs, or (more usually) twin Aden and two Firestreaks, began arriving, February 1968, the F.2s being progressively returned to BAC Warton, 1968-69, for modification to F.2A standard and re-issue to RAF Germany. Disbanded 31.12.70 at Gütersloh. Reformed Wildenrath 1.1.77 with the Phantom FGR.2.

23 Squadron

Motto: *Semper agressus* ('Always on the attack')
Command Assignments: Fighter Command Interceptor Alert Force; UK Air Defence Region (Northern)
Aircraft: F.3 (08.64-11.67); F.6 (05.67-10.75)
Stations: Leuchars (08.64-31.10.75)

Above: Wattisham TFF (Target Facilities Flight) F.1 taking off. Note the winged cat on the fin, a stylized rear view of a cat with its tail raised and its whiskers the horizontal points at the side. TFF pilots chose the badge because that is what they showed the intercepting pilots – their backside! The cat's tail represented the fins and the whiskers, wings and tailplane. A puckered orifice was painted beneath the tail in place of the No.1 jet pipe (No.1 was left off). (BAe)

Above and below: F.1A XM177 of the Wattisham TFF (Target Facilities Flight). This Lightning served this unit between 23 April and September 1971 (when this picture was taken) and again between May 1972 and 14 September 1973. XM177 first flew on 20 December 1960 and was first issued to 56 Squadron in March 1963. This Lightning, which also served in 226 OCU, Leuchars TFF, and 23 Squadron, was scrapped in 1974. (Dick Bell)

History: Re-equipped from the Javelin to the Lightning F.3 at Leuchars in August 1964. XP707 and XP708 first to arrive on 18.08.64; full squadron complement reached, end of October 1964. Became operational early in 1965, when in-flight refuelling exercises with USAF KC-135 tankers took place. Replacement with the (interim) F.6, from May 1967, followed by full production-standard F.6s. Won Dacre Trophy that same year (and again, 1969 and 1975, also winning the Aberporth Trophy, 1970 and 1971). F.6 SX938, the last Lightning to be built for the RAF, was flown from Warton to Leuchars on 28.08.67. Squadron fully equipped with F.6 by beginning of 1968. XR725/A and XS936/B flew non-stop to Toronto, Canada, in 7 hours 20 minutes in August 1968 using in-flight refuelling, returning to Leuchars on 03.09.68. Became operational with Red Top missile that same month. Detachments flown to Beuvechain, Belgium in July 1969; Malta, April 1970; Sweden, 1971; and to Cyprus, February 1971 – this to take part in practice air defence of Cyprus and ACM. First successful trial of twin 30mm Aden gun packs on 26.03.71. Replaced in the QRA role at Leuchars by Phantom FGR.2s of 111 Squadron and disbanded 31.10.75, before reforming as a Phantom FGR.2 squadron at Coningsby, 01.11.75, moving to RAF Wattisham, 25.02. 76.

29 Squadron

Motto: *Impiger et acer* ('Energetic and keen')
Command Assignments: Fighter Command Interceptor Alert Force; UK Air Defence Region (Southern)
Aircraft: F.3 (05.67-12.74).
Stations: Wattisham (05.67-12.74)
History: Equipped with Javelins, was relieved of air-defence duties on Cyprus in May 1967 by 56 Squadron's Lightning F.1s, which had arrived from RAF Wattisham that April. Returning to England, 29 Squadron reformed at Wattisham on 01.05.67 to become the last RAF unit to equip with the Lightning. The first aircraft (XV328, a T.5) was taken on charge on 10.05.67 followed, 08.66-05.67, by F.3s, mostly 'hand-me-downs' from 74 and 23 Squadrons at Leuchars, then beginning conversion to the F.6. Fully operational by September 1967. Awarded Dacre Trophy on 19.07.74. Disbanded on 31.12.74 at Wattisham, reforming as a Phantom FGR.2 squadron at Coningsby, 01.01.75.

56 (Punjab) Squadron

Motto: *Quid si coelum ruat* ('What if Heaven falls?')
Command Assignments: Fighter Command Interceptor Alert Force; UK Air Defence Region (Southern); and to Cyprus (1975)
Aircraft: F.1 (12.60-04.65); F.1A (1961); F.3 (03.65-12.71); F.6 (09.71-06.76)
Stations: Wattisham (12.60-28.6.76); Akrotiri (05.67-12.74); Wattisham (1975-28.06.76)
History: Conversion to the Lightning F.1 began in December 1960, to become only the second Lightning squadron in the RAF and the first to receive the F.1A (XM172 being the first to arrive, December 1960). Work-up to operational status took place at Wattisham, then, while the runways were resurfaced, continued at Coltishall. Full complement of F.1As received by March 1961. Undertook intensive in-flight refuelling trials in 1962, first using USAFE F-100Cs tanking from KC-50s, then with their Lightning F.1As with Valiants. Two F.1As flew non-stop to Cyprus on 23.07.62 in 4 hours 22 minutes, refuelled from two Valiants of 90 and 214 Squadrons. Became the official Fighter Command aerobatic team, 1963, being named the '*Firebirds*'. First

AAR detachment to Cyprus, *Forthright One*, took place in 02.64. F.3s began arriving at Wattisham in 02.65, the F.1As being transferred to 226 OCU at Coltishall. Took part in *Unison 65* in September 1965, and a year later in the Malta air defence exercise ADEX 66. Moved to Akrotiri, Cyprus, in April 1967, replacing 29 Squadron's Javelins, a posting which lasted seven years (05.67-09.74). Meanwhile, F.6s had been acquired from 74 Squadron, which disbanded at Tengah, Singapore, in 08.71. Following the Turkish invasion of Cyprus in 1974, 200 operational sorties were flown to protect the Sovereign Base Area airspace. Finally returned to Wattisham, the first of thirteen F.6s (and the Squadron's three Canberra TTs) arriving at Wattisham on 21.01.75. Awarded Dacre Trophy in 06.75, 56 (Designate) Squadron formed on the Phantom FGR.2 at Coningsby on 22.03.76, the actual squadron disbanding, 28.06.76, at Wattisham, being reformed the next day at Coningsby on the Phantom.

74 (Trinidad) Squadron

Motto: *I Fear No Man*
Command Assignments: Fighter Command Interceptor Alert Force; UK Air Defence Region (Southern and Northern) (1960-05.67); FEAF Air Defence (06.67-25.08.71)
Aircraft: F.1 (06.60-04.64); F.3 (04.64-09.67); F.6 (09.66-08.71)
Stations: Coltishall (06.60-04.64); Leuchars (02.06.64-05.67); Tengah (06.67-01.09.71)
History: Became the first RAF squadron to introduce the Lightning into service. XM165 (the first F.1) taken on charge at Coltishall on 29.06.60. In September 1960 Squadron Leader John F.G. Howe led formation flypasts of four aircraft at the Farnborough Air Show. A nine-ship formation was flown at Farnborough 1961, when the first public demonstration of nine Lightnings rolling in tight formation took place. In 1962, the *Tigers* became the official Fighter Command aerobatic team. Moved to Leuchars on 28.02.64, then in April became the first operational RAF squadron to operate the F.3, XP700 being the first to arrive, on 14.04.64. From 1965 onwards shared the northern IAF defensive duties at Leuchars with 23 Squadron's F.3s. Air-to-air tanking became a feature of these interception missions, operational range and endurance being improved from August 1966 by the introduction of the Lightning F.6, XR768/A being the first. From August 1966 full production F.6s, the first to reach an operational squadron, were received. In June 1967 thirteen Lightnings transferred to Tengah, Singapore, in Operation *Hydraulic*, the longest and largest in-flight refuelling operation hitherto flown, staging through Akrotiri, Masirah and Gan and using seventeen Victor tankers from Marham, for a four-year tour of duty in the tropics. During this time, three 2,000-mile deployments were made to Australia non-stop using Victor tankers, the major one being Exercise *Town House* (16.06-26.06.69). Also participated in *Bersatu Padu* ('Complete Unity'), a five-nation exercise in Western Malaya and Singapore in July 1969. Regular exchanges were also flown with RAAF Mirages at Butterworth, Malaysia, and two Lightnings were flown to Thailand for a static display in Bangkok. Squadron finally disbanded, Tengah on 25.08.71. All remaining Lightnings were flown on the 6,000-mile, 13-hour trip, to Akrotiri, Cyprus, from 02.09.71, staging through Gan and Muharraq and completing seven in-flight refuellings with Victor tankers for transfer to 56 Squadron. Reformed as a Phantom F-4J squadron at Wattisham on 19.10.84.

92 (East India) Squadron

Motto: *Aut pugna aut morere* ('Either fight or die')
Command Assignments: Fighter Command Interceptor Alert Force; UK Air Defence
   Region (Southern) (1963-65); RAF Germany (29.12.65-31.03.77)
Aircraft: F.2 (04.63-07.71); F.2A (08.68-03.77)
Stations: Leconfield (04.63-12.65); Geilenkirchen (29.12.65-12.67); Gütersloh
   (24.01.68-31.03.77)
History: Late in 1962 began equipping with the Lightning F.2, the first (XN783/A)
arriving on the squadron on 17.04.63. Declared fully operational that summer; a
team of F.2s displayed at Farnborough that September. Movement to Geilenkirchen,
Germany, began in December 1965, replaced 11 Squadron's Javelins. Moved to
Gütersloh in February 1968, to join 19 Squadron. Re-equipment with the F.2A
followed and was concluded in 1969. Disbanded on 31.03.77, reforming as an FGR.2
Phantom squadron at Wildenrath, 01.04.77.

111 Squadron

Motto: *Adstantes* ('Standing by')
Command Assignments: Fighter Command Interceptor Alert Force; UK Air Defence
Region (Northern)
Aircraft: F.1A (04.61-02.65); F.3 (12.64-09.74); F.6 (05.74-09.74)
Stations: Wattisham, (04.61-30.09.74)
History: Re-equipment with the Lightning F.1A began on 06.03.61 with delivery
of XM185. XM216, the last F.1A built, was delivered in August. Re-equipment
with the F.3 began in late 1964. In 01.65, formed the leading box in a formation of
sixteen aircraft for a final salute and flypast over the funeral barge of Sir Winston
Churchill. In 1965, formed a formation aerobatics team of twelve Lightnings. USAF
U-2 reconnaissance aircraft from Lakenheath, previously thought immune to fighter
interception, were successfully intercepted late that summer. F.3s continued to be used
until disbandment at Wattisham on 30.09.74, 111 Squadron (designate) forming on
the Phantom FGR.2 at Coningsby in July 1974. Full squadron complement followed
on 01.10.74.

AFDS (Air Fighting Development Squadron)/CFE (Central Fighter Establishment)

Command Assignments: CFE (Central Fighter Establishment)
Aircraft: F.1/F.1A/F.2/F.3/T.4
Stations: Coltishall (08.59-09.62); Binbrook (10.62-01.02.66)
History: Formed on 01.09.59 under the command of Wing Commander Jimmy Dell after
moving from West Raynham, whose runways were unsuitable for Lightning operations.
Its role was to carry out tactical and operational trials of all new fighter aircraft types and
to investigate all equipment and aircraft systems. First F.1 aircraft, 335 and 336, delivered
December 1959. XG334 lost, 05.03.60. Four more F.1s were delivered in May 1960 and
used in Exercise *Yeoman* that same month while on detachment to Leconfield. Moved
to Binbroo in 1962 with the CFE. First F.2 (XN771) delivered in November 1962,
followed by three more (XN726, 729 and 777 (lost 21.12.62). XP695 (first F.3 to enter
service) arrived on 01.01.64. First interim version F.6 (XR753) arrived on 16.11.65. CFE
disbanded on 01.02.66, AFDS becoming the FCTU (Fighter Command Trials Unit).

FCTU (Fighter Command Trials Unit)

Command Assignments: Fighter/Strike Command
Aircraft: F.2/F.3/T.4
Stations: Binbrook (01.02.66-30.06.67)
History: Renamed from the disbanded AFDS on 01.02.66. Developed the concept of supersonic targets for the front-line Lightning squadrons. Continued to operate from Binbrook until disbandment on 30.06.67, all aircraft going to the Binbrook Station Target Facility Flight.

LCS (Lightning Conversion Squadron)

Aircraft: F.1A/F.3/T.4/T.5
Stations: Middleton St George (29.06.62-31.05.63)
History: Formed on 29.06.62 using initially a few single-seat Lightnings from 56, 74 and 111 Squadrons on a daily-return basis. The first Lightning T.4 (XM970) arrived on 29.06.62 and the LCS had equipped with nine more by late 1962. Became 226 OCU on 01.06.63.

LCU (Lightning Conversion Unit)/LTF (Lightning Training Flight)

Aircraft: F.3/T.5/F.6
Stations: Binbrook (10.74-03.76); Coningsby (03.76-1977); Binbrook (1977-01.08.87)
History: LCU formed from 'C' Flight, 11 Squadron, in September 1974 becoming the LTF in the beginning of October 1974. Using initially four F.3s and four T.5s (from 1979 F.6 was added for target facilities purposes with a radar reflector usually carried in place of AI 23 radar), directed to provide conversion training for new pilots arriving from Tactical Weapons Units with fast-jet experience on Hawks, for onward posting to front-line Lightning squadrons. A T.5 flight was followed by two weeks of ground school, including approximately fourteen 'flights' in a simulator, followed by five flights in T.5, before first solo in the F.3. First phase of conversion training involved concentrated flying up to IRS (Instrument Rating Standard), followed by a series of exercises, including battle formation flying, culminating in a handling test on the T.5. A weapons phase, involving air combat training with Red Top acquisition rounds, followed, before a final check ride, normally with the CO. After about forty-two Lightning flying hours the new pilot was assigned to either 5 or 11 Squadron. In addition to conversion training, shorter, refresher courses for lapsed Lightning pilots were run. Flight Lieutenant Ian Black, a former Phantom navigator, became the last pilot to he trained to fly the Lightning before the Flight disbanded on 01.08.87. 5 Squadron and 11 Squadron operated some of the aircraft for some months after.

226 OCU (Operational Conversion Unit)

Motto: *We Sustain*
Command Assignments: CFE
Aircraft: F.1A/F.3/T.4/F.5.
Stations: Coltishall (04.01.60-08.61); Middleton St George (08.61-12.04.64); Coltishall (04.64-17.06.74); Leconfield (1966) and Binbrook (1972) used during runway repairs at Coltishall

History: Formed at Coltishall on 04.01.60 under the aegis of CFE with the task of training Lightning pilots, aircraft being borrowed from 74 Squadron. Moved to Middleton St George in 08.61 to become miscellaneous Lightning Conversion Squadron (LCS) using mainly Lightnings from 56 and 111 Squadrons. First T.4 (XM970) received on 27.6.62, followed by seven more before the end of 10.62. Re-titled 226 OCU on 01.6.63, receiving seven ex-74 Squadron F.1 aircraft shortly thereafter. Now took designation 145 (Shadow) Squadron (disbanded in 05.71; 65 [Shadow] Squadron being formed in its place). 226 OCU moved to Coltishall on 13.04.64. First T.5 (XS419) arrived on 20.04.65, being followed by fourteen more. Became last unit in the RAF to receive the F.3 (XP696, XP737, XR716 and XR718), on 06.07.80. Formed within 226 OCU (04.05.71) were No.1 (Conversion) Squadron with T.4/F.lA (adopting markings of 65 Squadron); No.2 (Weapons) Squadron using T.4s/F.1A/T.5 (also adopting 65 Squadron markings) and No.3 (Advanced) Squadron with F.3/T.5 in No.2T Squadron markings. 226 OCU disbanded on 17.06.74 and was replaced by the LTF. Reactivated late 1974 at Lossiemouth as the Jaguar Conversion Unit.

Binbrook TFF (Target Facility Flight)

Command Assignments: FCTIJ
Aircraft: F.1
Stations: Binbrook
History: Formed in 1966 on disbandment of the FCTU. Two F.1s (XM164 and XM137) were delivered (22.02.66 and 15.03.66 respectively). Disbanded in December 1973.

Wattisham TFF (Target Facility Flight)

Command Assignments: FCTU
Aircraft:F.1/F.1A
Stations: Wattisham
History: Formed in April 1966. Complement of three Lightnings, two pilots, one engineering officer and fifty ground crew. Disbanded in December 1973.

Leuchars TFF (Target Facility Flight)

Command Assignments: FCTU
Aircraft: F.1/F.1A
Stations: Leuchars
History: Formed in April 1966. Complement of three Lightnings, two pilots, one engineering officer and fifty ground crew. Absorbed into 23 Squadron, in 1970. Disbanded in December 1973.

60 MU Leconfield

Command Assignments:
Aircraft: All marks
Stations: Leconfield
History: Carried out all major servicing at all marks of Lightning.

Akrotiri Station Flight

Command Assignments:
Aircraft: T.5
Stations: Akrotiri, Cyprus
History: Formed from 'C' Flight, 11 Squadron, in 1974.

Lightning Conversion Unit (RSAF)

Command Assignments: Saudi Arabia
Aircraft: T.5
Stations: Khamis Mushayt Air Base
History: Operated as the Lightning Conversion Unit for the RSAF.

2 Squadron RSAF

Command Assignments: Saudi Arabia (Eastern and Northwestern Sectors)
Aircraft: F.53, T.55.
Stations: Tabuk Air Base (1969-?); King Ahd al-Aziz Air Base, Dhahran (?-1976); King Feisal Air Base (08.76-1986).
History: Formed mid-1969 from a small number of pilots trained at 226 OCU Coltishall in 1968. These were supplemented by officers who had graduated from miscellaneous transitional training course. F.53s delivered by RAF and BAC pilots began to arrive on 01.07.68. A Canberra was used to tow targets for firing practice. Joint exercises aimed at the air defence of the Eastern Sector were carried out. Last RSAF squadron to operate the Lightning, up until 22.01.86.

6 Squadron RSAF

Command Assignments: Saudi Arabia (Southern Zone)
Aircraft: F.52/F.53
Stations: King Abd al-Aziz Air Base, Dhahran (1967-1978)
History: Formed in 1967 from a group of Hunters and F.52 Lightnings. Used in air defence until the arrival of F.53 Lightnings. Lightning Flight declared operational on 13.11.66. From January 1967 onwards, used its air defence along the Yemini border area. Role changed to attack and defence in 1969, taking part in miscellaneous defence of the Southern Zone until the other types were withdrawn in 1974. With the arrival of F.53 Lightnings, carried out the entire defence of the Southern Zone during 1974-78, by which time the Lightnings were redistributed between 13 Squadron and 2 Squadron.

13 Squadron RSAF

Command Assignments: Saudi Arabia (Fastens Zone and North-West Sector)
Aircraft: F.5, F.53, T.55
Stations: King Abd al-Aziz Air Base, Dhahran (1978-1982); King Feisal Air Base
    (March 1982-)
History: Formed in 1978 at the King Abd al-Aziz Air Base at Dhahran from the transitional Lightning training unit and part of 6 Squadron. Using F.53 and T.55

Lightnings, along with the F.5, shared in training and joint exercises in the defence of sectors of the Eastern Zone of Saudi Arabia. With the arrival of F-15 Eagles in 1981, Lightning operations began to diminish and transfer to the King Feisal Air Base in the North-West Sector took place during 1981-03.82.

Kuwait Air Force

Command Assignments: Kuwait
Aircraft: T.55K/F.55K
Stations: Kuwait International Airport, Ahmed al Jaber and Jakra.
History: Deliveries of miscellaneous first of twelve F.53 fighters begun December 1968. Operated Lightnings until 1977, when replaced by Mirage F.1Ks.

APPENDIX 2

Lightning Specifications

Model	Span	Length	Height	Wing Area(sq ft)	Power Plant	Empty Weig
P.1A	34ft 10in	49ft 8in	17ft 3in	458.5	Armstrong Siddeley Sapphire 5	22,221lb
P.1B	34ft 10in	55ft 3in	19ft 5in	458.5	RR Avon 200R	24,816lb
F.1	34ft 10in	55ft 3in	19ft 7in	458.5	RR Avon 200R	25,753lb
F.1A	34ft 10in	55ft 3in	19ft 7in	458.5	RR Avon 210R	25,757lb
F.2	34ft 10in	55ft 3in	19ft 7in	458.5	RR Avon 210R	27,000lb
F.2A	34ft 10in	55ft 3in	19ft 7in	458.5	RR Avon 2110R	27,500lb
F.3	34ft 10in	55ft 3in	19ft 7in	458.5	RR Avon 3010R	26,905lb
F.3A	34ft 10in	55ft 3in	19ft 7in	458.5	RR Avon 301R	28,041lb
T.4	34ft 10in	55ft 3in	19ft 7in	458.5	RR Avon 210R	27,000lb
T.5	34ft 10in	55ft 3in	19ft 7in	458.5	RR Avon 301R	27,000lb
F.6	34ft 10in	55ft 3in	19ft 7in	458.5	RR Avon 301R	28,041lb
F.53	34ft 10in	55ft 3in	19ft 7in	458.5	RR Avon 301	28,041lb
T.55	34ft 10in	55ft 3in	19ft 7in	458.5	RR Avon 301	28,041lb

ed Weight	Max Speed	Service Ceiling	Armament
7lb	Mach 1.53 (1,011mph) @36,000ft	55,000ft	2 x 30mm Aden cannon
1lb	Mach 2.1 (1,390mph) @36,000ft	55,000ft	2 x 30mm Aden cannon
	Mach 2.3 (1,500mph) @36,000ft	60,000ft	2 x 30mm Aden cannon & 2 x Firestreak AAM
	Mach 2.3 (1,500mph) @36,000ft	60,000ft	2 x 30mm Aden cannon & 2 x Firestreak AAM
	Mach 2.3 (1,500mph) @36,000ft	60,000ft	2 x 30mm Aden cannon & 2 x Firestreak AAM
	Mach 2.3 (1,500mph) @36,000ft	60,000ft+	2 x 30mm Aden cannon & 2 x Firestreak AAM
	Mach 2.3 (1,500mph) @36,000ft	60,000ft+	4 x 30mm Aden cannon or 2 x 30mm cannon
olb	Mach 2.3 (1,500mph) @36,000ft	60,000ft+	2 x Firestreak AAM or 2 x Red Top AAM
	Mach 2.3 (1,500mph) @36,000ft	60,000ft+	2 x Firestreak AAM
	Mach 2.3 (1,500mph) @36,000ft	60,000ft+	2 x Firestreak AAM or 2 x Red Top AAM
	Mach 2.3 (1,500mph) @36,000ft	60,000ft+	2 x Firestreak AAM or 2 x Red Top AAM + 2 x 30mm Aden cannon in ventral tank, 48 x 2' rockets in place of missiles
	Mach 2.3 (1,500mph) @36,000ft	60,000ft+	As F.6 + 2 x 1,000lb bombs, 4 SNEB Matra rocket packs and Vinten camera recce pack
	Mach 2.3 (1,500mph) @36,000ft	60,000ft+	2 x Firestreak AAM or 2 x Red Top AAM

P.1A Two non-afterburning Armstrong Siddeley Sapphire 5 engines rated at 7,500lb (later rated at 9,200lb in re-heated version). VHF radio (later replaced by UHF). Martin-Baker 4BS ejection seat. First flown (WG760), 4 August 1954 at Boscombe Down. Became first British aircraft to exceed Mach 1 in level flight on 11 August 1954.

P.1B Two Rolls-Royce RA.24 Avon engines rated at 11,250lb dry, later increased to 13,300lb with installation of a four-stage afterburner (Avon 200R). Martin-Baker 4BS ejection seat. X6307 became the first aircraft built at Salmesbury and first of the Development Batch (twenty aircraft) to fly, on 3 April 1958.

F.1 Two Rolls-Royce Avon 210R engines rated at 14,430lb. First production version. Flew for the first time on 29 October 1959. First aircraft (XM135) released to the CFE on 29 June 1960. First Squadron delivery (XM165) to 74 Squadron. Ferranti Airpass AI 23 radar and fire-control system, VHF radio (later replaced by UHF). Martin-Baker 4BS ejection seat. Two 30mm Aden cannon with 130 rounds each in nose and two Firestreak missiles.

F.1A Two Rolls-Royce Avon 210R engines with revised, four-position re-heat throttle control. First flown (XM169) on 15 August 1960. F.1A first entered service (XM172) with 56 Squadron on 4 December 1960. First version with detachable in-flight refuelling capability, probe being fitted beneath port wing. UHF radio, external cable ducts to missile pylon positions. Martin-Baker 4BSA Mks.1 and 2 ejection seat. Airpass AI 23 radar and fire-control system. Two 30mm Aden cannon with 130 rounds each in nose and two Firestreak missiles.

F.2 Two Rolls-Royce Avon 210R engines with revised tailpipes. First flown (XN723) on 11 July 1961. First F.2 (XN771) delivered to the CFE on 4 November 1962. Entered service (XN775) with 19 Squadron on 17 December 1962. Revised cockpit including partial CR946 Flight Control System specification, liquid oxygen breathing system, stand-by turbo generator for DC electric supply (identified by small cooling scoop on dorsal spine). Steerable nose wheel in place of the earlier fixed nose wheel. Airpass AI 23 radar and fire-control system. Martin-Baker 4BSA Mks.1 and 2 ejection seat. Two 30mm Aden cannon with 130 rounds each in nose and two Firestreak missiles.

F.2A Two Rolls-Royce Avon 211R engines. F.2 rebuilt to incorporate some F.6 features, including kinked and cambered wing, square-cut tail fin, enlarged ventral fuel tank. Airpass AI 23 radar and fire-control system. F.2A released on 1 January 1968. Martin-Baker 4BSA Mks.1 and 2 ejection seat. Two 30mm Aden cannon with 130 rounds each in nose and two Firestreak missiles. Last F.2A (XN788) delivered to RAF Germany on 22 July 1970.

F.3 Two Rolls-Royce Avon 301R engines, 12,690lb dry thrust and 16,360lb re-heat. First flown (XP693) on 16 June 1962. First delivery (XP695), to the CFE on 1 January 1964. First entered service (XP700) with 74 Squadron on 14 April 1964. (First flight of F.3 to F.6 standard [XP697], 17.4.64.) Square-cut fin of 15 per cent greater area, built-in cannon armament deleted, more advanced AI 23B radar and fire-control system which allowed equipment with either two Red Top collision-course missiles or two Firestreaks. Full OR.946 Integrated Flight Control System instrumentation. Martin-Baker 4BSB Mks.1 and 2 ejection seat. Last F.3 (XR751) delivered to the RAF on 16 January 1968.

F.3A Two Rolls-Royce Avon 301R engines. Kinked and cambered wing of greater area and enlarged ventral fuel tank. Airpass AI 23 radar and fire-control system. Martin-Baker 4BSB Mks.1 and 2 ejection seat. Two Firestreak or Red Top missiles.

T.4 Two Rolls-Royce Avon 210R engines. Two-seat, dual-controlled trainer version of the F.1A. Aden cannon deleted. Airpass AI 23 radar and fire-control system. Two Martin-Baker 4BST Mks.1 and 2 ejection seats. Two Firestreak missiles normally carried.

T.5 Two Rolls-Royce Avon 301R engines. Two-seat, dual-controlled trainer version of the F.3, able to carry two Firestreak or Red Top missiles. Airpass AI 23 radar and fire-control system. Two Martin-Baker 4BST Mks.1 and 2 ejection seats.

F.6: Two Rolls-Royce Avon 301R engines. First production F.6 (XR752) flown on 16 June 1965. Released to the CFE (XR753) on 16 November 1965. Entered service with 5 Squadron on 10 December 1965. Full production version of the F.3A with provision to carry overwing fuel tanks. Some small improvements to equipment, such as Airpass AI 23 radar and fire-control system. Martin-Baker 4BSB Mks.1 and 2 ejection seat. Two 30mm Aden cannon with 130 rounds each in ventral pod; plus two Firestreak or Red Top missiles, or forty-eight 2in rockets in place of the missile pack. Last F.6 (XS938), delivered to RAF on 25 August 1967.

F.53 Two Rolls-Royce Avon 302C engines, 11,100lb static thrust, 16,300lb with re-heat. Export version of the F.6 with capability to carry a wide range of ordnance from overwing or underwing pylon hard points: two Firestreak or Red Top: Two 30mm Aden cannon with 130 rounds each in ventral pod; forty-four 2in rockets in place of missile pack; two 1,000lb HE bombs; thirty-six 68mm SNEB rockets in two Matra Type 155 launchers; or five Vinten Type 360 70mm cameras (1 x 6in f2.8 lens; 2 x 3in f2.0 lens; 2 x 1.75in f2.8 lens or 2 x 12in f2.0 lens) in reconnaissance pack. Ferranti Type AI 238 radar (export version of the AI 23B; approach and attack computers; search and attack display unit [CRT]; radar control and mode selector switch; and visual display cine recorder. Light fighter sight). Martin-Baker 4BSB ejection seat.

T.55 Two Rolls-Royce Avon 3020 engines. Export version of the T.5, with enlarged ventral fuel tank, kinked and cambered wing and Type AI 238 radar. Martin-Baker B840 ejection seat. Two Firestreak or Red Top missiles.

Jet fuel for the Lightning was AVTUR 50 (NATO AVTAG) with FS11 (fuel systems icing inhibitor).

APPENDIX 3

De Havilland Firestreak Dimensions

Length:	10ft 5.5in
Diameter	8.75in
Wingspan	2ft 5.5in
Weight:	300lb
Speed:	Mach 3
Range:	0.75-5 miles

De Havilland Red Top Dimensions

Length:	11ft 5.5in
Body diameter:	8.75in
Wingspan:	2ft 11.375in
Weight:	330lb
Speed:	Mach 3
Range:	7 miles

Lightning Production Airframes

Mark	Serial	Notes
P.1A	WG760	Preserved, Aerospace Museum, Cosford, Shropshire.
P. 1A	WG763	Preserved, Museum of Science and Industry, Manchester.
P.1A	WG765	Structural test specimen.
P.1B	XA847	Stored, Southampton area by Wensley Haydon Baillie.
P.1B	XA853	Second of the three P.1B prototypes, flown on 05.09.57. Mostly used on gun trials and gas-concentration tests and was last flown on 03.05.63 before SOC 10.02.65.
P.1B	XA856	First flown 03.01.58. SOC 06.67.
P.1B/F.1	XG307	First flown 03.04.58. Bedford fire dump 04.72.
P.1B/F.1	XG308	First flown 16.05.58. To Bedford 29.06.66.
P.1B/F.1	XG309	First flown 23.06.58. Dismantled, 03.67, for scrap.
P.1B/F.1	XG310	First flown 17.07.58. Converted to serve as F.3 prototype.
P.1B/F.1	XG311	Abandoned, 31.7.63, after undercarriage failure. Crashed into the sea off Lytham. Test pilot, D.M. Knight, ejected safely, EE Co.
P.1B/F.1	XG312	First flown 29.12.58. SOC 04.72.
P.1B/F.1	XG313	First flown 02.02.59. To Saudi Arabia as G-27-115. Preserved, Dhahran.
P.1B/F.1	XG325	First flown 26.02.59. Used for Firestreak trials. Nose section at 1476 Squadron ATC, Rayleigh, Essex.
P.1B/F.1	XG326	First flown 14.03.59. SOC 1971.
P.1B/F.1	XG327	First flown 10.04.59. Modified to F.3 standard, 1960.
P.1B/F.1	XG328	First flown 18.06.59. Scrapped 05.72.
P.1B/F.1	XG329	First flown 30.04.59. Preserved, Norfolk and Suffolk Aviation Museum, Flixton, Bungay, Suffolk.
P.1B/F.1	XG330	First flown 30.06.59. Last flown 05.01.65.

P.1B/F.1	XG331	Nose section in Gloucestershire Aviation collection, Staverton, Glos.
P.1B/F.1	XG332	Abandoned, 13.09.62, on approach to Hatfield, after double engine fire. Test pilot, George P. Aird, ejected safely but broke both legs crashing through a greenhouse. DH.
P.1B/F.1	XG334	Abandoned, 05.03.60, off Wells-next-the-Sea after hydraulics failure. Squadron Leader Ron Harding ejected safely. AFDS.
P.1B/F.1	XG335	Abandoned, 11.01.65, Larkhill Ranges, after undercarriage failed to lower, Crashed Woodborough, Wilts. Squadron Leader J. Whittaker, A&AEE, ejected safely.
P.1B/F.1	XG336	First flown 25.08.59.
P.1B/F.1	XG337	Preserved, Aerospace Museum, Cosford, Shropshire.
T.4/P.11	XL628	(Prototype) Abandoned by Test Pilot, J.W. Squier, 01.10.59, over the Irish Sea.
T.4/P.11	XL629	(Prototype) Gate guardian at RAF Boscombe Down, Wiltshire.
F.1	XM131	Static test airframe.
F.1	XM132	Static test airframe.
F.1	XM133	Static test airframe.
F.1	XM134	Abandoned, 11.09.64, after starboard undercarriage leg failed to fully lower, crashed off Happisburgh, Norfolk. Flight Lieutenant Terry Bond, 226 OCU test pilot, ejected safely.
F.1	XM135	First flown 14.11.59. Flown into IWM Duxford, 20.11.74, for permanent display.
F.1	XM136	Abandoned, 12.09.67, after cockpit fire. Crashed Scottow near RAF Coltishall. Jock Sneddon, Wattisham TFF, ejected and landed safely.
F.1	XM137	First flown 14.12.59.
F.1	XM138	Written off after engine fire on runway at RAF Coltishall, 16.12.60. Flight Lieutenant Bruce Hopkins, AFDS, evacuated aircraft safely.
F.1	XM139	First flown 12.01.60.
F.1	XM140	First flown 25.01.60.
F.1	XM141	Damaged in take-off accident, 16.05.61. Subsequently reduced to spares.
F.1	XM142	Abandoned, 26.04.63, after hydraulic power loss, crashed off Cromer, Norfolk. Flight Lieutenant J.M. Burns, 74 Squadron, ejected safely.
F.1	XM143	First flown 27.02.60.
F.1	XM144	First flew on 14.03.60, and saw extensive service with several units. It last flew on 07.11.73 and was used as a decoy at

Leuchars until it was refurbished in 1979
for gate guard duty as 'J' of 74 'Tiger'
Squadron. Nose section with South-West
Aviation Heritage, Eaglescott Airfield,
Devon.

F.1	XM145	First flown 18.03.60.
F.1	XM146	First flown 29.03.60. Scrapped 11.66.
F.1	XM147	First flown 07.04.60.
F.1	XM148	Cancelled.
F.1	XM149	Cancelled.
F.1	XM163	First flown 23.04.60.
F.1	XM164	First flown 13.06.60.
F.1	XM165	First flown 30.05.60. Scrapped 10.66.
F.1	XM166	First flown 01.07.60. Scrapped 10.66.
F.1	XM167	First flown 14.07.60. SOC 10.66.
F.1	XM168	Structural test airframe. Cancelled(?)
F.1A	XM169	Preserved, nose section with North Yorks Aircraft Recreation centre and Museum, Chop Gate, N. Yorks.
F.1A	XM170	Mercury spillage caused by heavy landing on first flight, 12.09.60. Written off. EE Co.
F.1A	XM171	On 06.06.63 was involved in a collision after a collision over Great Bricett with XM179. Flight Lieutenant 'Mo' Moore, 56 Squadron, safe.
F.1A	XM172	Preserved, gate guard, RAF Coltishall, Norfolk.
F.1A	XM173	Preserved, RAF Bentley Priory, Greater London.
F.1A	XM174	Abandoned, 29.11.68, after fire in air, aircraft crashing into a quarry at Bulmullo near Leuchars, Flight Lieutenant Edward Rawcliffe, Leuchars TFF, ejected safely.
F.1A	XM175	First flown 23.11.60.
F.1A	XM176	First flown 01.12.60.
F.1A	XM177	First flown 20.12.60.
F.1A	XM178	Preserved with the *Association des Amis du Musée du Château*, Savingny-Les-Beaune, France.
F.1 A	XM179	Lost, 06.06.63, in mid-air collision with XM171 during practice formation aerobatics. Crashed at Great Bricett near Wattisham. Flight Lieutenant Mike Cooke, 56 Squadron, seriously injured during ejection sequence.
F.1A	XM180	First flown 23.1.61.
F.1A	XM181	First flown 25.1.61.
F.1A	XM182	First flown 06.02.61.
F.1A	XM183	First flown 09.02.61.
F.1A	XM184	Fire on landing at RAF Coltishall, 17.04.67

Flight Lieutenant Gerry Crumbie, 226 OCU, safe.

F.1A	XM185	Abandoned near Wattisham, 06.03.61, after undercarriage failed to lower. Flying Officer Pete Ginger, 56 Squadron, ejected safely.
F.1A	XM186	Lost, 18.07.63, over Wittering during aerobatic presentation. Flying Officer Alan Garside, 111 Squadron, killed.
F.1A	XM187	Undercarriage collapsed at Wattisham, 19.09.63. Cat 4.
F.1A	XM188	At RAF Coltishall, 21.06.68, Squadron Leader Arthur Tyldesley, 226 OCU, taxied in with no brakes and ran off taxiway before striking No.1 Hangar.
F.1A	XM189	First flown 30.03.61. It left the runway during take-off roll at night on 18 January 1962. Later served with 226 OCU and was finally scrapped in 1982.
F.1A	XM190	Abandoned, 15.03.66, after ECU fire. Crashed in North Sea off Cromer. Captain Al Peterson USAF 26 OCU, Coltishall, ejected safely.
F.1A	XM191	Crashed on landing at RAF Wattisham, 09.06.64, after in-flight fire. Flight Lieutenant N. Smith, 111 Squadron, uninjured. Nose section now used as a travelling exhibit with RAF Exhibition, Production and Transport Unit.
F.1A	XM192	Preserved by Charles Ross at Binbrook, Lincolnshire.
F.1A	XM213	Crashed, 06.05.66, at RAF Coltishall after aborted take-off. Squadron Leader Paul Hobley, 226 OCU, uninjured. Cat 5.
F.1A	XM214	First flown 29.06.61.
F.1A	XM215	First flown 11.07.61.
F.1A	XM216	To 111 Squadron, 29.08.61.
F.1A	XM217	Cancelled.
F.1A	XM218	Cancelled.
T.4	XM966	Crashed in the Irish Sea, 22.07.65, after fin disintegrated at Mach 2. Jimmy L. Dell and Graham Elkington, English Electric, ejected safely.
T.5	XM967	Began build on T.4 line but transferred to BAC Filton for conversion to prototype T.5. First flown 29.03.62.
T.4	XM968	Abandoned, 24.02.77, near Gütersloh, Germany after total hydraulic failure led to loss of control. Squadron Leader M.J. Lawrance, 92 Squadron, and Squadron Leader Christopher Glanville-White, Harrier Squadron CO, ejected safely.

T.4	XM969	First flown 28.03.61.
T.4	XM970	First flown 05.05.61. First T.4 in RAF service.
T.4	XM971	Abandoned, 02.01.67, RAF Coltishall, after radome collapsed and debris entered air intake. Crashed at Tunstead. Squadron Leader Terry Carlton, 226 OCU and Flight Lieutenant Tony Gross, student, ejected and landed safely.
T.4	XM972	First flown 29.04.61.
T.4	XM973	First flown 17.05.61.
T.4	XM974	Abandoned, 14.12.72, near Happisburgh, after ECU/re-heat fire. Crashed in North Sea. Squadron Leader John Spencer and Flying Officer Geoffrey Philip Evans, 226 OCU, ejected safely.
T.4	XM987	First flown 13.07.61.
T.4	XM988	Abandoned, 05.06.73, near Great Yarmouth after Wing Commander Christopher Bruce of 74 Squadron entered a spin followed by loss of control.
T.4/T.54	XM989/54-650	Converted from T.4 for *Magic Carpet*. Re-serialled as 54-607 in 1967.
T.4	XM990	Crashed South Walsham, Norfolk, on 19.09.70 after aileron control failure during Battle of Britain Air Show at Coltishall. Both Flight Lieutenant John Leslie Sims and Flight Lieutenant Alfred Brian Fuller, 226 OCU, ejected safely.
T.4	XM991	Written off (Cat.5) after ground fire at Gütersloh, 06.75.
T.4/T.54	XM992/54-651	Converted from T.4 for *Magic Carpet*. Re-serialled as 54-608 in 1967. Written-off at Khamis Mushayt, 26.10.70, after starter fire.
T.4	XM993	Written-off after overrunning runway at Middleton St George, 12.12.62. Al Turley and student, Wing Commander C.M. Gibbs, escaped before aircraft caught fire and burned out. LCS.
T.4	XM994	First flown 12.03.62. To 19 Squadron 06.11.62.
T.4	XM995	First flown 25.F.62. To 92 Squadron 29.11.62.
T.4	XM996	First flown 13.04.62. To LCS Middleton St George 08.01.63.
T.4	XM997	First flown 22.05.62. To LCS Middleton St George 14.01.63.
T.4	XN103-112	10 a/c. Cancelled.
F.2/F.3	XN724	First flown 11.09.61. To Boscombe

		Down 22.05.62. Converted to F.2A. To 19 Squadron.
F.2	XN723	Abandoned on 25.03.64 near Hucknall after in-flight fire. Crashed at Keynham near Leicester, Mr. D. Witham, Rolls-Royce, ejected safely.
F.2/F.3	XN725	First flown 31.03.62. Converted to F.3 prototype.
F.2/F.2A	XN726	First flown 29.09.61. To CFE, Binbrook, on 14.02.63. To 19 Squadron, 07.06.68. Cat. 4 damaged by lightning strike, 27.03.72. Nose section now with the Cockpit collection, Rayleigh, Essex.
F.2/F.2A	XN727	First flown 13.10.61. To 92 Squadron.
F.2/F.2A	XN728	First flown 26.10.61. To 92 Squadron 01.04.63. Undercarriage collapsed 03.04.68. Now derelict at the former Al Commercials Yard, Balderton, Notts.
F.2/F.52	XN729/52-659 RSAF	Delivered 09.05.67 (as replacement for XN796/52-657). Re-serialled as 52-612 in 1967. Crashed near Khamis Mushayt, 02.05.70.
F.2/F.2A	XN730	First flown. 23.11.61. To 19 Squadron 12.03.63. Later 92 Squadron. Now preserved, *Luftwaffenmuseum*, Gatow, Berlin, Germany.
F.2	XN731	First flown 08.F.62. Later served with 92 and 19 Squadrons.
F.2	XN732	First flown 19.F.62. To 92 Squadron, 30.4.63.
F.2/F.2A	XN733	First flown 01.02.62.
F.2	XN734/G27-239	Converted from F.2 for *Magic Carpet* but never sent to Middle East.
F.2/F.2A	XN735	First flown 23.02.62.
F.2/F.52	XN767/52-655 RSAF	Converted from F.2 for *Magic Carpet*. Delivered 1966. Re-serialled as 52-609 in 1967.
F.2	XN768	First flown 14.3.62.
F.2	XN769	Nose section with Russell Carpenter, Sidcup, Greater London.
F.2/F.52	XN770/52-656 RSAF	Converted from F.2 for *Magic Carpet*. Delivered 1966. Re-serialled as 52-610 in 1967.
F.2/F.2A	XN771	First flown 29.08.62.
F.2/F.2A	XN772	Abandoned, 28.01.71, near Diepholz, Germany after entering spin at 36,000ft. Flying Officer Peter George Hitchcock, 92 Squadron, ejected.
F.2/F.2A	XN773	First flown 13.06.62.
F.2/F.2A	XN774	First flown 27.09.62. Involved in a mid-air collision with XN727 on 16.09.71. Repaired. SOC 01.01.77.
F.2/F.2A	XN775	First flown 01.10.62.

F.2/F.2A	XN776	Preserved, Museum of Flight, East Fortune, Lothian.
F.2/F.2A	XN777	Damaged, 21.12.62, Binbrook, when nose leg broke off after overshooting runway. Air Commodore Millington, CO AFDS, uninjured.
F.2/F.2A	XN778	First flown 09.11.62.
F.2/F.2A	XN779	First flown 20.11.62.
F.2/F.2A	XN780	Destroyed in ground fire at Gütersloh, 29.09.75.
F.2/F.2A	XN781	First flown 12.12.62.
F.2/F.2A	XN782	*Luftfahrtausstellung* in Hermeskill Museum, Germany.
F.2/F.2A	XN783	First flown 26.F.63.
F.2/F.2A	XN784	Preserved, Air Classic, Monchengladhach, Germany.
F.2/F.2A	XN785	Crashed, 27.04.64, on approach to disused airfield at Hutton Cranswick, East Yorkshire following a problem during an in-flight refuelling. Flying Officer George Davey, 92 Squadron did not eject and was killed.
F.2/F.2A	XN786	Destroyed in ground fire at Gütersloh, 04.08.76. 19 Squadron.
F.2/F.2A	XN787	First flight 15.02.63.
F.2/F.2A	XN788	First flight 25.02.53.
F.2/F.2A	XN789	First flight 11.03.63.
F.2/F.2A	XN790	First flight 20.03.63.
F.2/F.2A	XN791	First flight 04.04.63.
F.2/F.2A	XN792	First flight 19.04.6.3
F.2/F.2A	XN793	First flight 01.05.63.
F.2/F.2A	XN794	First flight 16.05.63.
F.2/F.2A	XN795	Nose section, Cockpit Collection, Rayleigh, Essex.
F.2/F.52	XN796/52-657 RSAF	Converted from F.2 for *Magic Carpet*. Delivered 07.66. Crashed on take-off from Mushayt, 20.09.66.
F.2/F.52	XN797/52-658 RSAV	Converted from F.2 for *Magic Carpet*. Delivered 1966. Re-serialled as 52-611 in 1967. Crashed whilst practising single engine approaches to Khamis Mushayt, 28.11.68. Major Essa Ghimlas killed.
F.2	XN798-808	11 aircraft cancelled.
F.3	XP693	G-FSIX. Barry Pover, Exeter, Devon.
F.3	XP694	Scrapped 04.88. Used as target, Otterburn ranges, Northumberland.
F.3	XP695	First flight 20.06.63. Last flight 15.03.84. Airfield decoy, then Scrapped 9.87.
F.3	XP696	First flown 02.07.63.
F.3	XP697	First flown 18.07.63.
F.3	XP698	In collision with XP747, 16.02.72, off Harwich. Flight Lieutenant Paul Cooper,

		29 Squadron, killed.
F.3	XP699	Abandoned, 03.03.67, Wethersfield, Suffolk after fuel-line failure/fire. Crashed just north of RAF Wethersfield. Flying Officer Stuart Pearse, 56 Squadron, ejected safely.
F.3	XP700	Abandoned, 07.08.72, on take-off from RAF Wattisham after engine fire. Crashed Great Waldringfield, Suffolk. Flight Lieutenant George Nicol Fenton, 29 Squadron, ejected.
F.3	XP701	First flight 14.09.63. Scrapped late 1987. Nose section, Robertsbridge Aviation Society, Robertsbridge, East Sussex.
F.3	XP702	First flight 19.09.63. Last flight 28.08.82. Stored, then scrapped, 04.88. Remains used as target, Otterburn ranges, Northumberland.
F.3	XP703	Nose section, Mick Jennings.
F.3	XP704	Crashed, 28.08.64, near Leuchars after spinning during practice aerobatic display. Flight Lieutenant Phil Owen, 74 Squadron, killed.
F.3	XP705	Abandoned near Akrotiri, Cyprus, 08.07.71, after jet fire. Flight Lieutenant Graham H. Clarke, 29 Squadron, ejected safely.
F.3	XP706	First flight 28.10.63. Last flight 07.85. Preserved, Lincolnshire Lightning Preservation Society, Strubby, Lincolnshire.
F.3	XP707	First flight 13.11.63. Crashed 19.03.87 near Binbrook, during practice aerobatics. LTF. Flight Lieutenant Barry Lennon ejected safely.
F.3	XP708	Target, Pendine ranges, Dyfed.
F.3	XP735	First flown 04.12.63.
F.3	XP736	Crashed into the sea thirty miles off Lowestoft, 22.09.71. Flying Officer Phil Mottershead, 29 Squadron, killed.
F.3	XP737	Ditched in Irish Sea off Valley, Wales, 17.08.79, after port undercarriage failed to lower. Flying Officer Raymond T. Knowles, 5 Squadron, ejected safely.
F.3	XP738	Written off (Cat.5) after wheels-up landing at RAF Wattisham, 10.12.73. 111 Squadron.
F.3	XP739	Abandoned 29.09.65 on approach to Wattisham after a double engine flame-out. Flight Lieutenant Hedley Molland, 111 Squadron ejected safely.
F.3	XP740	First flown 01.02.64.

F.3	XP741	First flight 04.02.64. Last flight 09.87. Delivered to Manston for fire training.
F.3	XP742	Abandoned, 07.05.70, in North Sea off Great Yarmouth, Norfolk, after ECU fire. Flying Officer Stuart Richard Tulloch, 111 Squadron, ejected safely.
F.3	XP743	First flown 18.02.64.
F.3	XP744	Abandoned 10.05.71 near Akrotiri, Cyprus after zonal fire warning. Flight Lieutenant Robert David Cole, 56 Squadron, ejected safely. Crashed eight miles South-East of Akrotiri.
F.3	XP745	Nose section, Vanguard Haulage, Greenford, Greater London.
F.3	XP746	First flown 26.03.64 and was issued to 56 Squadron on 12.11.69. It joined Treble One Squadron on 04.08.70 and operated for four years before going into store at Wattisham in October 1974. SOC in April 1975 and was used as a target aircraft for gunnery at Shoeburyness in 1976.
F.3	XP747	In collision 16.02.72 with XP698 over North Sea. Flight Lieutenant Paul Reynolds, 29 Squadron, ejected safely.
F.3	XP748	First flight 04.05.64. Last flight 02.75. Stored for two years. Used as gate guardian until summer 1988. Target, Pendine ranges, Dyfed.
F.3	XP750	First flight 03.F.64. Last flight 11.84. Scrapped 12.87.
F.3	XP751	First flight 16.3.64. Last flight 10.86. Scrapped 12.87.
F.3	XP752	Collided with FAF Mirage IIIE near Colmar, France, 20.05.71. Flight Lieutenant Tony Alcock, 111 Squadron, landed safely but aircraft written-off (Cat 5) due to damage.
F.3	XP753	Crashed into the sea off Scarborough, 26.08.83, during unauthorized aerobatics. Flight Lieutenant Mike Thompson, LTF, killed.
F.3	XP754	First flown 05.06.64.
F.3	XP755	First flown 15.06.64.
F.3	XP756	Abandoned 25.01.71 after re-heat fire. Crashed off Great Yarmouth. Captain Bill Povilus USAF attached to 29 Squadron, ejected safely.
F.3	XP757	First flown 04.07.61
F.3	XP758	First flown 10.07.64
F.3	XP759	First flown 14.08.64
F.3	XP760	Abandoned 24.08.60. ECU failure.

		Crashed North Sea 35nm off Seahouses, Fife. Flight Lieutenant Al Turley, 23 Squadron, ejected safely.
F.3	XP761	First flight 03.11.64. Last flight 11.10.74. Scrapped 01.88.
F.3	XP762	First flown 03.09.64.
F.3	XP763	First flown 11.09.64.
F.3	XP764	First flight 19.09.64. Last flight 10.86. Scrapped 01.88.
F.3	XP765	First flown 26.09.64.
F.3	XR711	Crashed on take-off at RAF Wattisham, 29.10.71. Flight Lieutenant Eric Steenson, 111 Squadron, uninjured.
F.3	XR712	Crashed, 26.06.65, near Padstow, Cornwall, after shedding pieces of tailpipe during Exeter Air Show. Flight Lieutenant Tony Doyle, 111 Squadron, ejected safely.
F.3	XR713	First flight 21.10.64. Last flight 11.03.87. Preserved, RAF Leuchars, Fife. 111 Squadron.
F.3	XR714	27.07.66, sank back on runway at RAF Akrotiri after being caught in jet blast during formation take-off. 111 Squadron.
F.3	XR715	Abandoned, 13.02.74, after ECU fire forced Flight Lieutenant Terence Taff A. Butcher, 29 Squadron, to eject. Aircraft crashed at Watermill Farm, Mells, near Halesworth, Suffolk.
F.3	XR716	First flight 19.11.64. Last flight 09.87. Fire training, RAF Cottesmore.
F.3	XR717	First flown 25.11.64.
F.3	XR718	First flight 14.12.64. Last flight 02.02.87. Battle damage repair aircraft at Wattisham. Preserved, Blythe Valley Aviation Collection, Walpole, Suffolk.
F.3	XR719	First flown 18.12.64. 56 Squadron 16.03.65-08.66. Used at Shoeburyness 09.08.66-1973. Declared Cat.5 after heavy landing at Coltishall, 05.06.73.
F.3	XR720	First flight 24.12.64. Last flight 6.2.85. Scrapped 01.88.
F.3	XR721	Crashed, 05.01.66, in the garden of Elm Tree Farm Cottages on the B1079, Otley to Helmingham Road, near Woodbridge, Suffolk, after engine flame-out. Flying Officer Derek Law, 56 Squadron, tried to eject but the canopy jammed and he was killed by ejection after a successful belly landing.
F.3	XR722	Converted to F.53 (53-656 RSAF) and allocated to 2 Squadron RSAF. Crashed

		06.02.72 while on loan to 6 Squadron, RSAF. Captain Mohammed Saud uninjured.
F.3	XR723	Abandoned, 18.09.79, near Akrotiri, Cyprus after engine fire. Group Captain Pete Carter, Station CO ejected safely. Crashed fifteen miles south of Akrotiri.
F.3	XR724	First flight 10.02.65. Last flight 29.07.92. G-BTSY. Preserved, Lightning Association, Binbrook Airfield, Lincolnshire.
F.3/F.6	XR725	First flight 19.02.65. Last flight 17.12.87. Preserved, Charles Ross, Chestnut Farm, Binbrook, Lincolnshire.
F.3/F.6	XR726	First flight 26.02.65 Last flight 24.08.87. Scrapped. Nose section, private collector, Harrogate, North Yorks.
F.3/F.6	XR727	First flight 08.03.65. Last flight 10.05.88. Flown to RAF Wildenrath.
F.3/F.6	XR728	First flight 17.03.65. Last flight 24.06.88. Preserved, Lightning Preservation Group, Bruntingthorpe, Leicestershire.
F.3/F.6	XR747	First flight 02.04.65. Last flight 14.08.87. Nose section, Barry Plover, Plymouth, Devon.
F.3	XR748	Abandoned, 24.06.74, near Coltishall after total hydraulic failure. Crashed in North Sea off Great Yarmouth. Flying Officer Kevin Mason, 111 Squadron, ejected.
F.3	XR749	First flight 30.04.65. Last flight 09.82. Preserved, Ken Ward, Teeside Airport, Durham.
F.3	XR750	First flown 10.05.65.
F.3	XR751	Preserved, Roy Flood, Lower Tremar, Cornwall.
F.3A/F.6	XR752	First flight 16.06.65. Last flight 08.01.86. Suffered in-flight fire and was finally Scrapped 09.87.
F.3A/F.6	XR753	First flight 23.06.65. Last flight 24.05.88. Preserved, 11 Squadron, RAF Leeming, North Yorks
F.3A/F.6	XR754	First flight 08.07.65. Last flight 24.06.88. Delivered to RAF Honington as battle damage repair airframe, scrapped 1992. Nose section preserved, Blythe Valley Aviation Collection, Walpole, Suffolk.
F.3A/F.6	XR755	First flight 15.07.65. Last flight 12.87. Preserved, Ernie Marshall, private collector, Cailington, Cornwall.
F.3A/F.6	XR756	First flight 11.08.65. Last flight 12.87.
F.3A/F.6	XR757	First flight 19.08.65. Last flight 12.87. Nose section, NATO Aircraft Museum,

F.3A/F.6 XR758
New Waltham, Lincolnshire.
First flight 30.08.65. Last flight 12.05.88. Used at RAF Laarbruch as battle damage repair airframe.

F.3A/F.6 XR759
First flight 09.09.65. Last flight 29.09.87. Scrapped. Nose section, Andrew Eaton, Haxey, Lincolnshire.

F.3A/F.6 XR760
Abandoned, 15.07.86, near Whitby after rear fuselage fire. Crashed in North Sea seven miles north of Whitby. Flight Lieutenant Bob Bees, 11 Squadron, ejected safely.

F.3A/F.6 XR761
Abandoned, 08.11.84, over North Sea after pitch trim failure followed by re-heat fire. Crashed North Sea, three miles off Donna Nook. Flight Lieutenant Mike D. Hale, 5 Squadron, ejected safely.

F.3A/F.6 XR762
Crashed into the sea off Akrotiri, Cyprus, 14.04.75, after Squadron Leader Hampton, 11 Squadron, misjudged height above sea during tail chase. Pilot killed.

F.3A/F.6 XR763
First flight 15.10.65. Abandoned 01.07. 87 near Akrotiri, Cyprus during APC after double engine flame-out following ingestion of part of the target banner. Flight Lieutenant D.K.M. 'Charlie' Chan, 5 Squadron, ejected safely.

F.3A/F.6 XR764
Abandoned, 30.09.71, near Akrotiri, Cyprus after jet pipe fire. Crashed into Limassol Bay, southeast of Akrotiri. Flight Lieutenant Richard Arthur Bealer, 56 Squadron, ejected safely.

F.3A/F.6 XR765
Abandoned, 23.07.81, over North Sea after double re-heat fire. Crashed into the North Sea, fifty miles North East of Binbrook. Flight Lieutenant J.G. Wild, 5 Squadron, ejected safely.

F.3A/F.6 XR766
Abandoned, 07.09.67, near Leuchars after uncontrollable spin. Crashed in North Sea, twenty miles east of Montrose. Squadron Leader Ron Blackburn, 23 Squadron, ejected safely

F.3A/F.6 XR767
Lost at night, 26.05.70, in the Straits of Malacca off Tengah, Singapore after Flight Lieutenant John C. Webster of 74 Squadron became disorientated. Pilot killed.

F.6 XR768
First full production standard F.6. Abandoned, 29.10.74, near Saltfleet, Lincolnshire after possible double re-heat fire. Crashed in North Sea three miles off Mablethorpe. Flight Lieutenant T.W. 'Tex'

		Jones, 5 Squadron, ejected safely.
F.6	XR769	First flight 01.12.65. Abandoned over the sea 11.04.88 near Easington, Lincolnshire, after engine fire. Crashed ten miles east of Spurn Head. Flight Lieutenant Dick Coleman RAAF attached to 11 Squadron ejected safely.
F.6	XR770	First flight 16.12.65. Last flight 04.88. Nose section, NATO Aircraft Museum, New Waltham, Lincolnshire.
F.6	XR771	First flight 20.01.66. Last flight 04.88. Preserved, Midlands Air Museum, Coventry, Warwickshire.
F.6	XR772	Abandoned, 06.03.85, near Spurn Head after possible structural failure. Crashed in North Sea, twenty miles northeast of Skegness. Flying Officer Martin 'Tetley' Ramsey, 5 Squadron, ejected but he was dead when recovered from the sea.
F.6	XR773	First flight 28.02.66. Last flight 23.12.92. G-OPIB. Lightning Plying Club, Barry Pover, Exeter, Devon.
F.3	XR774/795	Twenty-two aircraft cancelled.
T.5	XS416	First flight 20.08.64. Last flight 21.12.87. Preserved, NATO Aircraft Museum, New Waltham, Lincolnshire.
T.5	XS417	First flight 17.07.64. Last flight 18.05.87. Preserved, Newark Air Museum, Winthorpe, Nottinghamshire.
T.5	XS418	First flight 18.12.64. Crashed, 23.08.68, while landing at Stradishall, when undercarriage retracted on landing. Flight Lieutenant Henry Ploszek and SAC Lewis were uninjured. Last flight 09.74. Used as surface decoy until Scrapped 09.87.
T.5	XS419	First flight 18.12.64. Last flight 27.02.87. Scrapped 07.93.
T.5	XS420	First flight 23.F.65. Crashed on night take-off from Coltishall, July 1973. Captain Gary Catren, Instructor and Flying Officer George Smith uninjured. Last flight 05.83. Preserved, Fenland and West Norfolk Aviation Museum, Wisbech, Cambridgeshire.
T.5	XS421	Nose section, Cockpit Collection, Rayleigh, Essex.
T.5	XS422	Stored, Southampton area, Wensley Haydon-Baillie.
T.5	XS423	First flight 31.05.65. Last flight 1974. Used as airfield decoy. Scrapped 09.87.
T.5	XS449	First flight 30.04.65. Last flight 9.74. 87. Used as airfield decoy. Scrapped 9.87.

T.5	XS45C	First flight 25.05.65. Last flight 01.75. Scrapped 09.87.
T.5	XS451	G-LTNG. Barry Paver, Plymouth Devon.
T.5	XS452	First flight 30.06.65 Last flight 30.06.88. Airworthy, for Mike Beachy-Head, South Africa.
T.5	XS453	Abandoned, F.06.66, near Happisburgh, Norfolk, after hydraulics failure. Crashed into North Sea. 226 OCU. Flying Officer Geoff Fish, on his first T-5 solo, ejected safely.
T.5	XS454	First flight 06.07.65. Cat 3 damage, 07.03.67, when main undercarriage collapsed on Coltishall runway. Flight Lieutenants Mike Graydon and Bob Offord unhurt. Last flight 06.75. Used as decoy until 09.87. Scrapped.
T.5	XS455	Abandoned near Spurn Head, 06.09.72, after hydraulic failure caused loss of control. Crashed in North Sea off Withensea. Squadron Leader T.J.L. Gauvain, 226 OCU and Lieutenant R. Verbist, Belgian Air Force, both ejected, both injured.
T.5	XS456	First flight 26.10.65. Last flight 01.87. Gate guardian, Elms Golf Centre, Wainfleet, Lincolnshire
T.5	XS457	First flight 08.11.65. Written-off after undercarriage collapsed at Binbrook, 09.12.83. 5 Squadron. Nose section on display at NATO Aircraft Museum, New Waltham, Lincolnshire.
T.5	XS458	First flight 03.12.65. Last flight 30.06.88. Preserved, Tony Hulls, Cranfield, Bedfordshire.
T.5	XS459	First flight 22.12.66. Suffered an undercarriage collapse on landing at Binbrook, 27.3.81. LTF. Repaired. Last flight 15.03.87. Now at Fenland and W. Norfolk Aviation Museum, Wisbech, Cambridgeshire.
T.5/T.55	XS460/55-71C for RSAF	Written-off in crosswind landing accident at Warton, 07.03.67. Jimmy Dell and P. Williams, BAC, unhurt.
T.5	XS851/855	Five aircraft cancelled.
F.6	XS893	Ditched in sea off Tengah, Singapore, 12.08.70, when port undercarriage failed to lower. Flying Officer Mike Rigg, 74 Squadron, ejected safely.
F.6	XS894	Crashed in the sea five miles off Famborough Head, 08.09.70. Major W.B. Schaffner, USAF, attached to 5 Squadron, killed.

F.6	XS895	First flight 06.04.66. Last flight 12.87. Scrapped. Used at Pendine ranges, Dyfed, as a target.
F.6	XS896	Crashed on approach to Tengah, Singapore, 12.09.68, after fire in rear fuselage. Flying Officer P.F. Thompson, 74 Squadron, killed
F.6	XS897	First flight 10.05.66. To 74 Squadron, 21.12.66. Flown to 56 Squadron by Flight Lieutenant Roger Pope 04-06.09. 71. Last flight 14.12.87. Preserved, South Yorks Aviation Museum, Firbeck, South Yorkshire.
F.6	XS898	First flight 20.05.66. Last flight 30.06.88. Scrapped at Cranfield, 12.94. Nose section, Tony Collins, Lavendon, Buckinghamshire.
F.6	XS899	First flight 08.06.66. Last flight 30.06.88. Scrapped at Cranfield, 12.94. Nose section preserved by Mick Jennings.
F.6	XS900	Abandoned 24.01.68 after take-off from Lossiemouth when controls were jammed by FOD caused by total loss of power. Flight Lieutenant Stuart Miller, 5 Squadron, ejected safely.
F.6	XS901	First flight 01.07.66. Last flight 12.05.88. Delivered to RAF Bruggen as battle damage repair airframe.
F.6	XS902	Abandoned near Grimsby 26.05.71 after re-heat fire. Crashed nine miles east of Spurn Head. Flight Lieutenant Alastair MacKay RCAF attached to 5 Squadron, ejected safely.
F.6	XS903	First flight 17.08.66. Last flight 10.05.88. Preserved, Yorkshire Air Museum, Elvington, North Yorkshire.
F.6	XS904	First flight 26.08.66. Last Lightning to fly. Preserved, Lightning Preservation Group, Bruntingthorpe, Leicestershire.
F.6	XS918	Abandoned over the sea off Leuchars 04.03.70 after jet pipe fire. Crashed Firth of Forth. Flying Officer Anthony David Doidge, 11 Squadron, ejected and was killed.
F.6	XS919	First flight 28.09.66. Last flight 15.03.88. Dismantled in yard at Torpoint Shipping Co. Ltd, Torpoint, Devon.
F.6	XS920	Crashed 13.07.84 near Heuslingen, Germany after hitting power cables during ACM. Flight Lieutenant Dave Frost, 5 Squadron, killed.

F.6	XS921	Crashed thirty miles off Flamborough Head, 19.09.85, after uncontrolled spin. Flight Lieutenant Craig Penrice suffered leg injuries during the ejection.
F.6	XS922	First flight 06.12.66. Last flight 14.06.88. Delivered to RAF Wattisham as battle damage aircraft, then scrapped. Nose section, Air Defence College, Salisbury, Wiltshire.
F.6	XS923	First flight 13.12.66. Last flight 30.06.88. Scrapped at Cranfield 12.94. Nose section with Sue and Roy German, Welshpool, Powys.
F.6	XS924	Stalled in stream turbulence during formation take-off for the RAF 50th Anniversary Display and crashed at Beelsby near Binbrook, 29.04.68. Flight Lieutenant Al Davey, 5 Squadron, killed.
F.6	XS925	First flight 28.02.67. Last flight 09.87. Preserved (XS8961M) RAF Museum, Hendon.
F.6	XS926	Abandoned over North Sea, 22.09.69, after spinning during ACT. Crashed 51m E of Flamborough Head. Major Charles B. Neel USAF, attached to 5 Squadron, ejected safely.
F.6	XS927	First flight 15.02.67. Last flight 10.86. Scrapped by 03.88.
F.6	XS928	First flight 28.02.67. Last flight 08.92. Gate guardian, BAe Warton, Lancashire.
F.6	XS929	First flight 01.03.67. Last flight 20.05.88. Gate guardian, RAF Akrotiri, Cyprus.
F.6	XS930	Crashed, 27.07.70, into Malay village following take-off from Tengah, Singapore, after Flight Lieutenant Frank Whitehouse, 74 Squadron, climbed too steeply after take-off. Pilot killed. 100 buildings destroyed and three villagers injured.
F.6	XS931	Abandoned, 25.05.79, near Flamborough Head after control restriction after take-off caused by FOD. Crashed off Hornsea. Flying Officer Pete Coker, 5 Squadron, ejected.
F.6	XS932	First flight 09.04.67. Last flight 10.86. Nose section, Lightning Preservation Group, Bruntingthorpe, Leicestershire.
F.6	XS933	First flight 27.04.67. Last flight 10.86. Nose section, Terrington Aviation Collection, Terrington St. Clement, Norfolk.

F.6	XS934	Abandoned near Akrotiri, Cyprus, 03.04.73, after ECU fire. Flight Lieutenant Frederick A. Greer, 56 Squadron, ejected safely.
F.6	XS935	First flight 29.05.67. Last flight 09.87. Scrapped.
F.6	XS936	First flight 31.05.67. Last flight 10.87. Preserved, Castle Motors, Liskeard, Cornwall.
F.6	XS937	Ditched off Flamborough Head, 30.07.76, after undercarriage failure. Flying Officer Simon C.C. 'Much' Manning, 11 Squadron, ejected safely.
F.6	XS938	Abandoned, 28.04.71, near Leuchars after re-heat fire during take-off. River Tay, Fife. Pilot Officer Alastair Cameron MacLean, 23 Squadron, ejected.
F.6	Twelve aircraft cancelled.	—
T.5	XV328	Cockpit section, Phoenix Aviation, Bruntingthorpe, Leicestershire.
T.5	XV329	Sent by sea to Singapore from Sydenham, Belfast, June 1967, when 74 Squadron deployed to Tengah from Leuchars. Returned by sea to the UK, August 1971 and to be written-off in December when it was discovered that acid spillage from the batteries had corroded the airframe.
F.52	52-655 RSAF	(see XN767) to 52-609. Converted from F.2 for *Magic Carpet*. On display, Technical Services Institute, Dhahran.
F.52	52-656 RSAF	(see XN770) to 52-610. Converted from F.2 for *Magic Carpet*. Stored for display, Riyadh.
F.52	52-657 RSAF	(see XN796) Converted from F.2 for *Magic Carpet*. Written-off after excessive rotation at low speed 20.09.66. Pilot unhurt.
F.52	52-658 RSAF	(see XN797) Converted from F.2 for *Magic Carpet*. Re-serialled as 52-611 in 1967. Crashed whilst practising single engine approaches to Khamis Mushayt, 29.11.68 inbound to Khamis. Major Essa Ghimlas killed
F.52	52-659 RSAF	(see XN729) Converted from F.2 for *Magic Carpet*. To 52-612. Crashed Khamis Mushayt, 02.05.70, after hydraulic failure.
F.53	53-412 KAF G-27-80.	'C' Displayed, Kuwait International Airport.
F.53	53-413 KAF G-27-81	—
F.53	53-414 KAF G-27-82	Crashed, 10.04.71, after fire. Pilot Razzack died en route to hospital

F.53	53-415 KAF G-27-83	'H' Displayed on pole in vic formation, Al Jaber AFB
F.53	53-416 KAF G-27-84	'J' Displayed on pole in vic formation, Al Jaber AFB
F.53	53-417 KAF G-27-85	'K' Displayed on pole in vic formation, Al Jaber AFB
F.53	53-418 KAF G-27-86	Derelict, Al Salem.
F.53	53-419 KAF G-27-87	Crashed, 02.08.71, on take-off from Rezayat. Lieutenant Nasser unhurt
F.53	53-420 KAF G-27-88	'N' Displayed at Kuwait Technology Institute.
F.53	53-421 KAF G-27-89	'O' Presented to Air Museum, Kuwait International Airport.
F.53	53-422 KAF G-27-90	'P' Badly damaged at Messila Beach and dumped at Ali Al Salem APB
F.53	53-423 KAF G-27-91	Gate guardian at Ali Al Salem APB.
F.53	53-666 RSAF G-27-2	Lost 06.02.72. Details unknown.
F.53	53-667 RSAF G-27-37	Crashed, 03.09.85, 28m north of Tabuk. Double re-heat fire.
F.53	53-668 RSAF G-27-38 ZF577	Portsmouth Marine Salvage (ex-Haydon-Baillie Collection).
F.53	53-669 RSAF G-27-39	Crashed, 21.04.79, near Tabuk after running out of fuel.
F.53	53-670 RSAF G-27-40 ZF578	Ex-Wales Air Museum, Cardiff Airport, exhibit.
F.53	53-671 RSAF G-27-41 ZP579	Portsmouth Marine Salvage (ex-Haydon-Baillie Collection).
F.53	53-672 RSAF G-27 42 ZF580	Gate guardian, BAe Salmesbury airfield.
F.53	53-673 RSAF G-2743	Crashed, 22.09.80, Khamis Mushayt after colliding with 53-680.
F.53	53-674 RSAF G-27-44	Crashed off coast of Bahrain, 28.09.72. Pilot, Abdul Jussef, killed.
F.53	53-675 RSAF G-27-45 ZP581	Portsmouth Marine Salvage (ex-Haydon-Baillie Collection).
F.53	53-676 RSAF G-27-46 ZF582	Portsmouth Marine Salvage (ex-Haydon-Baillie Collection).
F.53	53-677 RSAF	Crashed at night, 04.09.83.
F.53	53-677 RSAF G-27-47	Crashed at night, 04.09.83. Written-off.
F.53	53-678 RSAF G-27-48	Crashed near Tabuk, 21.04.79, during sandstorm after running out of fuel.
F.53	53-679 RSAF G-27-49 ZF590	Portsmouth Marine Salvage (ex-Haydon-Baillie Collection).
F.53	53-680 RSAF G-27-50	Crashed, 22.09.80, Khamis Mushayt after colliding with 53-673.
F.53	53-68 1 RSAF G-27-51 ZP583	Solway Aviation SOC, Carlisle Airport, Cumbria.
F.53	53-682 RSAF G-27-52 ZP584	Gate guard, GEC-Marconi Ltd, South Gyles Works, Edinburgh.
F.53	53-683 RSAF G-27-53 ZF585	Portsmouth Marine Salvage (ex-Haydon-Baillie Collection).
F.53	53-684 RSAF G-27-54	Crashed on take-off from Dhahran, 30.06.80.

F.53	53-685 RSAF G-27-55 ZF591	Portsmouth Marine Salvage (ex-Haydon-Baillie Collection).
F.53	53-686 RSAF G-27-56 ZP592	Portsmouth Marine Salvage (ex-Haydon-Baillie Collection).
F.53	53-687 RSAF G-27-57	On display, Khamis Mushayt.
F.53	53-688 RSAF G-27-58 ZP586	Crashed Tabuk, 27.07.84. Portsmouth Marine Salvage (ex-Haydon-Baillie Collection).
F.53	53-689 RSAF G-27-59	—
F.53	53-690 RSAF G-27-60	Crashed, 04.09.68, Stakepool, Pilling, twelve miles north of Warton after total control failure. John Cockburn, BAC, ejected safely.
F.53	53-691 RSAF G-27-61 ZF587	Portsmouth Marine Salvage (ex-Haydon-Baillie Collection).
F.53	53-692 RSAF G-27-62 ZP593	Robins APB, Highway 247, near Macon, Ga. USA.
F.53	53-693 RSAF G-27-63 ZP588	Midlands Aeropark, Castle Donnington Airport.
F.53	53-694 RSAF G-27-64	Crashed, 11.09.76, forty miles north of Khamis Mushayt after spin.
F.53	53-695 RSAF G-27-65	Crashed fifty-five miles South East of Tabuk, 28.09.81, on training sortie.
F.53	53-696 RSAF G-27-66 ZP594	North East Air Museum, Usworth, Sunderland, Tyne & Wear.
F.53	53-697 RSAF G-27-67	Crashed, 03.05.70, near Yemeni border during reconnaissance sortie after being hit by ground fire. Pilot ejected.
F.53	53-698 RSAF G-27-68	—
F.53	53-699 RSAF G-27-69	On display, Tabuk.
F.53	53-700 RSAF G-27-233	Portsmouth Marine Salvage (ex-Haydon ZF589 Baillie Collection).
T.54	54-650 RSAF XM989	First flown 30.08.61. On display, Dhahran.
T.54	54-651 RSAF XM992	First flown 13.12.61.
T.55	55-410 KAF G-27-78	First flown 24.05.68.
T.55	55-411 KAF G-27-79	First flown 03.04.69.
T.55	55-710	Crashed landing at Warton, 07.03.67, in strong crosswind. BAC.
T.55	55-711 RSAF G-27-70 ZP597	Damaged, 13.03.71, Portsmouth Marine Salvage (ex-Haydon-Baillie Collection)
T.55	55-712 RSAF G-27-71	Crashed, 21.05.74, into Half Moon Bay after inverted low-level pass over sand dunes. Colonel Ainousa and Lieuteant Otaibi killed.
T.55	55-713 RSAF G-27-72 ZF598	Midland Air Museum, Coventry Airport.
T.55	55-714 RSAF G-27-73 ZF595	Portsmouth Marine Salvage (ex-Haydon-Baillie Collection).
T.55	55-715 RSAF G-27-74 ZF596	Portsmouth Marine Salvage (ex-Haydon-Baillie Collection).
T.55	55-716 RSAF G-27-75	First flown 14.07.69. Scrapped 1985.

Lightning Production Totals/ Production By Mark

Model	Registrations	No	Manufacturer
P.1A	WG760, WG763	2	EE
P.1A	test airframe (WG765)	(1)	EE
P.1B	XA847, XA853, XA856	3	EE
P.1B (Pre production batch)	XG307/XG337	20	EE
P.1B	test airframes	(3)	EE
F.1	XM134/XM147	—	EE
—	XM163/XM167	19	EE
F.1A	XM169/XM192	24	EE
—	XM213/XM216	4	EE
F.1A	test airframe	(1)	EE
T.4/P.11	XL628/XL629 (prototype)	2	EE
T.4	XM966/XM974	9	EE
F.2A	XM987/XM997	11	EE
F.2	XN723/XN735	13	EE
—	XN767/XN797	31	EE
F.3	XP693/XP708	70	BAC
—	XP735/XP765	—	BAC
—	XR711-XR728	—	BAC
—	XR747-XR751	—	BAC
F.3 ER/6 interim	XR752/XR767	16	BAC
F.6	XR768/XR773	38	BAC
—	XS893/XS904	—	BAC
—	XS918/XS938	—	BAC
T.5	XS416/XS423	22	BAC
—	XS449/XS460	—	BAC
—	XV328/XV329	—	BAC
T.55.	55-711/716	6	BAC
—	55-410/411	2	BAC
F.53	53-667/699	33	BAC
—	53-700	1	BAC
—	53-412/423	12	BAC

Total 333 (5)

Production By Mark

P.1A	2 prototypes
P.1B	3 prototypes
—	20 development batch aircraft
F.1	19
F.1A	28
F.2	13 (5 converted to F.52)
F.2A	31
F.3	63
T.4	21
T.5	23
F.6	62
F.53	46
T.55	8

Lightning Write-Offs by User/Type

Type	RAF	Contractors/Test Aircraft	KAF	RSAF	Total
P.1B/F.1	1	3			4
P.1	5				5
F.1A	9	1			10
P.2		1			1
F.2A	4				4
P.3	19				19
P.6	31			1	32
T.4	7	2			9
T.5	4				4
T.55		1		1	2
P.52				3	3
P.53		1	2	13	16
Totals	80	9	2	18	109

Loss Record (Write-Offs) by Year (All Users)

Type	RAF	Contractors/Test Aircraft	KAF	RSAF	Total
1959	1	1969	1	1979	5
1960	3	1970	9	1980	3
1961	3	1971	13	1981	2
1962	2	1972	8	1982	0
1963	4	1973	3	1983	3
1964	5	1974	4	1984	3
1965	4	1975	3	1985	3
1966	7	1976	3	1986	1
1967	6	1977	1	1987	2
1968	6	1978	0	1988	1

N.b. Write-off figures include crashes, abandoned aircraft, collision, enemy action and Cat.5 (written off after severe damage caused by any of the above, or corrosion, etc.).

RAF/RSAF/KAF Transfers

Aircraft Transferred from the RAF to the RSAF

RAF Registration	Model	RSAF Registration
XM989	T.54	54-650 RSAF
XN729	F.52	52-612/52-659 RSAF
XN767	F.52	52-609/52-655 RSAF
XN796	F.52	52-657/52-657 RSAF
XM992	T.54	54-651 RSAF
XN734	G-27-239	F.3A
XN770	F.52	52-610/52-656 RSAF
XN797	F.52	52-611/52-658 RSAF

Aircraft Transferred from the RSAF to the RAF

RAF Registration	Model	RSAF Registration
ZF577 G-27-38	F.53	53-668 RSAF
ZF579 G-27-41	F.53	53-671 RSAF
ZE581 G-27-45	F.53	53-675 RSAF
ZF583 G-27-51	F.53	53-681 RSAF
ZF585 G-27-53	F.53	53-683 RSAF
ZF587 G-27-61	F.53	53-691 RSAF
ZF589 G-27-233	F.53	53-700 RSAF
ZE591 G-27-55	F.53	53-685 RSAF
ZF593 G-27-62	F.53	53-692 RSAF
ZF595 G-27-73	T.55	55-714 RSAF
ZF597 G-27-70	T.55	55-711 RSAF
ZF578 G-27-40	F.53	53-670 RSAF
ZF580 G-27-42	F.53	53-672 RSAF
ZF582 G-27-46	F.53	53-676 RSAF
ZF584 G-27-52	F.53	53-682 RSAF
ZF586 G-27-58	T.55	53-688 RSAF
ZE588 G-27-63	F.53	53-693 RSAF
ZF590 G-27-49	F.53	53-679 RSAF
ZF592 G-27-56	F.53	53-686 RSAF
ZE594 G-27-66	F.53	53-696 RSAF
ZF596 G-27-74	T.55	55-715 RSAF
ZF598 G-27-72	T.55	55-713 RSAF

APPENDIX 8
Civilian Registrations

RAF Registration	Model	RSAF Registration
G-AWQN	F.53	53-686 RSAF
G-A	F.53	KAF
G-B	F.6	XR724
G-A	F.53	53-687 RSAF
G-B	F.3A	XN734
G-FSIX	F.3	XP693

Glossary

ADEX	Air Defence Exercise
AFCS	Automatic Flight Control System
AFDS	Air Fighting Development Squadron
AGL	Above Ground Level
AI 23	Airborne Intercept Radar
APC	Armament Practice Camp
ASI	Airspeed Indicator
ASR	Air Sea Rescue
ATC	Air Traffic Controller/Control
AVM	Air Vice Marshal
AVPIN	isopropylnitrate (starter fuel)
BAC	British Aircraft Corporation
'Badger'	Soviet Tupolev Tu-16 bomber
'Bear'	Soviet Tupolev Tu-20 (95) bomber
'Brackets'	in-flight refuelling
Categories	

Cat 3: The aircraft damage is considered to be militarily beyond unit resources (but may be repairable accidents) on site by a service working party or a contractor's working party.

Cat 4: The aircraft is considered to need special facilities or equipment for repair which is not available on site.

Cat 5: The aircraft is considered to be damaged beyond economical repair.

CGI	Chief Ground Instructor
Chief Tech.	Chief Technician
C-in-C	Commander-in-Chief
CFI	Chief Flying Instructor
CI	Chief Instructor
'cobblestones'	buffeting caused by compressibility
dive circle	Recovery area centered on a point 18 nautical miles from the airfield, on the extended centreline of the duty runway. Its radius in nautical miles equated to approximately the altitude of the aircraft in thousands of feet (where the pilot would descend from 36,000ft to 3,000ft)
DOCFW	Deputy Officer Commanding Flying Wing
ECU	Engine Control Unit
F-100C	USAF Super Sabre fighter aircraft
Firestreak	air-to-air heat-seeking missile
g	acceleration of free fall due to gravity

GCI	Ground Controlled Interception
GCA	Ground Controlled Approach
HE	High Explosive
IAS	Indicated Air Speed
IIFIS	Interim Integrated Flight Instrument System
ILS	Instrument Landing System approach aid
IWI	Interceptor Weapons Instructor
JPT	Jet Pipe Temperature
KAF	Kuwait Air Force
KC-50	Boeing in-flight refuelling aircraft
knot	unit of speed of 1nm (about 1.15 statute miles) per hour.
LAC	Leading Aircraftsman
'linies'	flight line crewmen
LCU	Lightning Conversion Unit
LOX	liquid oxygen
TANKEX	In-flight refuelling exercise
Ten Ton Club	A club for those who have flown at 1,000mph, with its own special tie and badge
TFF	Target Facility Flight
TFW	Tactical Fighter Wing
TMN	True Mach Number
'Trappers'	Examining Team of instructors
tropopause	The height at which the stratosphere begins. It varies with latitude and season but can be taken as approximately 36,000ft, above which the temperature remains constant.
USAF	United States Air Force

Bibliography

Air Clues

Barnato Walker MBE, Diana *Spreading My Wings* (PSL, 1994)

Beamont, Roland *English Electric P1 Lightning,* (Ian Allan, 1985)

Beamont, Roland *Testing Early Jets* (Airlife, 1990)

Bendell, Anthony 'Bugs' *Never In Anger* (Orion, 1998)

Bowman, Martin W. *English Electric Lightning,* (Crowood Aviation Series, 1997 & 2005)

—*English Electric Lightning, The, Images of Aviation* (Tempus, 1999)

—*Fast Jet Fighters 1948-1978* (Airlife, 2001)

—*Lightning Strikes; English Electric's Supersonic Fighter In Action,* (Airlife, 2001)

—*RAF Marham; Bomber Station* (The History Press, 2008)

Caruana, Richard J. *Close Up Classics: The BAC Lightning* (Modelaid International Publications, 1990)

Cossey, Bob *Tigers: The story of No.74 Squadron RAF* (Arms & Armour Press, 1992)

Fairclough, Robert & Ransom, Stephen *English Electric Aircraft And Their Predecessors* (Putnam, 1987)

Halpenny, Bruce Barrymore *EE/BAC Lightning* (Osprey, 1984)

Jackson, John & Scott, Stewart *Offence To Defence! The History of RAF Binbrook* (GMS, 1990)

Jennings MBE, Mick *RAF Coltishall Fighter Station: A Station History* (Old Forge, 2007).

Lightning Review

Lindsay, Roger *Aircraft Illustrated Special: Lightning* (Ian Allan, 1989)

Moulds MBE RAF, Squadron Leader (Compiled by) *The Lightning Conversion Units 1960-1987.* (Prospect Litho, 1993)

Oliver, David *British Military Aircraft Accidents. The Last 25 Years,* (Ian Allan, 1990)

Philpott, Bryan *English Electric Lightning* (PSL, 1984)

Reed, Arthur *Modern Combat Aircraft 5, BAC Lightning* (Ian Allan, 1960)

—*BAC Lightning,* (Ian Allan, 1980)

—*RAF Aircraft Today: 2 Lightning* (Ian Allan, 1984)

Ross, Charles (Edited and published by) *Lightning Review July 1991-July 1996*

Scott, Stewart A. *English Electric Lightning; Birth of A Legend* (GMS, 2000)

—*English Electric Lightning; Vol.2.* (GMS, 2002)

Sharman, Sarah *Sir James Martin* (PSL, 1996)

Tecklenborg, Marc & Rydzynski, Werner *No.226 OCU Lightning Instructors Handbook RAF* (Flottman Verlag GmbH., 1995)

Telegraph Sunday Magazine 1965

The History and Development of Martin-Baker Escape Systems (Martin-Baker, 1978)

Trevor, Hugh *Lightnings Live On!* (Lightning Preservation Group, 1996)

Wynn, Humphrey *RAF Nuclear Deterrent Forces* (HMSO/MoD) Air Historical Branch (RAF), 1994)